WITHDRAWN

W9-BPO-774

ILLINOIS CENTRAL COLLEGE
PN4121.L45
STACKS
Speaking and listening

A12900 282333

11713

PN
4121      LEWIS
.L45      Speaking and listening

Illinois Central College
Learning Resource Center

# SPEAKING
## and
# LISTENING

## A GUIDE TO EFFECTIVE
## ORAL-AURAL COMMUNICATION

by

## Thomas R. Lewis
Professor of Speech
Associate Dean of the Graduate School
Florida State University

with

## Ralph G. Nichols
Head, Department of Rhetoric
University of Minnesota

Illinois Central College
Learning Resouce Center

11713

**WM. C. BROWN COMPANY PUBLISHERS**
135 SOUTH LOCUST STREET • DUBUQUE, IOWA 52003

PN
4121
.L 45

Copyright © 1965
by
Wm. C. Brown Company Publishers

Library of Congress Catalog Number: 65-21885

All rights reserved. No part of this book may be
reproduced in any form or by any process without permission in writing from the copyright owner.

*Manufactured by* WM. C. BROWN CO. INC., Dubuque, Iowa
Printed in U. S. A.

# Contents

## Part I

## Part II

## Part III

# Foreword

In recent years the educational philosophy training in oral communication has stressed the importance of training for listening as well as training for speaking. The authors of this book agree completely with this approach and believe the objective will be achieved best by coordinating the instruction in the two skills. Classroom instruction is most efficient when every moment of every class period is economically used. Many speech classes, however, do not use the time available in fully effective fashion. One student while speaking perhaps draws the attention of the instructor and a few classmates, but the attention of many classmates is largely lost. Some will be practicing their own speeches which are to be called for later during the class period. Others will be following mental tangents of a wide variety and scope. This diversion of attention occurs even though we recognize the possibility of acquiring many techniques and principles while listening to a classmate talk. A central objective of this text is to help every student expedite his learning through listening and thereby use every moment of the speech class period better.

Moreover, the authors wish to emphasize to the student in the strongest possible way that oral communication is an instantaneous two-way process. When it is not a two-way process, it is pure exhibitionism or display. The interest of the speaker must be in "getting through" to the receiver, and the interest of the listener must be in "accurate reception" of the message from the sender. In the past too little attention has been given to the listening part of this dual process. It is hoped that serious attention to underlying principles of listening training and motivated practice built upon these principles will be equally emphasized with the principles and practice of speaking skills. In the chapters to follow, the reader will note the emphasis which has been placed upon the importance of listening.

A course in oral communication training, however, must do more than disseminate a body of subject matter about the skills of listening and speaking. The student must be able to demonstrate in guided practice what he has learned. Through methods of scoring and grading the teacher must be able to point out weaknesses and strengths in these student demonstrations. Each student performance is really a test of progress and he needs the help of his instructor and classmates as a guide to improvement. To help in evaluation and criticism of performance, the authors have provided sample criticism blanks for individualized use.

Since ours is a serious world for the most part, the argument is sound which says that serious subject matter, on the whole, should engage the attention of the speakers and listeners in their oral communication training. Immediately following the exercises for gaining experience in various types of speech performance, the authors have provided lists of topics on several "eternal" problems. Even though these specific subjects are not used by a class, it is to be hoped that other serious problems will be chosen as the general subject matter for the training performances.

The authors wish to acknowledge their indebtedness to colleagues Russell Barton, Wayne Minnick, Harold Ostvold, Gregg Phifer, and Elizabeth Thomson. Ideas of theirs have influenced many sections of this book.

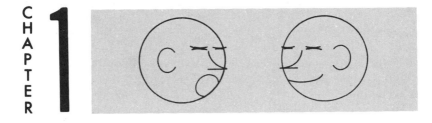

# Speaking and Listening . . .

# . . . the educational system

## Part A: Subject Matter and the Curriculum

With the exception of the presently favored natural and physical sciences, every elementary, secondary and collegiate course discipline is under constant pressure to state its case and show why it should continue to be a part of the total curriculum. If it cannot do this job well, it may not disappear completely but it will certainly fail to expand and grow to the same extent that the safely established disciplines will grow and develop. This is as it should be. There are so many things for a student to learn in this twentieth century that a reshuffling of course disciplines must always be taking place and the subject fields of the communicative arts are no exception. Those who are most closely associated with the training programs in speaking, writing, listening, and reading skills are the ones to state the case for these programs to the curriculum builders.

**The Communicative Arts**

The communicative arts will be a prominent part of the various curriculums in direct relation to the generally acknowledged importance of communication in man's development in his changing environment. Mathematics, another communicative skill although frequently thought of as a science, is an example of a course discipline which has already achieved a prominent place in every school program from the elementary level through graduate school. It should be in that important position. Without the communicative skill in mathematics, the physical sciences could not exist and the natural sciences would be seriously hampered. Anyone who attempts the study of physics or chemistry realizes quickly the need of mathematics through calculus. Even successful business management lies more in the realm of the computer equation than in what was once termed "business acumen." Do the expressive skills of speaking and writing, and the receptive skills of reading and listening hold the same high position as the skills of mathematics? In terms of most curriculums, they do not.

**Lag in Language Arts**

There are three outstanding reasons why the language arts skills lag behind the mathematical skills in curricular importance. The first lies in an accepted, if not expressed, assumption that the language arts skills can be obtained with a minimum amount of training. Reading training is largely completed during the elementary school program and writing training gets meager attention in elementary and secondary schools because of the adverse pupil-teacher ratio for the effort needed for proper instruction, and a one- or two-semester writing program in college usually completes the training. This amount of learning time might be sufficient under ideal conditions involving highly qualified and inspired teachers and a class load maximum of 15 to 18 students.

The second reason lies in the operational acceptance of a worse assumption that in the natural course of maturation the language art skills will develop without specific training. Speech training, for example, gets little attention in the elementary schools, training for the talented few in secondary schools, and still less attention for most students at the college level. Today, many college administrators take the position that incoming students who have deficiencies in the language arts skills merely demonstrate that they are not ready for college programs. If the reference is to the oral communication skills, then many indeed are not ready for their college careers. But the fault is not that of the student. Most of them have had no formal training in the principles of oral communication and very little in the way of unguided practice. All who have studied seriously the principles of speaking and listening know only too well that incidental learning will not do the job.

The third reason lies in the false but frequently held assumption that the language arts skills are not very amenable to training. Listening training has no doubt been long delayed because of this assumption, and, as a consequence, only now has begun to appear frequently in the programs at the elementary, secondary, or college level.

It should be pointed out that the last decade has shown a re-awakening of the educational world to the importance of language-arts instruction. The need to repair a real gap in the educational processes was emphasized in the 1953 publication of the National Council of Teachers of English, *The English Language Arts*. With improvement in the techniques of instruction, the attention to these programs will undoubtedly increase. Students in elementary and secondary schools as well as colleges will benefit from this new emphasis.

# Part B: Speech in the Curriculum

No thinking individual would deny the importance of speaking ability in the development of man to his fullest potentialities. This function of thought through language, transmission of ideas to others through language, and cooperation of others through language is one power that sets off man from the remainder of the animal kingdom. We might go further to say that it is in the differentiation of language ability, as much as anything else, that one human being is distinguished from another. This importance of the development in language skills is widely recognized. Apparently nearly everyone has imagined himself on many occasions in a performance in which he is the central figure as he holds the attention of others with his powers of speech. With this general acceptance of speaking ability as a skill in thinking, communication, and social control, why is it that speech as a course subject has occupied such a minimal place in the curriculum hierarchy?

**Natural Gift?**

It would appear that a primary reason lies in the unestablished but generally accepted idea that skill in speaking is largely a matter of innate ability. This assumption is often expressed in such statements as "He is a born speaker," or "Speaking comes to him quite naturally." And yet, anyone able to demonstrate proficiency in speaking would deny this assumption categorically. These individuals know best the effort that has gone into their training; they also know best that good speakers are made and not born. The ones most ready to accept and promote the idea of innate ability are those who never have had speaking and listening training.

## Is Training Necessary?

A less widely accepted generalization, but nevertheless important reason for the lag in providing speech courses for the curriculum, is that if anyone has anything important to say, he will be able to talk about it effectively. This is another way of saying that the art of speaking lies only in having something important to say. Nothing could be further from the truth and nothing more easily refuted. Many individuals with good minds and important thoughts fail to achieve recognition of their abilities because they are unable to operate effectively in the speaking opportunities which would, if handled properly, give them the recognition they deserve.

The ability to express one's self is certainly something more than the matter of having important ideas to talk about. Effective speaking is the expression of important thoughts to others in a fashion interesting enough to insure their reception. The factors of interestingness include selection of language, use of voice, and control of bodily action, all of which grow out of guided training and practice. Unless we are able to convince the important figures in the schools and colleges of the necessity of these training courses for the development of speech skills, our educational system will continue to produce individuals who cannot express their thoughts effectively.

Thousands of individuals who have gone though our schools come to the realization of this weakness in their training. Their abilities in the oral situations which they have to face simply do not meet the needs of those occasions. That is why we have Toastmaster's clubs all over the nation and why so many private speech training organizations have maintained a flourishing business. These adults are trying desperately to secure the training which they failed to get in the elementary, secondary, and college programs.

## Error in Emphasis

Upon careful reflection it would appear that another very unfortunate development has occurred in the educational patterns of this country which has retarded the development of speech as a serious discipline. Speech activities became associated with the extracurricular programs attached to educational training, and soon were identified in the minds of the public as "contests" or "public performances." In a similar way the physical education activities became associated with its by-products. Both disciplines are struggling to recover from this initial setback.

**Contests and Entertainment**

In the little red school house, speech activities were largely for entertainment. Reciting and declaiming were things to do on Friday afternoon after the last recess. These exercises grew easily into county contests in oratory and declamation. With the development of secondary schools, these contest activities became full-blown as they became county, state, regional and even national in breadth. In both elementary and secondary schools the dramatic activities became a source of funds, a way to get extra money for items not supported by school budgets. Even in college programs, speech activities have gone the same route with the emphasis on winning contests and making money through public performances. Under such a system it was almost inevitable that the activity, whatever it was, became the end. Winning contests or making money became the goal rather than the development of expressional skills for all the youth. The number of students participating in these speech activities became a small fraction of the total student body. The result has been that speech has failed to become an integral part of the educational plan even though it deserves a top priority in curricular importance.

**New Emphasis**

Recent developments, however, seem to indicate a realization of the importance of aural-oral communication. Our world is relying more and more on the spoken word and the demand for educational emphasis is spreading rapidly at all school levels. Schools of business are asking for courses in speaking and listening for all their students. Schools of education are beginning to require of all prospective teachers a specified competence in speaking and listening skills. Many departments in the colleges of arts and sciences are encouraging their majors to take certain speech courses.

This new emphasis is an encouraging movement to teachers of speech everywhere. It appears the time is at hand when speech and listening training is to be considered an important area of study throughout the educational system. Perhaps aural-oral communication is assuming a new place which will provide a training experience for all students, not just a training for the very talented or the very handicapped.

# Part C: Listening in the Curriculum

At the outset of a discussion of listening training in the curriculum, it seems desirable to determine just what is meant by the term listening. In a sense it is a combination of what we hear, what we understand, and what we remember. Obviously hearing and listening are not identical. They are most clearly conceived as two distinguishable phases, the hearing of sound and the interpreting of sound, of a total process usually called aural assimilation. If the first phrase, hearing, is identified as the perception of sound only, then it is the second phase of the process — the attachment of meaning to the aural symbols perceived — which has come to be widely accepted as the definition of listening.

This definition will serve our needs well enough if three qualifications are understood: (a) since much listening is done in intervals of quiet, and since silence frequently carries meaning, silence itself must be accepted as an aural symbol; (b) since the assimilation of meaning sometimes starts before a speaker says a word, and since it very frequently continues long after he has said his final one, listening is not necessarily limited to the immediate speaking situation; and (c) although meaning may be attached to aural symbols with or without the presence of visual ones, listening as a medium of learning usually implies the presence of speakers in person, in "live" situations in which visual and aural cues complement each other in the mode of presentation.

**Listening Training**

Listening and reading, the two media through which most of us do almost all of our learning, are in many ways parallel skills, and they are definitely related skills, Despite their similarity, it is a mistake to assume that improvement in one will automatically assure corresponding improvement in the other.

Training in visual reception of language symbols simply does not result in a significant carry-over to aural reception. Perhaps similarities in these skills are outweighed by some very marked differences. Certainly it is true that the receptive mechanisms are distinctly different. Listening is the assimilation of aural plus visual cues, reading the assimilation of visual cues alone. Moreover, listening is usually a group activity; reading usually an individualized one. Finally, listening demands considerable adjustment to a pace set by the speaker; reading only an adjustment to the pace desired by the reader.

Today there is a real awakening in education to the importance of listening, that is, to the importance of learning through listening. In every state in the Union, people in the business of education are recognizing that the real function of listening is to learn; that the all-important, central contribution to be made to individual growth and development is that of making learning easier, more pleasant and more economic.

**Integrated Approach**

The best approach to classroom training in listening appears to be through a coordination of listening and speech instruction. In schools where no immediate opportunity exists to institute a course labeled "listening," the next best alternative has frequently seemed to be the dovetailing of listening assignments into routines already established in speech classes. There are many desirable aspects to this method. Many instructors are finding it so productive and contributory that they refuse ever to give a speech-making assignment without an accompanying listening assignment designed to develop one or more of the underlying skills inherent in effective aural assimilation. This will be the method in the assignments for this course.

Effective listening and effective speaking are so closely woven together as to be inseparable. When we spot the best speakers in a class, we have at the same time spotted those who are most successfully improving their speech by listening attentively to their mates.

In view of the widespread significance accorded to listening comprehension today, it is difficult to understand why training programs have been so long in forthcoming. The answers seems to be that four unfounded — but widely held — assumptions have been largely responsible. Those four assumptions, and some of the evidence now suggesting how badly we have been misled by them, are well worth our consideration.

**Listening and Intelligence**

False assumption number one is that listening is largely a matter of intelligence. There is, of course, a positive correlation between listening ability and intelligence. For that matter, our intelligence to a degree limits and controls what we do or think. But the relationship between these two attributes is not nearly as close as many have assumed. For generations it has been widely accepted that listening ability and intelligence are almost identical commodities. How many times, for instance, have we heard something like this? "He's so stupid! You can tell him and tell him. He still won't get it." While it is true that we do in a sense "listen with our intelligence," it is even truer that we "listen with our experience." How well we listen with our experience is largely determined by our application of definite and specific skills in receiving material and evaluating it in terms of our experience.

**Listening and Hearing**

The second assumption is that listening ability is closely related to hearing acuity. A rather vaguely held notion that hearing acuity significantly controls listening ability has undoubtedly played a part in retarding educational development in this area. What could be done except send the defective to an otologist? That this assumption is unfounded is evident when one discovers that only from three percent to six percent of the nation's school population suffers from hearing defects severe enough to impair learning in a classroom situation.

**Guided Training**

The third assumption, perhaps even more vital than the first two in the failure to develop listening in the curriculum, is that daily practice eliminates the need for training. The feeling that we all get enough practice in listening outside the school room and need no formal training inside it has retarded progress in developing listening courses. The truth is that unless we are carefully guided we apparently tend to practice, develop, and reinforce assimilative faults rather than skills.

**Reading Training vs. Listening Training**

Finally, some few believe that learning to read is more important than learning to listen. The rather vague impression that human behavior is more influenced by what is read than by what is heard may well be the most significant of the four assumptions which in past years have combined to retard listening training. It now begins to appear as unfounded and false as the other three. Not only do we listen three times as much as we read, but the former may also have more influence upon human behavior.

| **The New Emphasis** |

It seems probable that in the years ahead the significance of listening comprehension will increase as our knowledge about this medium of learning — its significance and its economy — develops. Certain comparative facts about the eye and the ear serve to increase our respect for the latter organ. It is important to know that assimilation through the ear is multidirectional while that through the eye must be focused; that the ear is more sensitive than the eye, requiring a smaller amount of energy for activation; that reaction time for sound is faster than for light; and that the ear appears to be much more durable than the eye, with a much greater capacity for continuous use.

At this time the best judgment that we can make of the four foregoing assumptions is that they not only are unfounded, but also are essentially false. As their falsity becomes more widely recognized, more and more training programs to refine listening comprehension are certain to appear. Fortunately, professional literature is today supplying abundant reports of research leading to the conviction that other factors than intelligence influence listening performance; that most of these factors far outweigh hearing acuity; that this assimilative skill can be taught; that to be taught well it must be taught directly; and that in the years ahead it seems certain that we shall be influenced even more by the things we hear than by the things we read.

# CHAPTER 2

## Speaking and Listening . . .

# . . . the communication process

## Part A: Development of the Oral and Aural Skills

In its broadest concept, interpersonal communication is the sharing of ideas and feelings. This transference takes place through a system of symbols which may range all the way from spoken and written words to musical sounds, designs, colors, and motions. The degree of success in a communication act depends upon the agreement between the expressor and receptor of the meaning of the symbols used.

The type of communication used in speaking and writing is called linguistic communication because words are the basic symbols used in these processes. It should be understood, however, that other elements also play an important part in the transference of ideas and feelings. The vocal quality and the physical gestures of the speaker may be as important as the words he uses. The punctuation marks and the visual aids are important to the writer. In developing the oral and aural skills of communication, we must be concerned with improving our use of the nonverbal as well as the verbal elements in both the expressive and the receptive sense. Efficient oral-aural communication demands sight as well as hearing. It has been found that listeners comprehend and retain a significantly greater quantity of information when they can see as well as hear the speaker.

## Need for Communication

The desire to develop these skills of communication is an innate characteristic of man. He is more than a gregarious creature; he is a communicating creature. Expressing himself and listening to the expressions of others is one of his greatest needs. Ideas which arise within his mind must be brought outside so others can know what he is thinking about, what his wishes are, and how he is reacting to what he senses. He starts on his progress towards this accomplishment at an early age and he ordinarily progresses in his development as he matures in years. For his communicating needs, he has developed this refined set of sound symbols which, when combined in certain set patterns, carry meanings, and as he grows in intellectual development, his use of the symbol system becomes complex and more encompassing. If this growth in language power is halted, there man's progress stops and his full contribution to society is never realized.

## Language and Social Control

So, for all of us, speech enables us to play our roles as men and women. We begin these roles in early childhood and continue on as adolescents, lovers, parents, and citizens of community and state. In all these roles oral language is the primary social instrument which enables us to play our parts to the limit of our abilities. Our progress in language use must be one of continuous growth in expression and reception skill if we are to function adequately in our human relationships. The simple language techniques of childhood will not meet the needs of the mature individual of a democratic society.

## Speech Needs

It is at the college level that we should determine what place we expect to hold in society and to develop our communication needs for that position we wish to achieve. It is true that we have been talking and listening all our lives and have become quite skilled in certain elements of language usage.

We have become reasonably versatile in many of the aspects of simple conversation; we are able to meet friends easily and to introduce one individual to another; we are able to make polite conversation at mealtime or when we meet an acquaintance; and we are able to ask questions and to answer questions asked of us. However, in stating a case and proving it, we aren't quite so adept.

| Listening Needs |
| --- |

We have become reasonably skilled in the simple listening situations of everyday life. We have developed a certain amount of listening *ability* for those occasions when we know we will be tested in some way on the results of our skill. In listening *performance,* when no immediate testing is foreseen, we are not nearly so adept. And yet it is exactly in the latter type of listening that so much of our ultimate development as a mature individual depends.

It is to the continuation of our development in expression and reception skills that this course in speaking and listening experiences is directed. To have a thought about a serious subject is only the first step. We must be able and willing to put our ideas up for review and criticism. To fail to have ideas is irresponsible; but the failure to express them is cowardly. We must also be willing and able to listen to the ideas of others so that we can advance our own learning and can compare our thoughts with those of others.

The student who learns to speak with a purpose, clearly and interestingly, to properly structuralize his ideas, and to adapt his ideas and materials to his audience is better prepared to become an intelligent, effective citizen able to accept the common responsibility of living in a free society. The student who has learned to discern the purpose of the speaker, his organization of ideas, and his use of developmental materials is likewise better prepared to resist double talk and meaningless generalization and to acquire new information.

# Part B: The Speaker's Role

The speaker's role varies from the informal conversation with an intimate acquaintance to the highly formal public speech with a large audience. There are the in-between performances of directed conversations, set public discussions, and somewhat informal public speeches to small audiences. For the purpose of simplification we will discuss these situations in which a speaker may find himself in the roles of conversationalist, discussant and public speaker. Public speaking is the situation in which most persons find themselves least often and the situation which requires the most skill. Conversation is the most common situation and the one where we operate with the least pressure because little is demanded of us in that role. In spite of this lack of pressure for effective performance, it is a very important situation for us on many occasions. The skills required for effective discussion are less restrictive than those required of the public speaker but more restrictive than those required for good conversation. We will consider each of these roles in turn in the order of their frequency of use.

## Importance of Conversation Skills

A few years ago, a research student in speech asked of several thousand persons, "What language skills does the public want and most need?" The ability to carry on an interesting, worthwhile conversation was the answer most frequently given. That answer was indeed a sensible one. Most of our speaking will occur in this form. Our conversations must be hundreds of times as voluminous as our formal speeches.

Our social integration with our fellows demands almost constant use of "talk" in one form or another; social situations, business interviews, discussions, communications in work and play all involve conversational skill which many of us need to improve. It is in such talking that the skills of listening and speaking are brought into rapid interplay as in no other type of oral communication. A sense of timing, when to speak and when to listen, becomes an invaluable asset to the good conversationalist. The larger the group participating, the more difficult the process becomes.

## The Social Need

Wherever two persons meet there is this normal exchange of talking and listening. We converse with our fellow man to entertain and be entertained, to express friendliness, to share experiences and ideas, and to influence or determine attitudes and actions. Although the chief earmark of colloquy is its spontaneity and informality, it requires at the same time both the thoughtful and effective statement of ideas. It has been called a way of living with other persons, a means of social control. Specifically, it is a spontaneous utterance of thought apparently coming to the mind for the first time, as when ideas are expressed to a friend. With such spontaneous utterance the listener becomes as absorbed and takes as much part as the speaker. Listening to conversation is an equally important skill.

Perhaps the most satisfying conversations occur among relatively small groups of persons who are interested for the moment in the same subject or subjects. On these occasions the successful participants use the same resources, the same speaking and listening skills, which they employ in any oral situation. The nature of the subject, the number of persons present, and the surroundings guide the converser in rate of speech, loudness of voice, and placement of emphasis. To increase the meaningfulness, the speaker uses facial expression, vocal inflections, gestures and other body movements which are appropriate to the ideas being expressed.

| **Ability in Conversation Not Accidental** |
| --- |

The ability to carry on an interesting, worthwhile conversation can be acquired and is a skill most definitely needed. How many would-be salesmen have failed because they lacked the ability to converse intelligently and interestingly with their prospective customers? How many interviews have fallen flat because the interviewer was unable to catch clues for conversational development from the interviewee's answers to set questions? How many jobs have been lost because the candidate for the position became tongue-tied when confronted by his prospective employer? How many individuals have been classed as socially maladjusted because they could not converse effectively? The purpose of this unit is to consider some principles that will help us carry on effective conversation. Although class exercises will be confined to selected subject matter, some of the qualities we will acquire can be carried over into life situations.

We may have no extensive opportunity to participate in speaking in public during our lives, but whether we wish it or not, we must communicate with our fellows on a conversational level day in and day out. Consequently, we ought to be able to say the effective thing at the proper time in a gracious way. We know from experience that we learn most readily and become most vitally interested and active through conference relationships. Within a group, opinions are exchanged and we often have our eyes opened to entirely new aspects of a question. Perhaps we change our opinions; perhaps we are content with our original views; but the influence of the exchange of opinion on the group as a whole is immeasurable. We should not avoid these opportunities of social intercourse; we must learn how to meet them. Since true conversation occurs in unplanned situations only, classroom practice must be through participation in discussion exercises.

---

**Skills of Conversation Undergird All Speech**

Most important of all, we should study and exercise good conversational practices as the undergirding force for successful speaking and listening in the formal situation. What we do in such communication situations will either reinforce or undercut the specific elements of our speech training. As someone has wisely said "practice does not make perfect; perfect practice makes perfect." If we are careless in speech habits as we talk informally with others, we cannot expect to display good speech skills on the special occasions. Here is our best and almost only opportunity for frequent practice of effective speaking and listening skills.

Conversations are of either a social nature or a business nature. Every such discourse serves some useful purpose. The light and trivial chat relaxes us. Other types help develop opinions and points of view on many questions of varied importance. Some are arranged specifically to complete a business transaction.

Many of the best of these informal chats are indulged in primarily for mental and spiritual fellowship. We talk to other people to help ourselves adjust to various social situations and to help others adjust themselves to us. Through this social adjustment we live together harmoniously for minutes or hours, as the case may be. Have we not often begun a conversation with a chance acquaintance, say on the bus, train, streetcar, just to make the time pass more pleasantly? Pleasure, social adjustment, mental and spiritual companionship — these are the objectives of social conversation.

---

**Information in Conversations**

Many people think themselves qualified to discuss any subject without taking the trouble to become informed about it. The informality of conversation is no excuse for lack of information. Pooling common ignorance through group discourse will not produce enlightenment on the subject being discussed; information and thought on a question are prerequisites to rational discussion. Hence it is imperative that intelligent people keep themselves informed about questions likely to arise through day-to-day observation of their immediate worlds, listening to lectures, radio and television, and reading current publications, particularly newspapers, and magazines. Such activities must be directed towards true learning situations. Poor choice of radio and television programs or printed material produces waste of effort.

**The Sales Situation**

Verbal interplay takes other forms than that which arises spontaneously from chance meetings and social occasions. Light discourses are used in business as well as social situations. The simplest form of such dialogue might be in the nature of inquiry. If we want to know about the quality of a piece of wearing apparel or the features of a new lawn mower, we expect the salesgirl or salesman to know enough about the fabric or the machine to give us correct information. A more complex element in a business situation might hinge on such a subject as the open-end mortgage or term life insurance. Whether we seek to give or to obtain information, we must know something about the area under discussion in order to speak intelligently.

**The Interview and Conference**

One of the most common forms of business discourse is the interview. Here, usually by prearrangement, two persons come together, one to receive and the other to give information or opinion or both on some definite topic. While the purpose of an interview is usually the exchange of information or opinion, it may well be that the interview may have a persuasive end, such as would be the case if we were interviewing someone to obtain either a position or a special privilege. Another type of parley common to the business world occurs in the conference room. A business of any size at all requires frequent meetings between management personnel and between management and labor. These meetings usually involve the conversation method (unorganized discussion) for the interplay of ideas.

Not all people are good conversationalists, but conscious efforts to improve such discourse have been neglected. As with listening, it is probably assumed that since we are all so familiar with such informal discourse there is no real need for specific training in it. Many prominent schools, however, have denied this assumption and have added a rather extensive unit in conversation to their courses in communication. It is difficult to prescribe a formula for the preparation or conduct of good conversation, but there are a few principles we might observe that will help us improve. Some of these skills may be practiced through our use of free discussion exercises in the classroom. Probably the better method will be to practice the skills in real conversations in outside the classroom situations.

**Good Ideas in Direct Language**

In the first place, we must have ideas to exchange. We can't talk if we haven't anything to talk about. Then what we have to say must be worth saying; our contribution should always be stimulating. Finally, our manner of speaking should invite the exchange of ideas. Our language should be that of good idiomatic expression. This does not mean that we are to indulge in sloppy expressions and poor grammar. Our language should be simple, direct, and to the point.

We can improve our own participation by analyzing conversations we hear, increasing our discussion resources, and taking advantage of practicing in every opportunity we have. We must be alert, interested in others, good listeners, interesting, sincere and straightforward. When we are talking, we should observe the reaction to what we are saying, sense the willingness of the group to continue on the subject, and by all means observe the desire of others to speak. The courteous conversationalist respects the ideas and privileges of his companions. Lacking an appointed leader, such discourse depends on the good social instincts of all who engage in it. Some specific things we can avoid; some we can cultivate in our attempts to improve our conversational ability.

*Talk Must Contribute Ideas*

We should certainly avoid glibness. Being able to talk glibly will not make us good conversationalists. Do not let it be said of us, "He talks a lot but he never says much." Everything we say should promote mutual understanding and satisfaction. The only desirable contribution is that which makes all participants comfortable together. Very uncomfortable situations arise when one or more of the participants make flat contradictions of statements made by others. Even though evidence available would support the contradiction, these dissenting statements should be offered in good taste. Too direct refutation antagonizes everyone and particularly the person being chastized.

We should never engage in gossip. Social discourse is no place for strife or bitterness, or unkind gossip, or for sharp and biting comments. We should in general avoid criticism of anything that will hurt the listener. Unkind remarks about others, whether present or not, whether true or not, are evidence of bad social taste and of a mean spirit as well.

*Avoid Monopoly*

We should not do all the talking. One of the most common social errors is monopolizing conversation. The individual who cannot bear to remain silent while others talk, who fidgets uneasily as he waits his turn to say something, who is anxious to show his own information and erudition, and who obviously cares more about himself and his own interests than he does for others and their problems can scarcely be expected to be appreciated in any company. Josh Billings once said, "A man is a bore when he talks so much about himself that you can't talk about yourself."

*Cultivate Good Humor*

There are several things we can train ourselves to do in conversation. We should cultivate humor. Humor is a most useful and pleasant element of social discourse. However, if we can't tell a joke well, and many cannot, we must be content to enjoy the jokes of others. Much of the best humor is not in the form of jokes or stories; it is in the turn of a phrase or wording of a sentence. All humor should be kindly, not biting; it should be not achieved at the expense of someone else. People do not always appreciate what they laugh at.

*Keep Up To Date*

At most social functions the conversations will move in many directions. As we move from group to group we find ourselves faced with abrupt changes in the drift of ideas being discussed. There is no way to be fully prepared for these various situations; in some, our part will be played primarily as a listener. However, if we are fully acquainted with local and world affairs by regular reading of at least one good newspaper and several news magazines, we will not feel uninformed. If we can be expert in several items of current interest, we will be able to participate better as both speaker and listener.

*Be Friendly and Concerned*

We should have a friendly attitude. We must create a genuine liking for people and an interest in them if we would converse well. We should be ready to respond to them, to share with them our wishes, desires, opinions, ideas. More than half of good conversation is good listening. By our manner, our facial expression, our interpolation of an occasional word judiciously designed to draw out reaction from others, and our evidence of sympathetic concern and understanding, we become a desirable partner in these social relationships.

If we wish to succeed in such informal communication, we must be sincere, consider and talk about the interests of others, give others a chance to talk, use our best action, voice, and language, analyze conversation habits — our own and those of others, and practice diligently and intelligently with a will to improve.

## The Speaker's Role in Discussion

The second most active role of the speaker involves some form of public discussion. Discussion differs from conversation in that it is a planned situation. Groups gather with a definite purpose of talking about a topic of common interest. Their ultimate purpose may be to reach a decision regarding a course of action or the solution of a problem. Conversations are made up of many pieces of discussion woven into a pattern that befits the moods and minds of the performers. The average conversation has frequent changes of topic in a highly unorganized manner of selection. When system and preparation become a planned part of group participation, we have advanced to discussion.

## Free Discussion Versus Public Discussion

Discussion as a type of speech situation ranges from the highly informal activity called free discussion to the highly formalized activity known as public discussion. Most of the discussion in which men and women engage will be that of free discussion. In most high school and college classes this method is used to some extent. In college classes particularly, it is used to implement the lecture sections where the sheer numbers in the class prohibit discussion during the regular class period.

When the groups become too large for all to participate freely, some type of public discussion has to be adopted. Such public discussions may take the form of a panel of active participants who carry on a conversation about a specified topic. On other occasions a symposium of speakers on divisions of a specific topic will be used to open up the issues involved. In some cases, as with the forum method, one speaker stimulates the audience with a set speech. The last method is always followed by an audience participation and the other types of formal discussion frequently allow the audience to participate after the panel or symposium has done its job. No matter which type of public discussion selected for classroom use, careful preparation for the participation is essential for a successful demonstration.

**Panel Discussion**

For classroom work the informal panel method of discussion seems to meet the needs best. From four to six students will be assigned a discussion topic, and the rest of the class will get an opportunity to voice their thinking at the end of a prescribed panel period. Such panels may or may not have a leader assigned for their period of performance. However, a leader, when assigned, will usually keep the discussion moving, direct the course of the discussion, and bring the whole business to a satisfactory conclusion with a summary. Without a leader, the total result is sometimes unsatisfactory.

Such informal group participation is an ideal way to begin classroom exercises for a class in speaking and listening training. The individual is less tense when he performs in a group than when he carries the whole responsibility for the total performance as in a public speech. Moreover, the use of the discussion method tends to unify the class and mold it into a closely knit learning unit. Skills developed in discussion exercises transfer nicely to everyday conversation situations.

**Speech Skills in Discussion**

The use of the discussion method in a speech and listening course is important for a very sound reason over and above the content material considered. Our speech faults tend to show up more vividly because we are less in the spotlight and so tend to grow careless. We should try to be as fluent in this situation as in any other and our words and sentences should be carefully selected for the expression of our ideas. We should speak out clearly without mumbling the sounds and we should be intense in our desire to communicate. As listeners we must keep our minds upon what others are saying and give deep consideration to the ideas presented by others in the group. By their words, discussants sometimes reveal that they have not heard all that has gone on but have been off in reveries of their own choosing.

Those who participate in discussion must remember that their purpose is to consider a topic or problem for exploration and understanding. It becomes a mutual effort not only to explore but to share these explorations so that all will understand and know the topic. Moreover, those who engage in this group effort should realize that they are not trying to get acceptance of a personal point of view. However, they have every right to present for consideration any and all points of view.

The success of the informal group discussion method will depend considerably upon the topics selected by the panels. Each group should spend enough time on this aspect of the preparation to be sure that all members of the panel have an interest in the suggested topic, some foundation knowledge about the topic, and a real desire to present materials about the subject to the rest of the class. In addition the purpose of the discussion must be determined. Is it the purpose to exchange ideas on the topic so that greater understanding will result? Is it to determine the best solution to a problem? Probably most classroom discussions should take the first purpose as a goal rather than the second. This determination can best be made after the topic has been selected. Topics for classroom discussion will come from three general areas: the college campus, the current interests of our people, and life's eternal problems.

**Preparation for Discussion**

Once the topic has been selected and the purpose of the discussion determined, each member of the panel is on his own resources in preparation for the coming class exercise. He should read about the subject and he should converse with others about it. In this preparation he will find out several things. First, he will acquire a body of knowledge for himself; second, he will find out what others know about the topic as well as what they would like to know — what their questions are. Both of these things prepare him for the classroom presentation.

The effective participation by each member of the panel will depend upon the same general patterns of action described for the effective conversationalist. Each must be sure that all important information is presented, that he remains objective and unemotional about his own beliefs as well as the beliefs of others, and that he stays on the subject and does not monopolize the time. Above all, he must listen effectively while others are presenting information or points of view.

**The Speaker's Role in Public Speaking**

The role of the speaker in which he finds himself least often but the role which requires by far the most skill is that of the public speaker. All speech roles are public in a sense but the term public speaking has come to be applied to the situation in which the single speaker faces an audience of few or many to express ideas which have been thought through carefully, organized with a specific plan in mind, and rehearsed for final oral delivery.

The role is an easy one to describe but a difficult one to carry out effectively. It is a role to which most of our effort and attention in practice needs to be given. For, if we can learn this most difficult of the speaker's roles, we will be prepared to handle the more common roles of conversation and discussion in a satisfactory fashion. Except for the last chapter in this book, each succeeding chapter will have some material devoted to an element of effective communication through public speaking.

**Common Elements in All Speaking**

It should be pointed out now, however, that the best elements of conversation and discussion are also important elements of good public speaking. These have to be dignified, energized, and amplified for the formality and spaciousness of the public speaking situation but they must not be lost in the transformation. If the public speaker wishes to be effective, he must show the same sincerity, ease of performance and desire to communicate as is demonstrated by the effective conversationalist or discusser.

**Sincerity — the Desire to Communicate**

Let us consider the element of sincerity as an example. We cannot fool our audiences on this element. True convictions and the desire to communicate them are revealed by the speaker in many ways. He speaks in a conversational manner of bodily action and vocal change. He is burning up energy at an enormous rate as he tries to make the listener understand. The sincere speaker is direct in language and manner — he is alert and he looks the listener in the eye.

The informality spoken of here does not mean casualness on the part of the speaker. The sincere speaker could not sit on a desk and make a speech — he has to be on his feet and he communicates with his hands, body, head, and eyes as well as with his words.

What is the significance of this desire to communicate? It is the difference between something worthwhile and something unimportant. The conviction of the speaker is important to him by definition. He makes it seem so to the audience by the powerful way in which he unfolds his ideas on the topic being considered. The listener listens to this dedicated speaker because he cannot very well do otherwise.

## Part C: The Listener's Role

Loosely speaking, listening can be said to be of three types, with each serving a different end: (a) appreciative listening to any kind of stimuli gratifying to the senses of the hearer; (b) critical listening to persuasive speech for the purpose of evaluating the speaker's argument and evidence; (c) discriminative listening to informative speech (usually in an instructional situation) for the purpose of comprehension — and perhaps later utilization — of the ideas and information of the speaker.

Most of us will hear during our lifetime many times as many speeches as we will deliver. We will hear twenty to thirty in our speech class for every one we give ourselves. We need to discover how this differential can be turned to our advantage in the development of our communicating skills.

**Importance of the Listener**

The most important single psychological principle underlying all speech instruction is that of the "circuit response." The essence of the concept is that communication is always a two-way affair. The listener is always of equal importance to the speaker and makes an equally significant contribution to the successful sharing of material. Whatever a speaker says to an audience should cause some reaction in that audience. The change may be facial or more broadly physical. But in any case, if the speaker is studying his auditors as he talks, as he always should be, the visible change will immediately stimulate or depress him. Thus, the listeners always and immediately exert a tremendous influence upon the speaker. They increase or decrease his effectiveness. If each of us wants sympathetic and helpful audience response when we speak, we must always be willing to provide such response when the other chap is up front.

**Good Listeners Get Paid**

This kind of effort may at first thought seem extremely altruistic. Actually, it is as self-centered as it is generous. It is true that when a listener is animated, cooperative, and responsive, the first dividend is paid to the speaker who is stimulated by this contribution. But when the speaker, so encouraged, proceeds to communicate with improved effect, the listener immediately receives three dividends.

In the first place, he receives a more stimulating and meaningful message, with a chance for a fuller and more complete comprehension of it. Second, he gains the rewarding opportunity to analyze more completely and carefully the strengths and weaknesses of the presentation. Speech instructors know the value of getting students to observe closely any skill or fault of immediate concern. Often instructors will come to the front of the room and demonstrate the technique under consideration, not to "show off" but to convey their point in the shortest possible unit of time. Every such demonstration is evidence of the economy of improving our own speech by careful observation of the methods used by others. The vast majority of such demonstrations will be those of our classmates, of course, not those of our instructors. Third, he is rewarded for his obvious receptivity by an enlarged circle of friends. His whole personality may benefit from the process.

None of the foregoing implies that by helping the speaker do his best work the listener is committing himself in any way to accept the speaker's thesis or to vote for his proposition. The central purpose of responsive listening is to make as accurate as possible the eventual evaluation we shall want to make of the material presented. By helping the speaker to improve his proficiency, we help ourselves to improved comprehension of his message and our assessment of it.

**Interest and Listening**

All objective studies of listening ability point out the tremendous significance of the interest factor in aural assimilation. They reveal that good listeners seem to find interesting elements in almost any or all topics for discussion, and that poor listeners frequently find a topic "dry." Persons truly interested in the content of a presentation concentrate their attention very well and learn efficiently enough through listening. The central question becomes, of course, "What can we do when we are not interested? If a topic is boring, how can it be made less so?"

The fact is that every subject is interesting from certain points of view. The learner will discover the interesting aspects most rapidly and surely if he proceeds on a completely selfish basis. Whenever he is tempted to condemn the dryness of a presentation, he would do well to ask himself at once "Why am I here? What initial motive led me to get involved in this situation? Is that motive now dead, or does it still exist?" Then let him answer these queries soberly and honestly. The chances are that he came for selfish reasons, and justifiably on that basis, too. Honest introspection usually results in the realization that his initial motive still has foundation. Things are usually being said that he can use some way, somehow, at some time.

## Can We Afford Not to Listen?

In order that his self-analysis be complete, and his amplification of motive strengthened, let every learner consider carefully three pleas for selfish (interested) listening.

### Increased Knowledge

It is the easiest way to acquire needed information. Even if listening is hard — and well it may prove to be — it is still the easiest way yet found to learn most of the things we shall need to know in our lifetimes. The lecturer has probably spent several weeks in reading, studying, assembling, screening, and organizing the digest of his studies which he presents for our benefit all in one hour! He will use words new to us which we can learn through their contextual setting if we try, and which are invaluable in broadening our vocabularies and enhancing our chances for success in this world.

### Cultural Growth

It is the quickest way to grow culturally. Whether we confess it or not, most of us would like to know that we are growing culturally while we are in school. It is a logical and legitimate wish; and our fastest speed ahead depends on how well we use our ears!

### Social Maturity

Finally, it is the surest route to social maturity. Social growth depends upon our ability to reinforce the good ideas we hold and to screen out and eliminate our illusions and misconceptions. The most certain route is by ear! When one of our own ideas is given verbal expression — perhaps in better language than our tongue supplies — by a man we respect, confidence and strength in our idea is increased. Conversely, attentive listening in social situations helps us to recognize our own social quirks which, if not eliminated, cannot help but embarrass us sooner or later.

Courtesy, tact, acceptable standard of conduct — all can be learned in this way.

Can we afford to condemn a subject as dry and uninteresting? Obviously, we cannot. Effective listening is altogether too closely related to personal success. For selfish and personal reasons alone we need to explore every presentation for uses we can make of it; to assemble for our own use the accumulated knowledge of others. Our interest and proficiency in listening are directly related to how selfishly we "tune" in.

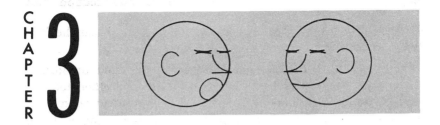

# CHAPTER 3

## Speaking and Listening . . .

## . . . the subject matter

### Part A:  The Purposes of Speaking and Listening

The communication process, depending on the media used, calls upon the cooperation of at least two persons. In written communication the two are writer and reader; in oral communication we have speaker and listener. The two media have similar goals but the tools used to reach the goals differ. In both forms of communication the core of the process involves information — the sending of it and the reception of it.

It would be useless to possess information and not be able to express it to others or to have skill in expression without thoughts worthy of communication. Obviously, then, it is impossible to teach communication without concern for thought processes and substance in subject matter. This text tries to have a real concern for both.

Moreover, the oral process of communication is cyclic, since it involves reciprocal responses from speaker and listener. These two skills are not unrelated, however. The mastery of the skills of speaking tends to improve the skills of listening. The improved skill in listening usually results in improved skill in speaking. This text tries to secure a balance in training for both skills.

The basic purposes of speaking and listening are demonstrated in the active process of communication when two or more individuals are expressing themselves concerning an idea, feeling, or desire. The speaker wishes through this speaking to impart knowledge, to reveal emotion, and to entertain. Through the imparting of knowledge and emotion, he may wish to persuade to a belief or a course of action. The listener, on the other hand, hopes that by listening he will increase his knowledge, understand the revealed emotion, and be entertained. Through the information gained and the reason for the emotion understood, he may accept a belief or decide upon a course of action.

## The Cyclic Process of Giving and Receiving Ideas

Conversation between individuals is an alternating process involving at least one speaker and one listener. In this simple conversation pattern the speaker becomes in turn the listener and the listener in turn the speaker. These exchanges in position as speaker and then as listener occur and reoccur as the process continues. When more than two individuals are carrying on a discussion these interchanges become complicated. Sometimes two or more individuals attempt to take the single speaker's position at the same time.

The very complexity of the oral communication process makes the description of it difficult and somewhat inadequate. We must necessarily describe a continuous process as though it were static. For example, we must recognize that what we say about the purpose of a speaker is not an accurate description of an active process because the purpose will be changing as the feedback from the respondees occurs. By similar logic we cannot describe the purposes of the listener in an active process of communication. Since we must look at the process if we are to describe the purposes of the speaker and the listener at all, let us keep these limitations in mind.

## The Social Purpose

Within the broad basic aim of communication the speaker operates to achieve a social or a serious purpose. If his purpose is social, and we will include here the intent to entertain, he is trying to create a pleasurable response. Conversation in chance meetings on the street or elsewhere are of this nature. Man is a social creature and he doesn't like to remain in silence with his friends and close acquaintances.

He makes talk of one kind or another. This talk may be completely light and frivolous or it may assume the aspects of serious discussion.

**The Serious Purposes**

In serious communications the purposes of the speaker become more defined and identifiable. Although these purposes can never be clearly separated as a speaker progresses on a topic, we can note a distinction between them. The distinction is created when we say a speaker is seeking either to inform or to persuade his listeners. If his purpose is to inform only, his emotional attachment to his topic is subdued and his real concern is that the listeners receive the information he is trying to give. Such a speech will, of course, have elements which entertain.

His purpose in persuasion is to convince his listeners with respect to some belief or to secure an action of some kind. In case this is the purpose of the speaker, there will be considerable emotional attachment displayed by him. He is so anxious that his listeners accept a belief or take an action that he demonstrates by word and action the importance to him of the listener response. This demonstration of feeling is the additional element added to the giving of information. Of course, all persuasive speeches should be based on sound information as well as elements which entertain.

**Social Listening**

In a similar way we can define the purposes of a listener. If he is listening in a social way, he is not too concerned about the material he hears although he has an opportunity to guide this somewhat by what he says when he is the speaker. His satisfaction as a listener in the social situation depends primarily on the degree to which he is entertained by the wit and congeniality of the occasion. Nothing in particular is expected of him as a listener either by the speakers or by himself. His performance in the social situation is judged by his responses when he becomes a speaker rather than by what he does as a listener. Naturally, he is expected to appear alive and alert and enjoying himself rather than sleepy, uninterested, or disgusted.

**Serious Listening**

In the serious listening situation, the listener has at least two distinct purposes in mind. First of all, he is anxious to understand the strong feeling displayed by the speaker. In this understanding he tries to analyze the motives of the speaker and so judge the soundness of those motives.

More fundamentally, however, the listener is trying to reach a belief or course of action, in case an action is prescribed. If we presume that beliefs and courses of action are the result of logical analysis, then we must presume that the listener wishes to receive from the speaker any information which will help in forming beliefs or reaching decisions as to action.

The second distinct purpose of the listener involves a less immediate need. Man is also an intellectual creature; he wants to know about many things. He secures information by reading, by observation, and by listening. He deliberately places himself in listening situations in order to learn. The college classroom becomes a listening post where the student learns by listening to the professor. The public lecture in an auditorium, on radio, or television becomes a source of information about whatever topic is being discussed. The listener in all these situations is interested in increasing his store of knowledge whether he knows of a need for this knowledge or not.

## Selection of Subject Matter By the Speaker

The subject matter employed by the speaker will grow out of the general purpose he has in mind. If his general purpose is entertainment, his specific subject matter will depend upon what he deems would be an acceptable choice for a particular audience and upon his ability to handle the subject in an entertaining fashion. If his general purpose is to give information, his specific subject matter will depend on his assessment of audience interest plus his command of knowledge on the subject contemplated. If his general purpose is persuasion to either belief or action, then his specific subject comes from his strong beliefs or convictions. These convictions must develop from earnest thoughts about important ideas.

We cannot speak or listen with any great concern about trivial matters which have little significance as to whether our society improves or goes backward. In thinking about and studying important ideas, the individual discovers what others have thought about these ideas and what facts lie behind them.

College and university years provide the time and place to form convictions on the important subjects of mankind. This is the one period when we have the time to study such as we will never have again. It is also the time when we have an adequate library of resource materials and listening occasions easily accessible. The foregoing does not mean that the convictions formed during college years will never change. In college we also learn that circumstances alter cases, that new knowledge may affect the foundation on which former convictions rested, and that pure rigidity in opinion has no value.

**Importance of Deep Convictions**

The depth of the convictions we reach depends on three things: (1) We come to deep belief in a particular idea because we feel it is important to mankind; it deals with significant materials which affect large numbers of people. (2) We believe in the idea as a socially, economically, or politically desirable step, an improvement for mankind. (3) We feel a personal reward in giving our support to the conviction. In other words, when we speak up in support of the status quo or for a change, we feel we are saying something important and we feel our message needs to be sounded.

*We Must Speak Up*

Under these conditions, a failure to speak up is bound to cause uneasiness within the individual — an actual loss of self-respect. In such instances nonpartisanship becomes an intolerable situation. In truth, nonpartisanship can come from only two directions: either the individual has *no* conviction or he is cowardly in his approach to others about the truth as he sees it. In the latter position, he speaks for what he knows is popular regardless of his personal belief and he refuses to speak against the unpopular and remains silent. In either case, we see a kind of mental perjury taking place. In these false positions the speaker cannot speak with sincerity — with the "power of conviction." On occasions we see this person let out a lot of emotional steam in order to cloak his lack of conviction, but he doesn't fool anybody. Such insincerity reads like an open book.

A note of caution must be made at this point. Even though an individual has a definite and deep belief about an idea, he doesn't sound off at every opportunity on any and all occasions; he is judicious in giving his support. The time may not be ripe for the expression. The speaker must respect his audience as well as his subject. In so doing, he should bide his time and "say his say" when he can do so with telling effect.

The speaker with the deep conviction is also easy to spot. His voice, his manner, the thoroughness of this thought all carry the weight of deep belief. His eye contact is direct, his gestures are vigorous, his voice is clear and strong. He seems to be concerned about the message he brings. If you were fortunate enough to have heard Charles Laughton read, you realized that no small part of his audience appeal came from the obvious pleasure he got from the material he was reading. In all these things, however, the sincere speaker is humble; never arrogant, never condescending, and his manner never denies his words.

**Classroom Subjects**

Students in speaking and listening courses frequently complain of difficulty in selecting the topic for their speeches. They seem to feel that the classroom is not a real speech situation. This is untrue. The speech topic for the classroom, just as in out-of-classroom situations, must arise from a general subject which is adapted to the speaker, the audience, the occasion, and the time limits available. What was said earlier in this chapter had to do with real life speaking situations but the same information applies to the classroom.

With a little imagination we can make our class assignment a real speech situation with respect to the duties about development of subject matter and in relation to an audience which has assembled to hear our speech just as we would observe them in any audience-speaker-occasion performance.

# Part B: Choosing the Subjects

The selection of the general subject is the starting point for finding the final speech topic. By luck or intuition, we may jump immediately to a suitable speech topic, but the chance of this happening is slight, and certainly we have given ourselves no opportunity to choose and evaluate among the many topics open to us.

**The Subject Materials**

What is a general subject? Any broad area or field constitutes the general subject. Examples of such fields might be education, sports, food, science, family, religion, entertainment, transportation, matrimony, or music. Some of these are broader fields than others but all open up a wide choice of speech topics.

In the back portion of this book will be found a selection of twelve general subjects which might be called some of man's eternal problems. From these general subjects a list of twenty-five topics for speeches has been drawn. These materials were developed for classroom use but only at the discretion of the teacher and students in any specific class. Much better topics may evolve through classroom discussion of the interests of the group.

Certain advantages arise when the whole class uses the same general subjects from which to draw the specific topics for speeches. The biggest advantage lies in the cooperative concern with the same subject area. Reading about and discussing the same general subject create a unity in interest which is highly desirable. A second advantage lies in the depth to which a single problem can be pursued. Many facets of a problem will be opened when twenty to twenty-five speak about it. A final advantage accrues from the possibility of comparison among the efforts extended in pursuit of the subject.

**Topic Suited to the Speaker**

Any topic chosen from a general subject should be one in which we have much interest. We must enjoy reading about it and discussing it with others. It is always good when we have had personal experiences in relation to the topic, but that is not a requirement. Vicarious experience, such as can be secured through reading and reflecting and talking to others, will serve. Certainly the topic must be within the range of our comprehension. Sometimes we try to discuss subjects about which we have too little information. The result can only be humiliating.

*Say Something New*

The topic chosen should allow a development with information beyond that which everybody already knows. The unprepared speaker usually talks about something which is common knowledge. A talk using materials of such general information will never be worthwhile. In fact, it is an almost total waste of time. The speaker may have gained a little practice in speaking but most of the audience will have gained nothing. As listeners in a speech class we have the right to demand of the speaker some real information. He has no right to waste our time! As speakers, we must accept this challenge from the listeners.

If nothing else can be said of our classroom speeches, it ought to be said that they are at least the result of our own creative efforts. In oral reading we deliberately appropriate some other person's words and ideas and attempt to recreate them for others. In speech making we are the creators and, although we may search for material out of which to build, the end production is something which we can call our own.

| Subject Suited to Audience |

Any topic chosen by a speaker should come within the interest range of a large part of the audience. A great deal of that interest will depend upon the material and manner of presentation. Aside from that, the speaker should take the limitations of his audience into consideration. Student speakers sometimes select technical topics outside the range of the audience's experience and background.

The classroom audience, except for the instructor, is made up of college students. Every student is aware of such factors as the approximate age, the proportion of men to women, the common interests, the probable moods, and the prejudices in his particular class. The student speaker has the duty of presenting material which will result in time profitably spent by the audience in the listening process. This does not imply that he must talk upon topics of national or international importance; topics of local interest concerned with the college or university, state, or region can certainly meet the requirements. It does imply a responsibility for people's time. If a classroom performer speaks for four minutes to twenty-five listeners, he has used a hundred minutes of time which should account for something achieved.

| Subjects Arising from An Occasion |

Speech topics may grow out of the occasion also. This is true primarily of real life speaking but true somewhat of the classroom situation too. Some speech topics, such as those at the back of this book, are almost undated in that they seem to go on through the years; some, however, are dated to season or situation. Many topics become alive and important because of local, state or nationwide interest. The newspapers, magazines, radio and television provide us with knowledge of what is being discussed now. Campus activities also dictate topics which are of immediate concern to students and therefore good ones for classroom use.

| Limitation of Subject |

Most speakers are held to a time limit for speeches. In the classroom, we will be held usually to a four or five-minute performance. All speeches should rigidly adhere to the time limits imposed. The simple statement of the central idea therefore must be something which can be adequately covered within the time limit.

# Part C:  Effective Listening

College students frequently indicate that one of the problems which makes school routine difficult is the inability to concentrate. Helpful advice on this problem is scanty and of dubious value. Surprisingly enough, psychological literature is not very helpful in suggesting how we can improve our powers of concentration. No doubt the vagueness of the term accounts for some of the superficiality in its discussion. We usually use the term loosely to mean "sustaining of attention," and believe that this can be done for some minutes at a time. This concept is not that of full and complete focusing of all mental faculties upon a single point; rather it is that of keeping one stimulus source in the forepart of the mind, but not necessarily to the complete exclusion of all others.

**Listening Control**

As a factor in listening efficiency, concentration is best conceived as an intentional isolation of a single sound source from the many aural stimuli besieging the learner. Abundant research has been published to show that most people can give satisfactory attention to a speaker whose discourse is no longer than fifteen to twenty minutes; that less satisfactory attention is given to a speech of thirty minutes' length; and that very poor communication results when the speech runs forty-five minutes or more. It does not follow that listeners cannot train themselves to follow a discourse of forty-five minutes or more. It merely shows that most untrained listeners have not developed the singleness of purpose nor the techniques which will enable them to do so.

It is entirely possible for man to control the direction of his thoughts. Indeed, this is one of his peculiar gifts — perhaps the finest of all he has been given. Many a person, in solitude, at times achieves this control without the help of guidance or previous training. Which one of us has not found himself unable to go to sleep at night because of worries and tensions, and then to have solved his problem by deciding to think of something pleasant until slumber comes? In classroom learning situations few of us, without training, possess the ability to control consistently the direction of our thoughts; but most of us, with training, readily achieve it. The acquirement of no other skill is more appropriately a concern of education, and particularly a course in speaking and listening.

### The Problem and Its Causes

College students may very well be correct in rating inability to concentrate as the greatest obstacle to learning. Certainly, it is the most important of all factors influencing listening comprehension. Inability to give full attention to sustained oral discourse is an almost universal problem. Why is this true?

Almost everyone these days is afflicted with a disease the semanticist would call multidirectional orientation. To put it simply, we all have too many things to keep track of. Some of us show many symptoms of the malady, others but few; but all of us display at least occasional evidence of its influence.

### Part-time Listening

Perhaps the most universal symptom of the ailment is "half-listening." It consists of pretending to hear what someone is saying to us, but reserving most of our thoughts for making personal decisions or pursuing other mental tangents. We may nod, and smile, and even mutter an "um" or an "Is that so?" while we attempt to follow two or more separate pathways at the same time. Actually the term "partial listening" is more accurate than "half-listening" for usually we are trying to keep a mental finger on several matters, not just two.

There is no denying that we suffer from multidirectional orientation. How do we contract the malady? Are all its influences evil ones? Are there certain occasions when our inattentive habits are particularly damaging? These questions deserve our thoughtful consideration.

We need only to watch a three-year-old youngster intently studying the action of ants around an ant hill to discover how we must have behaved before developing multidirectional orientation. The little toddler will demonstrate complete preoccupation in his scrutiny; his concentration upon a single source of stimulation is perfect, considering his age level and the limited experiential background with which he is doing his learning. Before many more years pass, however, he learns to look out warily and simultaneously for other stimuli — among which may be the disciplinary action of a heavy-handed parent — while pursuing the activity most immediately of interest and concern to him.

**Multidirectional Attention**

It is almost axiomatic to declare that partial listening is caused by the complexity of the culture and economy in which we live. Some writers estimate that the weight, volume, and complexity of our cultural heritage have increased at least fourfold in the last two hundred years alone. Most of us soon learn that if we want to stay alive and happy we must not become so deeply engrossed with any activity that we fail to hear the sound of a truck rapidly bearing down on us; to catch the hiss of escaping gas from an unlighted burner; to detect the snort of a male parent about to erupt emotionally; to interpret correctly the anticipatory giggle of friends about to play a practical joke; to recognize the wail of a police siren from down the street; to identify the sound of the heavy footsteps of our employer rapidly approaching our desk. To a large measure, therefore, multidirectional orientation is a defense mechanism which we carefully construct to protect our persons and our prospects. In this sense it has undeniable values. The damage it does results from building multiple-stimulus awareness into an unvaried habit of giving only short-lived attention to any single sound source, regardless of its character. Once the habit is formed, we are likely to practice it irrespective of time and place.

**Varied Attention and Classroom Listening**

In classroom learning situations the disastrous consequences of partial listening are most conspicuous. Here there are no moving vans to run us down; no male parents about to "blow their stacks." Here is a learning environment in which many distracting variables have been intentionally controlled and in which it is to be hoped we can give our full attention to the instruction provided. But often our ingrained practice of multiple-stimulus awareness makes it nearly impossible for us to concentrate fully upon the sound source we know is centrally important.

There are no internal switches we can throw which will automatically convert us from multidirectional to monodirectional orientation. Instead, we must increase our ability to give sustained attention to a single source by studying the nature of the thought process itself and by employing more fully the ingredient skills of concentration in a listening situation. Before examining these resources and their possible contributions, let us look at some results of multidirectional orientation.

Our inability to give sustained attention to any sound source for an appreciable length of time seems to have peculiar effects on many of us. The more closely these effects are scrutinized, the more depressing they appear.

**Superficiality of Interests**

One effect seems to be the nearly universal habit of cultivating a wide variety of extremely superficial interests. Many of us today have a little interest in scores and scores of things — and a truly deep and absorbing interest in none. Undergraduate college students, particularly, appear so inclined. Indeed, some wander along to the full completion of a four-year degree without ever deciding what they want to do in life — without ever determining a major field of interest. Developing a shallow interest in anything and everything we encounter has both advantages and disadvantages. It may make us appear well-informed to the nondiscerning; and socially, it may well serve to make us more adaptable, more easily integrated with any group.

When we participate in learning situations, however, our ingrained habit of building superficial interest proves only distinctly harmful. It is so easy to decide the immediate presentation is only moderately interesting; to drift off to a different area of moderate interest — and from that to still a third. It becomes harder to concentrate. Worst of all, we wander from one mental tangent to another without consciously knowing that we are doing so. If the discourse is so barren that we can conscientiously, consciously, and deliberately tune out the speaker and set sail on some preferable line of thought, such action is courageous and perfectly justifiable. *The great evil is that of pursuing mental tangents without a conscious awareness that we are so engaged.* More and more frequently, as we grow older, we may find moderate interest deteriorating to noninterest with respect to an increasingly large number of subjects. Such prior consideration we give the issues involved in these instances may well be so superficial as to make the subjects themselves seem sterile.

When ever-present, near-by distractions are combined with the shallow interest we may have for some topic, intense listening becomes nearly impossible. It is not that we cannot be attentive to anything. It is relatively simple, for example, to be attentive to a beautiful blond when dancing with her; but listening to instructive discourse is immeasurably more complicated. The topic under discussion may seem difficult; some previous and senseless admonition "to plunge right in" or "to be attentive" may be nagging away at some cortical center of thought; or a purely artificial motivation — such as the desire "to look good" by earning a high grade — may be impeding our development of a real and all-engrossing interest.

| *Learn to Concentrate* |

What can we do to battle successfully this effect of multidirectional orientation? It will help, of course, to keep reminding ourselves of the three great economies of learning previously examined: that listening is the easiest way to acquire needed information, to grow culturally, and to become socially mature. It will help to make a careful analysis of our own motives in being present; to get seated in a favorable position and to prepare to take notes; to remember that "I want to" must replace "I have to" if all-important, real interest is to develop. It will help to remind ourselves that everything is interesting from certain points of view; and that in a listening situation it is better to capitalize upon this fact than to drift off on some attractive mental tangent. But these steps are not in themselves enough. They must be supplemented with an understanding and application of several skills which in combination constitute our power to concentrate.

**Too Many Interests and Their Consequences**

A second effect of trying to keep track of all the obligations, appointments, assignments, records, and details in our daily routine has been to make us a nation of extremely tense people. Our commonest disease is mental disease. Although psychiatrists disagree on how many of us are neurotic, they come to rather close agreement on what proportion of our population is seriously mentally disturbed — or likely to become so. The consensus seems to be that one in every sixteen of us is mentally ill; that one of every seven of our people alive today will spend, or should spend, time in an institution providing psychiatric care. Regardless of the exact percentage of us seriously deviated mentally, it is obvious that the number is far too large.

**Procrastination**

The third apparent effect of our complexity of life is procrastination. Many of us put off things we know we must do until the last possible moment. We are prone to announce, usually with a bit of pride, that we "work best under pressure." An analysis of what we are really saying in this remark is revealing indeed. It seems to be a stratagem we employ, perhaps but half-consciously, to escape the multiple stimuli which normally distract us. By severely limiting the amount of time for finishing a necessary task we attempt to force ourselves to concentrate sharply on our problem. Sometimes the strategy works. All too often it fails because unanticipated and unavoidable interruptions occur which disastrously disrupt our delicately balanced time schedule. How do we then react, having learned that the necessary task cannot be finished? According to our individual natures, of course; but usually the result is one of worry, frustration, and a pyramiding of uncontrolled nervous tension.

All the foregoing general effects of multidirectional orientation are reflected in lowered performance while listening to informative speech. Usually the more diffuse our orientation, the more distraught and tense we become. Occasionally, though, two conflicting tensions within us, if they are of approximately even strength, will nearly tear us apart. One moment we will be trying hard to focus upon the speaker and to understand what he is trying to say. The next we will devote to worry over whether we may lose our part-time job at the student union for having come to work a full hour late the evening before. Back and forth our mind rushes, from one stimulus to the other. Each of the two tensions, nicely equated in strength, demands priority. Unless we are capable of taking time out to compare the two and to decide which deserves and shall have priority — to make a conscious and objective decision in this respect — our listening comprehension will suffer badly.

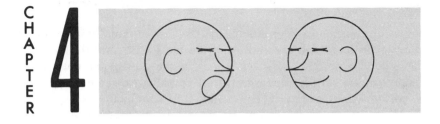

**Speaking
and
Listening . . .**

# . . . the content
# elements

## Part A: Content Materials and Audience Interest

The ideas which we present in expository or persuasive speeches need amplification for full development and for acceptance on the part of the audience. Without this development by use of illustrative detail, the listener is forced into an almost impossible situation. He is forced to accept our statements without the explanatory material upon which we arrived at the statement in the beginning. He is forced to jump from one idea to another without the materials which bridge the gaps. Moreover, he is forced to keep high interest in our remarks without encouragement from us to do so. In short, unless we present the content materials which serve to create interest, hold attention, clarify meaning, and demonstrate relationships, we do not have a speech. We are engaged in announcing a series of ideas or topics instead of making a speech. It would be fair to say that more speakers fail on this ground than on any other single element of speech making.

Even when beginning speakers know that a speech must be something more than a series of general statements, we still seem to find the building of a speech, the business of putting flesh on the skeleton, a difficult job. Our first inclination is to expand the outline primarily by definition, by further explanation, or by the addition of details in the form of bare facts and figures. This is the method of exposition and it is the straight line of support for the generalization stated. When produced verbally, however, this method is the greatest sleep producer since the introduction of morphine. It is dull. The indirect route to point support is far superior as a means of verbal reinforcement and several such methods of dressing up the evidence will be considered in this chapter.

## The Building Materials

The materials we use will depend upon the type of subject we select, whether our purpose in speaking is that of exposition or persuasion, and the audience before us. The effective speaker will use definitions, specific instances, illustrations, opinions of others, restatements, descriptions, contrasts and comparisons, statistics, figures, passages of literature — both prose and poetry — jokes or anecdotes, and visual aids. The kinds of materials which interest us will probably be of interest to our listeners when we speak. As speakers we should be constantly on the lookout for such content materials.

It would be well to maintain a speaker's notebook in which we keep such material as comes to us through our reading, observation, and listening. We must keep looking for these content elements out of which speeches are built and we must have some means of holding them for future use.

Out of all the possibilities in content materials, there are four which will hold the attention of an audience best. These are the straight narrative, the personal experience, the verbal picturization or description, and poetry. These content elements and all others as well are presented best in an aura of dramatization, or with some shock to the imagination. The selection and use of these various methods of dressing up your ideas is an index of your originality and creativity.

## Use of Definition

In expository speaking it frequently becomes necessary to define terms. In technical processes some of the terminology may be far from common and yet impossible to avoid. When we are forced to use strange terminology we must define these terms adequately the first time we use them in our speaking. Sometimes we use rather common words in a special sense and when we do we must let our listeners know how we are using them.

In defining words or phrases for our audience we can use one of several methods, whichever best suits the purpose of clarity. A word may be defined by etymology, the tracing of the word back to an earlier origin. This may be a useful method if the word still carries the original meaning, completely useless if it does not. Perhaps one of the best methods of definition is by illustration. Tunnel vision, for example, might well be defined by illustrating its meaning. A method commonly used in a dictionary is that of giving a synonym which may be more commonly known. This is a useful method where synonyms exist, but unfortunately many terms have no acceptable equivalent synonyms. A fourth type of definition has been called defining by negation, the pointing out what is not meant in the usage of a term. This method is extremely useful when a word has several distinct meanings. A final method of definition is that of classification, the placing of the term in its class and then distinguishing it within its class in some fashion. This is probably the least used method.

Whatever the method, the terminology used in speaking must be understood. We must always guard against a failure of communication because the words we use are misunderstood. These details of definition form a portion of the content. We should remember, however, that definition is used only when we cannot avoid strange or confusing terminology.

## Use of Specific Instances and Illustrations

We will frequently find specific instances and illustrations useful in supporting and developing our ideas. The specific instance differs from an illustration in that the former merely names the person, date, or place which supports the statement or declaration. In supporting a statement with instances we usually try to name a good many instances. In sustaining the declaration that "There is little relationship between I.Q. and listening ability," we would name a good many studies in verification of this statement.

An illustration is a development of a specific instance through the supplying of details of the instance given. In support of the statement that "Cities profit by long range planning programs," an extended instance with all the details should be used. Sometimes, as with specific instances, more than one illustration is developed.

These illustrations are usually based on fact but the occasion sometimes calls for a hypothetical illustration. With the use of hypothetical illustrations we move into the realm of prediction for what will happen or what might have happened.

Our use of specific instances and illustrations helps hold attention to our ideas. Without such details our listeners either go to sleep or wander off on some personal subject matter. With such materials interwoven with our general statements we will deserve attention for our ideas and we will get it. Moreover, we will be understood.

**Use of Personal Experience**

Any time we can introduce materials drawn from personal experience about the topic we are discussing, we have a distinct opportunity not only to hold attention but to strengthen our speech. There are qualifications to be made about the value of such experience, however. The listener must be made to feel that our experience was sufficient to enable us to speak with authority. The second qualification is that we present such experience with sufficient humility that attention is not drawn to our personality rather than to the ideas we are presenting.

**Use of the Opinions of Others**

The use of authorities to develop a point is usually thought of in terms of persuasive speaking. The testimony of others is just as useful in the field of exposition. Whether discussing the building of a pipeline or the weather conditions two miles above the earth, the speaker must presume to be giving honest, worthwhile information. Our audience gives more respect to our ideas when we can support them through the opinions of others. This testimony may be in the form of an individual or group report. Frequently it appears as a statement embodied in an agency report.

*Authority Must Be Specific*

The individual, individuals, or agency supporting our statement should be named and identified. "A man in a department of agriculture somewhere said" is practically useless, but the detail "Henry Tabor of the Agricultural Extension Division of Georgia said in the 1934 Forestry Bulletin that a slash pine seedling can be expected to start producing turpentine in 18 years" is important amplification. The offering of such testimony is valuable in making the audience feel they are listening to a speaker who has made considerable pursuit of his topic.

We should line up the best authority available behind our ideas. Our audience will not accept with any respect the testimony of one who is obviously unqualified to give a responsible report. The person quoted should be an expert in his field and either he or his agency should be known to our listeners. These quotations add vividness to our speeches as well as support to our ideas. We should learn to cite authority effectively.

**Use of Causal Relations**

Chapter 5 will discuss causal relation in terms of arrangement of materials; a whole speech can be developed by tracing causes and effects. It is well to remember, also, that explanation of a statement within a speech may be developed by details of causation. Ordinarily, a development within a process occurs because of certain operating factors; when undesirable things occur in a process there will be effects, perhaps undesirable.

If we have made the statement that "The giant clumsy reptiles of the Mesozoic era became extinct and were replaced by smaller running animals," we would amplify that statement by causal details. We would explain that during the Mesozoic period much of the ground was marshy and that, under these conditions, the matter of size and power were more important than speed. We would point out that geologic changes which drained off the water provided large areas of hard surfaced land suitable to running and that, under these conditions, the animals with speed and ability to range far in search of food supplanted the ponderous reptiles which were literally starved out of existence. The detailing of such causes and effects frequently makes up a sizable portion of our speech detail.

**Use of Restatements**

Often it is important that we give the audience time to absorb what we have said and sometimes a statement we have made is of such extreme importance that we wish it remembered. When such is the case we restate the same idea in several ways. This may seem like an invitation to wordiness and a waste of time. Ordinarily it is important for us to be concise, but in the instances mentioned such restatement is not only acceptable but extremely effective.

## Use of Descriptions

We use description when we wish to provide our listeners with the same impression which we ourselves have had of a person, place, or object. By using the right details of touch, sight, sound, taste, and smell we may induce a mood or create an image. In expository description we try to represent with accuracy the details of a person, place or object. The advertisements in newspapers describe with detail: "New 3-bedroom brick home; separate dining room; tile bath; fireplace; hardwood floors; plastered walls; tile window sills; water heater; space heater; attached garage; utility room; large screened porch; small study; total of 2200 sq. ft. under roof. Located on large, beautifully wooded corner lot, Magnolia Drive, near golf course. Price $31,500."

In speaking we have frequent use for descriptive detail. If we describe a place we should establish a definite point of view and maintain it consistently. We first choose a position which will enable us to observe advantageously and let our listeners know our position with respect to the scene. The point of view in time may also be important — time of day, time of week, month, and year.

## Use of Comparisons and Contrasts

Comparisons and contrasts serve to make our ideas clear and vivid. In comparison we attempt to show a relationship between the known and the less well-known. We assume that what applies in a known instance will apply in instances which have many similarities. In exposition we are concerned primarily with establishing this comparison. The shortened comparisons in the form of similes and metaphors also add color to our expression.

In the use of contrast we emphasize the differences between persons or instances which on the whole have like characteristics. "The Democratic and the Republican parties differ greatly in their aims" could be dramatically and colorfully explained by the method of contrast. Our informative and persuasive speeches will offer possibilities for using the device of contrast as well as that of comparison.

## Use of Figures and Statistics

In general an audience does not relish figures and particularly not long lists of them. It is important in many speeches, however, that we supply such data. When figures are needed we should give them in round numbers, the most acceptable fashion. If the area of timber in Canada is important data for a speech, we should say "a little more than one million square miles." Similarly we should say that the United States has "about 250,000 miles of railway." Moreover, when we present figures we should be sure that the listeners are able to recognize their significance. The cost of World War II in dollars is impressive but too large to be understood. Recognition of what the war really cost can be made on the basis of comparison. We should draw that comparison by pointing out how many miles of highway, how many $50,000 homes, how many Cadillac automobiles for every man, woman, and child in the United States such an amount of money would buy. The amount of soil lost by water erosion in Kentucky becomes significant when dramatized as so much land, ten feet deep, covering whatever expanse it turned out to be. These concrete comparisons to standards which the listener recognizes are of extreme importance to our technique of using figures.

Statistics differ from figures in that they are a compilation of instances from which we draw general conclusions. Public opinion polls, data about the number of unemployed, etc., are not made in the same way the census is taken — by an actual count. They are instead the result of sampling and need to be regarded with care. We must be particularly wary of averages. In many cases the mode is far more meaningful than the average. To illustrate, if four men make $50.00 per month and one makes $1,300 per month, the average is $300 per month for the five persons. The average wage wouldn't buy any groceries for the four $50.00 men, however. The mode, where most of the cases fall, would be $50.00 and in terms of general income would more accurately represent the economic situation of this group.

We should always give the source of figures or statistics when we use them. The listener is entitled to check for himself, if he cares to do it, and without such indication of source our figures and statistics are not worth much anyway.

**Use of Literary Passages** Sometimes it is possible for us to use striking quotations from prose or poetry which confirm the statements we have made. Speakers of past generations made frequent use of the Bible for such quotations. Whatever the source, they are most effective when well known by the listeners but not shopworn. We usually use such excerpts in introduction or conclusion but they may be used throughout the speech.

When quotations from literature are used, we should give the author's name and the literary work where the quotations appear. The quotations should be suited to the point they supposedly support. The notebook mentioned earlier in this chapter should be used to store away these quotes until we need them for our speeches.

## Use of Jokes and Anecdotes

As immature speakers we usually shy away from using jokes or anecdotes. Surely we do not wish to become known as jokers who never consider any subject seriously. Our speeches, however, usually benefit from the spice which a cleverly told joke will give. When we use such material, usually in the introduction, we must tell the joke well, keep it short, and time the gag line carefully. Nothing is quite so disastrous to a speech as a joke poorly told or one in which the punch line is mutilated or even forgotten.

Anecdotes are effective in making points clear. These are presented best when we draw them from our actual experience and they usually involve persons with whom we are intimately acquainted. The fictitious anecdote will sometimes serve our purpose but it is seldom as effective as an actual one drawn from our past experiences. As with jokes an anecdote must point up the statement which we have made and must be effectively told.

## Use of Straight Narrative

A longer narration of an actual event is employed as the basic organization of some speeches. The speaker uses a story or series of stories to draw a focus for a single statement or conclusion. The story method of developing a point is thus a method of arrangement in itself as well as content material for points within other types of speech arrangement.

The recognition that the story or narrative is an effective method of holding attention and in influencing thought is not new. In Mark 4:11 Jesus is reported to have said: "But unto them that are without (understanding) all these things are done in parables." Abraham Lincoln was an effective story teller and he used this method frequently in speech development because he realized that nothing holds attention and influences belief as well as a good story. These stories become the witness or authority for the generalization drawn.

The best stories are drawn from actual happenings but must sometimes be built from pure fantasy. If the story is a hypothetical one, we must let our audience know it has been so drawn. To relate a story which is purely fictional as though true will be fatal to the speaker when he is found out. Although hypothetical narrative is difficult to develop in such fashion as to be a powerful support, it is often worth the effort to try on occasion.

**Use of Visual Aids**

The authors of this text feel the use of visual aids as speech detail is a matter differing slightly from the foregoing types of detail considered. This visual reinforcement of our ideas is of tremendous importance in expository speaking. It will be given separate treatment in Chapter 6.

# Part B: Finding and Choosing Speech Materials

The finding and choosing of speech materials is a matter of reviewing your own interests, beliefs, and convictions. A section of Chapter 3 spoke of the importance of establishing deep convictions. If you believe anything strongly enough to argue about it, you have a source for one or for many speech topics.

The content of our speeches will be good or poor according to judgments about it relating to quantity and quality. In quantity it may be overweight, adequate, or underweight. In quality it is judged by its accuracy, its relevancy, its freshness, its specificity, and its originality. This section will discuss the matter of finding speech materials or content and how to reach selective judgments about the content secured.

**Sources of Speech Content**

Materials for our speeches come from several distinct sources. We may draw from our own personal experience, from campus courses we are taking, from conversations and interviews with other persons, and from materials we have read.

The good speaker pursues all these sources in preparation for a speech. We cannot afford to slight any possibility in gathering materials. Those who neglect the task invite failure; those who diligently dig out the facts are richly rewarded for their efforts. Our listeners will appreciate good detail.

We will never use all the materials gathered. We will examine and retain or discard what we have found on the basis of accuracy, adequacy, relevancy, freshness, and originality. Listeners will judge our content on these standards and we must apply the same critical evaluation of our product.

## Content from Personal Experience

Our own experiences constitute the bedrock of good speech materials, for these details from our own lives add vitality and freshness to the presentation. What we have seen and experienced for ourselves can be much more realistically presented to an audience than the thoughts and observations of others. If we have worked in a brickyard and were observant of the techniques used in the manufacture of bricks, we are in a much better position to tell of the process than one who has only read about such manufacturing. If we have seen the Taj Mahal, Washington's Monument, Lincoln's Tomb, or the Statue of Liberty, we should be equipped to describe them to others.

If we have bought and sold cars, houses, any consumer goods, we understood the details thoroughly and our knowledge gives us the ability to talk about those types of salesmanship. We can explain the main points involved in the purchase of an auto or a house and are able to illustrate our ideas with interesting and sometimes amusing details. If we have attended auctions — tobacco, household goods, bankruptcy — in short, if we have done anything, we have something to speak about. Our occupations, our hobbies, our school work should supply a great fund of information from which we can draw for speech content.

All too often, students underestimate the value of their personal experiences and knowledge. Our own private storehouse of information may not be enough to develop our speech topic completely, but its importance must not be overlooked. We should use what we have experienced whenever such information is applicable to the topic being discussed.

Someone has said, "Those who have lived excitingly always make the best speeches." Are we willing to admit we have not had exciting experiences? Unless we admit that we have lived rather drab lives, we must have from within our experiences a great deal of good speech content.

## Content from Campus Courses

A somewhat neglected but richly suggestive field for speech details is the local campus curriculum. In such courses as economics, political science, psychology, and philosophy, we should find a rich source of materials. The most valuable courses for this purpose, perhaps, are found in the social sciences but surely mathematics, the physical and biological sciences, and other courses will sometimes present the very materials we need for the development of a speech.

A music major might successfully compare composition in music with composition in speaking. A mathematics major might utilize the classroom situation as an opportunity to try out his powers of illustration and clarification. He might explain the mathematical theory of probability and give a concrete demonstration to his audience by means of a model slot machine. A language major might explain a method for learning four foreign languages simultaneously. These illustrations could be expanded indefinitely, for the courses on any college campus make available a wide variety of potential topics.

**Content from Conversation and Interviews**

Good speech materials often arise from conversations or interviews with other persons. In college we have an excellent opportunity to talk to specialists and semi-specialists who often can aid us in uncovering material which will help develop a topic we have chosen. We may want to interview some public official about affairs connected with local or state government. A student, interested in making a talk on the highway patrol system, might interview a state official on the subject, thereby receiving personal information and probably printed and illustrative materials for developing a first rate speech. We should be brief and courteous in such interviews.

In many cases it will be possible for us to get information we need by telephone. This method, when feasible, saves a great deal of time as well as energy.

Another source of speech material may come from visits to places where processes of manufacture are carried on. Most plant managers are anxious and willing to explain processes to us, and particularly so if they know we will carry this information to other groups of individuals. Should a student visit a local milk pasteurizing plant he could devise a speech both interesting and worthwhile. There is nothing like firsthand information as far as speech content is concerned.

**Content Through Reading**

While personal experiences, interviews, and conversations provide valuable sources for the content of speeches, there will be occasions when the speaker will have to resort to printed materials. Books and magazines, as well as newspapers, can provide abundant material for the development of topics where knowledge already gained is insufficient. Through reading we can experience life vicariously and thus be able to present what we have read to an audience. A student who has never seen a sulphur mine can make a speech on the sulphur-mining process which proves clear enough to create the impression that he has actually participated in the experience. Much more successful, however, is the use of such materials to supplement what has already been gained from actual experience.

When we do rely on printed materials, we must not be satisfied with anything less than a reasonably thorough examination of several articles on the subject, and, if necessary, one or more authoritative books. Actually we should read widely enough to have the content for several talks. We should be highly critical as we read; we should never assume that a thing is true because it appears in print.

The indexes of current literature such as the *Reader's Guide to Periodical Literature, Education Index, Industrial Arts Index,* and *New York Times Index* will give us the sources of articles about our topic. Also, we should investigate the library card catalog for possible books which cover the subject. The document collection in college and university libraries contains federal and state government pamphlets with which we should become familiar. In addition, there are encyclopedias and yearbooks which will yield important materials for speeches.

**Recording Materials**

The notes on selections read are probably kept most easily on 3 x 5 or 4 x 6 cards which can be purchased in any book store. Such cards are easy to handle and classify. Three helpful things can be put upon these cards: (a) a label indicating what the notes are about, (b) the source, and (c) the material — facts, opinions, and data of whatever kind desirable. With such a system of note keeping it is easy to select the material which we wish to use in developing our main ideas.

The gathering of the materials for a speech should begin early. Several different sittings should be used for thinking through and working out the materials. With a reasonable time left for practice in delivery, we should choose the details to be used and organize them into an acceptable pattern. The chapter on analysis and organization will help with the framing of the speech.

**Accuracy of Materials**

Material for speeches should be accurate and reliable. The speaker should consider himself responsible for statements made and any content of a questionable nature should be left out altogether or sufficiently qualified to allow for a possibility of minor inaccuracy. "John Smith told me that Mary Jones reported that some man said that he had heard" isn't dependable evidence. To repeat what we have not tested sufficiently for inaccuracies is mere "gossip" and should be avoided. "I realize that your experience has been to the contrary, but I want you to believe me when I say" doesn't do much in converting an audience to our way of thinking. We should submit our materials to the tests of consistency. Is this material consistent with human experience? Is it consistent with known facts? Is it internally consistent — consistent with itself? When carefully applied these tests should safeguard our content against the charge of inaccuracy.

In addition, we must be careful to state the materials used exactly. We should quote statistics accurately as far as round numbers are concerned; for example, "nearly 200" is sufficient for 197, and "approximately 150 thousand" is satisfactory for 151,296. We should be especially careful about taking material out of context; oftentimes a false impression is thereby given. One bad slip in accuracy of material tends to throw doubt upon the whole body of content used. It is certainly unrealistic for us to expect our listeners to accept information which is questionable and the responsibility for not asking them to do so lies directly with us as speakers.

**Relevancy of Materials**

The materials used may be accurate and yet be of little consequence because they are irrelevant to the topic being talked about. All the content offered must keep on the subject. If we are explaining methods of city slum clearance, what we might say about conservation of the soil will be irrelevant even though our materials are accurate. This matter of relevancy applies to humor as well as to serious thought. Everybody relishes a little humor but it must be applicable to the point being discussed. "This story about a college professor doesn't apply to the subject I am discussing, but it is so good I want to tell it to you" is not sufficient excuse for the joke.

Relevancy is probably more a matter of organization than of content. If we have carefully outlined our speech, we will be able to throw out that material which doesn't help advance the topic.

**Adequacy of Materials**

The amount of material needed to develop a speech topic depends upon the central idea used and the specific audience addressed. One central idea may take more in the way of illustration and facts than another because of its scope or nature. The same central idea may take more in the way of details, illustrations, and facts with one audience than with another. One audience might be confused with too many details; without the same number of details, another audience might fail to grasp the idea presented. We must adjust our content, then, to the idea we wish to present and to the intellectual and emotional state of our audience.

Unless we have adequate detail, our speech will be uninteresting and inconsequential. We will have a skeleton with little meat and people will refuse to listen to us as we repeat unnecessarily. On the other hand, if we have too much detail we will not have enough time to relate the detail to our central idea. The result will be an obscurity of main thought because the audience has gotten lost in the multitude of illustrations and facts offered. There are no rules for adequacy of content. It is a matter of personal judgment which one has to learn through trial.

**Freshness of Material**

Many times the speech topic chosen will be one of those which has frequently been used. In such cases, the student should attempt to find material that is not common knowledge. Such an attempt involves the location of new details not applied to the topic before. This type of content may be fresh in that it has just become known or it may be fresh because it has been forgotten. Whatever the development, it should not be too common or our classmates will not listen to it.

Freshness of material is largely a matter of using specific, concrete detail. We should not talk about "some schools have found"; we should talk about Georgia Tech, Iowa State, and Notre Dame. "Leading educators" will not hold attention as well as "Robert Hutchins" and "John Dewey." The use of concrete experiences will promote the central idea much better than "experience indicates that . . ."

| **Originality of Material** |
| --- |

Originality of material is concerned with a matter differing from freshness. The student receives criticism on originality when he develops a speech from a single newspaper or magazine article. In such case he has made no contribution to content which he can call his own. He merely repeats parrot-like the developmental materials used by another. Such poverty of sources is highly discouraged in this course.

The illustrations which we use to make our points clear should be colorful and exciting. This is partially a matter of language, which will be discussed in a later chapter, but also a matter of choice of material. The content of the speech should be within the experience and imagination range of our audience and we should proceed from the familiar to the less familiar. We should always supply the relationships between the material and the central idea being explained. "This illustration shows . . . ," "From these figures we can see . . . ," is the language which indicates the speaker is relating the material he has used to the central idea. The handling — selection, interpretation, application — of materials gives us the opportunity for originality.

# Part C: Listening to Content Materials

The close relationship between the skills of speaking and listening is forcefully demonstrated when we seek a description of the listener's job in respect to the content of the speeches to which he listens. If he has mastered the ability to create materials which are relevant, accurate, and specific, he will be able to judge those qualities in the speech materials of others. To the extent that he has developed creativity with speech content, he will be able to judge quantity and quality in speeches that he hears.

Listening for the content materials in persuasive speeches is more important and more difficult than in purely informative speeches. If the speaker is giving information only the important listening skill involves the matter of accuracy primarily. If the speaker is attempting to persuade, the listener is required to make important judgments about the materials presented far beyond accuracy.

| **The Art of Critical Listening** |
| --- |

The counter-art to the speech of deep conviction, in the inter-action of speaker and listener, is the act of critical listening. Today, more than ever before in history, we are assailed by the continuous stream of propaganda emanating from individuals whose living depends upon their salesmanship or from pressure groups trying to manipulate our beliefs. In a sense their discourse is persuasive, for surely their goals are belief or action; but this is persuasion at its lowest plane, with little effort to weigh, to balance, to reason objectively. The tools used range all the way from comic books, newspapers, and magazines to soap operas, campaign speeches, news commentaries, radio and television commercials. All seek to move us in one direction or another, to sell us something, to control our beliefs, our actions, and even our value systems.

The men employing propaganda are "committed" speakers; that is, they have personally declared allegiance to a certain product or point of view — sometimes with conviction, but many times without it. Their avowed intention is to influence us, with or without ethical considerations motivating their efforts. Unless we are to become helpless before their swelling tide, we must build some kind of self-defense against the waves of propaganda besetting us. In America perhaps our most precious possession — freedom of speech — is guaranteed by our Constitution to all men, whether their thinking be straight or crooked. Our best defense against the latter is rigor-ously critical listening and thinking.

| **Propaganda** |
| --- |

The methods employed by the propagandists are now well known. Let us examine them closely. The Institute for Propaganda Analysis has identified the several devices or basic techniques of propaganda.

| *Name Calling* |
| --- |

The nature of this device is evident from its title. Essentially it consists of denouncing a person or thing by giving it the label of something widely condemned. In this cate-gory would fall such labels as Red, Fascist, slacker, chiseler, sub-versive, fellow-traveler. Many a dictator has used name calling as a stepping stone on his rise to power. Unfortunately, many organiza-tions are today encouraging their members to brand as "red" any person disagreeing with their ideas. In this, they defeat the very democracy they claim to serve.

*Glittering Generalities*

This device seeks acceptance of ideas or propositions by associating them with words widely accepted and approved. Among the latter are such labels as American, democratic, Christian, freedom, business-like. Superficial though it may sound, the artifice often proves effective.

*Transfer*

Transfer is the device of citing respected sources of authority, prestige, or reverence in such a fashion as to make it appear they sanction the new proposal at hand. The purpose, of course, is to create favorable attitudes toward the latter. Respected sources would include such institutions as the home, the church, the flag, the Constitution, will of the people, public education. The technique has proved highly influential.

*Testimonial*

Most selling campaigns use testimonials from famous people to build confidence in a product or proposition. We hear and see illustrations of this technique every day of our lives, if indeed not every hour of the day. The universality of this method of appeal is fairly eloquent evidence of its successful employment.

*Plain Folks*

Presidential candidates photographed in Indian war garments, or politicians shown milking cows in order to prove their "dirt-farmer" background, are illustrations of the technique of seeking favor through establishing the candidate as being "just one of the boys." It is employed on every hand by those who would sell products or ideas through its appeal. With certain population elements it always seems to work.

*Card Stacking*

This technique of propaganda is one which is built upon half-truths. Through a careful selection of favorable evidence and an equally careful omission of unfavorable or contrary evidence, the listener or reader is deceived and led to a false conclusion. The technique may well be the most vicious of all those commonly employed.

*Band Wagon*

The band wagon appeal is based on the premise that if everybody else is doing some certain thing, we ought to climb aboard the movement ourselves. By and large this artifice is so successful that defense against it becomes extremely difficult. We would all do well, no doubt, to keep in mind Anatole France's "If fifty million people say a foolish thing, it is still a foolish thing."

**Improvement of Critical Listening**

Procedures to improve critical listening are quite similar to those designed to improve critical reading. Improving critical listening is, however, more difficult than improving critical reading. Additional problems are created through the face-to-face relationship of speaker and listener. The speaker's voice, his gestures, and the general reaction of the audience to the talk all tend to increase the difficulty any single listener faces in his attempts to remain completely objective toward the appeal being made. Moreover, oral communication requires the listener to digest what he is hearing at a pace set by the speaker. If the latter demands an immediate decision on his proposition, then the role of the critical listener is still further complicated. Nevertheless there are definite and specific safeguards we can apply.

Fortunately, the evidence used can be evaluated. Whenever a speaker makes an assertion he either does or does not support it with evidence. If no evidence is submitted, and no credible explanation for its absence is offered, then of course the assertion is suspect. If evidence is submitted, be it either testimonial or statistical in character, to be convincing it must be attributed to a specific source. As soon as the hearer identifies its purported source, he can and should immediately set about testing the value of it.

*Old or New?*

The *first question* we as listeners should mentally raise about any piece of evidence is the date of its origin. A quoted statement by President Franklin D. Roosevelt dated 1936, for instance, would in most instances carry much less weight than one dated 1944. Statistics gathered by the Bureau of Census in 1960 would in most instances and on most issues have more meaning for us than those gathered ten years earlier. Thus our first test of evidence is that of recency. Is the evidence the speaker is submitting too old to support adequately the point he would establish? Usually a quick answer can be given, and a partial evaluation of his argument can be made.

| |
|---|
| *Is it Sound?* |

The *second question* we should mentally raise on each piece of evidence submitted concerns the competency of its source. Testimony of a Hollywood starlet on the excellence of engineering in a late-model automobile is much less convincing than would be that of a mechanic employed for twenty years in an independently owned and operated garage. Statistics gathered by the Bureau of Census, or any independently operated fact gathering agency, are much more convincing than those produced through a small scale survey made by some local person or group. Thus our second test of evidence is that of competency of its source. Evidence simply cannot be more convincing than the source from which it comes. On this basis we can make our second assessment of the argument of the speaker.

| |
|---|
| *Is it Prejudiced?* |

The *third question* we should always mentally raise concerning each piece of evidence submitted concerns the neutrality or the lack of prejudice existing in its source. Suppose, for example, the speaker declares that one of our neighbors, Citizen Jones, has openly testified that the North Park addition contains only land which is certain to double in value within the next ten years. But suppose we happen to know that Citizen Jones himself owns one-fourth of all the lots in North Park addition. Immediately the evidence is suspect. It fails to pass the free-from-prejudice test, for Jones stands in a position to profit by having his testimony widely accepted. Or suppose that the Zee Wee Pump Company has offered testimony to the effect that every home should contain a Zee Wee Pump. Its obviously prejudiced source makes such evidence worthless.

This third test is the most important of the three. The way to apply it usually is to ask ourselves this question: "Does the person or organization supplying this evidence stand to gain something through its acceptance?" If the testimony is that of a single individual, good questions to ask ourselves are: "For whom does he work?" "Is his income-earning in any way related to the testimony he gives?" "Is there some way in which he personally stands to gain by having his evidence accepted?"

Independent, fact-gathering agencies — often a part of state or federal government — are usually neutral and free from prejudice. Normally, they are reliable sources. Of them all, the United States Bureau of Census is probably our best single source of statistical information.

Thus our third method of weighing evidence is based on the free-from-prejudice test. The application of this test will shed light on the motives of the speaker or his witnesses, or both. It will permit us to complete a sensible evaluation of the argument the speaker would have us accept. Wendell Johnson in *People in Quandaries* says that we should continually ask ourselves three questions concerning the speaker: "What does he mean?" "How does he know?" "What is he leaving out?" Surely these questions make sense, and lie at the very core of the whole process of critical listening.

It seems only fair to conclude by saying that not all propagandists are evil persons seeking to do us or the nation harm. Many of the persons and groups who employ propaganda methods no doubt are sincere in their convictions concerning their ideas and their products. It is the task of the listener to separate them; to divorce wheat from chaff. His major source for this purpose is critical listening, a process built upon an immediate and continual weighing and testing of the evidence (or lack of it) used to support each argument presented.

**Full Comprehension in Listening**

To achieve full comprehension of what a speaker is saying we must do much more than just absorb the literal content of his speech. We must supplement and reinforce his literal content: (a) by anticipating what he will say before he says it; (b) by noting the adequacy with which he supports each of his points; (c) by mentally reviewing, after each main point of the talk, the portion of the talk so far covered; and (d) by "listening between the lines" in our search for additional meaning. These four mental activities are the ingredients of concentration. Before we examine them individually, let us note their common characteristics.

*Staying on the Track*

The four skills of concentration permit the listener to think as rapidly as he likes, but at the same time they compel him to stay "on track" with the speaker. They are best understood if we think of their being used along a railroad track. At one end of a stretch of track is a speaker with a subject.

As his talk unfolds he will travel steadily down the track at a pace of one hundred words per minute. Starting out even with the speaker, at the beginning, is the listener. But normal and easy cruising speed for the listener will require his thinking at a pace four or five times as fast as that by which the speaker is progressing. Even if it were wise to do so, and it is not, the listener cannot synchronize his speed with that of the speaker. The listener's only out, therefore, if he is to keep tuned in on the discourse at all, is to dash down the track ahead of the speaker, make a quick survey of the direction being taken, look back from a distance to verify his judgment, and then make a quick return to the original starting point.

These swift excursions by the listener, back and forth along the the right of way, may be several times repeated during a single speech. But on every trip ahead and back he passes a score of sidetracks, the switches to which in every instance are wide open. These sidetracks are the mental tangents constantly appealing to the listener. They seem to lead in the most enchanting directions, too! To travel back and forth past all those open switches is no easy task. It would be impossible were it not for the fact that the trained listener is carrying out specific assignments; were it not for the fact that his mental activities, through training, have become fixed members of his habit pattern.

The trained listener keeps between the rails of the main line. He keeps "on track." He travels, and travels fast, but always in a horizontal direction — always shuttling back and forth. He evades all oblique or right angled departures from the speaker's route. He exploits and cashes in the inherent advantage of thought speed over speech speed. He is able to concentrate. He is a good listener.

**Anticipating the Speaker's Point**

Good speakers — and some of the poor ones, too, for that matter — build a number of points in each talk they give. Written essays and themes sometimes do not have a "point" organization, but the pattern is a conspicuous one in effective speech making. It automatically provides us, as listeners, with a chance to engage in a mental activity extremely valuable both in sustained attention and a more complete understanding of what is being said. This activity is to try to anticipate the speaker's next point — to dash down the track ahead of him, mentally, for this purpose.

After only a few introductory sentences at the beginning of his talk, it frequently is possible for us to guess quite accurately how the speaker's thesis will be stated. Once the thesis has been declared, it is both stimulating and profitable to anticipate each main point before its announcement. Each time, on the basis of what has already been said, we should keep asking ourselves: "What is this speaker trying to get at?" "What generalization is he trying to reach?"

Each time that we guess the speaker's next point correctly, our understanding and retention of that point is reinforced. In a sense it is twice assimilated by our brains, once when we anticipate it and again when our guess is confirmed by the communicator.

But what if we guess wrong? Suppose we anticipate point "X" only to discover a bit later that the speaker is developing point "Z." Fortunately, we profit anyhow. We have been making perhaps the one gamble in the world it is impossible to lose! As soon as we discover point "Z," not "X," is being developed we almost instinctively start to compare the two. One of the oldest known economies in learning is that of learning through contrast and comparison. It is one of the classical laws of association and dates all the way back to Aristotle. Thomas Brown (1778-1820), a psychologist exerting considerable influence upon present-day educational theory, did much to expound and elaborate this principle, a concept which is now widely accepted as one of the primary laws of learning.

Anticipating the speaker's point is perhaps as profitable as any mental activity which we ever employ to facilitate comprehension. Whether we guess right or wrong, it always pays good dividends.

**Identifying Three Kinds of Point Support**

When a speaker builds a point he must have raw materials of which to construct it. These raw materials—called "supporting elements" by standard speech textbooks — are at the very grass roots of both speech composition and of our comprehension of the speech when we listen to it. How many kinds of supporting elements are there? In an earlier section of this chapter the authors listed more than a dozen varieties, but from the standpoint of the listener they are best conceived to be of only three types.

Effective listening demands an ability to identify these three types of point support whenever we hear them. Such identification is tremendously important, for it does much to reveal how adequately each point is constructed. Often it discloses a good deal about the skill and motives of the speaker. Finally, it provides our best basis for ultimately making a sensible evaluation of the speech, and for deciding what our response to it should be. To speed up and make more accurate identification of these elements, we need every bit of objectivity we can obtain. To pursue our analogy of the railroad track, we need to "stand aside" along the right of way and study closely the speaker's efforts to support his point. To identify quickly the raw materials he is using will require an understanding of their character. Let us examine in more detail, then, the three kinds of supporting material conventionally used by speakers in building their points.

**Straight Exposition**

The most frequently used of all point-supporting material is straight exposition. It is all too true that about three of every four points we are destined to hear throughout our lives will be constructed of this kind — and only this kind — of material. The thought is most depressing, for unrelieved exposition is difficult for the listener.

Exposition is another word for explanation. It consists basically of explaining how something is made, how something operates, how something can be done. It is full of definition and classification. Despite every effort by the speaker to keep it out of his speech, it creeps in; just as quicksilver slips between our fingers when we try to pick it up, exposition slips in between the speaker's resolutions to keep it out. To the listener it is dry, tedious, seemingly interminable. As our minister pedantically "expounds his text," as our instructor belabors the difference between the law of unity and the law of coherence or as our senator reveals all the flaws in our present tax structure, a slow paralysis attacks our higher cortical centers. Our interest begins to waver; our heads to nod. Before long the speaker's words no longer get through to us. We have succumbed to reverie and are off on a pleasant mental tangent; or we are sound asleep.

*Ask Yourself Some Questions*

What is effective listener activity when we are subjected to sustained expository elements? First, of course, we need to identify what is happening as soon as possible. Having achieved this, we should immediately prod ourselves mentally with these questions: "Will it be necessary for me to do a lot of supplementary reading to understand this material?" "What has all this to do with me?" "How can I use this information?" Are things exactly as he says?" "Could I repeat what he is saying?" By continually confronting ourselves with these queries and by honestly trying to answer them, we may be able to stay "on track" with the speaker. Most helpful of all devices is probably the one of intending to report what we are hearing to someone else — a friend, a roommate, or spouse, perhaps. If we are determined to make such a report, and to make it a good one, our chances for full comprehension are greatly improved.

**Emotional Appeal or Harangue**

The second type of content used by speakers in building their points is highly emotional in character. It is loaded with appeals to us to do things for emotional reasons: for preservation of our own lives, our good names, our future prospects, for purposes of revenge, of getting even, of avoiding exploitation; for purely sentimental reasons — love of home, school, or country. Sometimes the appeal degenerates to the level of pure harangue, name-calling, and abusive language.

No sleep producer is emotional appeal! With this kind of content we shall have no trouble at all in staying awake. Our real problem is to identify as quickly as possible what the speaker is doing and to determine to assume a coolly objective attitude toward what the speaker is saying. We need to stay "on track" with the speaker, but at the same time attain enough mental detachment to keep free from disruptive emotional arousal. It helps to keep asking ourselves mentally: "Why is he so aroused?" Why is he trying to arouse us?" "Are his motives justifiable?" "What real evidence is he including to support his ideas?" Again, it helps greatly if we determine to report what we are hearing to someone else. The desire to make that report complete and accurate will add to our comprehension of what is being said.

**Illustrative Development**

The third way in which speakers build their points is through the use of illustrative material. The conventional steps the communicator takes with respect to each point he constructs are these: (a) He states the point. (b) He illustrates it. (c) He generalizes the illustration — that is, he submits evidence to show that his illustration is reasonably typical of the majority of cases bearing upon his point. Usually the illustrative method of point support is a highly effective one. It contains a nice balance of appeal to reason and appeal to emotion. The listener usually finds it easy to stay alert and to follow the thread of the discourse. Furthermore, when the supporting items are skillfully and honestly developed, the point is usually established to the satisfaction of both speaker and listener.

Speakers using the illustrative method of point support sometimes deviate from the three steps listed. If they are following rigidly a deductive pattern in developing the point, they will incorporate step three in step one by weaving the generalization they wish the listener to accept into the initial statement of the point. The three steps thus are reduced to two: a generalized statement of a point and the presentation of supporting illustrative materials. Conversely, when speakers follow a strictly inductive pattern in developing a point, they eliminate the initial statement of it entirely, again reducing the three steps to two: the presentation of illustrative materials and the making of a generalization on the basis of these materials.

What is illustrative material? Usually it is simply a story of a single case of the point being made. (Speech theorists use the phrase "narrative specific instance," which means precisely the same thing.) For example, if the speaker's main point is "Achilles Auto workers are underpaid," his illustration might well be the personal and dramatic story of Hughie Roberts, one of these workers. Following the telling of the story of Hughie, the speaker will generalize this single illustration of his point by showing that Hughie is reasonably typical of more than 70 percent of all the workers at the Achilles Auto Factory. In a longer talk the speaker may tell several stories, not one, to illustrate the point he is building.

As listeners, however, we must understand that illustrative material may include much more than strict storytelling. Upon occasion it may include any form of an example — general, specific, or hypothetical; it may include short anecdotes, fables, parables, figures of speech, and analogies. Conceivably, any one or all of these items could be used to illustrate a point.

Furthermore, the final generalization used to summarize and conclude the illustrative items presented can itself be of two kinds. It may be either statistical or the quoted testimony of an accepted authority upon the point being constructed. All of this makes the illustrative method of point support appear more complicated than it really is. With a bit of practice and guidance we can soon learn to recognize illustrative elements used for point support, and to distinguish between them and the other two great kinds of material used, straight exposition and emotional harangue.

What is effective listener activity during the moments devoted by the speaker to illustrative point development? First, of course, we need to identify the method as soon as possible. Then we should note the degree of skill with which the speaker presents each illustrative idea. If he is relating a story, does he have a hero, villain, action, bloodshed, a wealth of familiar and intimate detail? Are other illustrative items clearly, vividly, and colorfully worded? Finally, we should study closely how fairly and reasonably the speaker generalizes his illustrative items and states the conclusion he feels we should draw from them.

| **Recapitulating What Has Been Covered** |
|---|

Periodically, in listening to a speech, we should seek an opportunity to recapitulate mentally the main points so far covered. It will require but a few seconds to do this, and such mental reviews are invaluable in reinforcing the elements we shall want later to be able to recall. An opportunity to recapitulate may come when the speaker pauses to take a drink of water, to manipulate some kind of visual aid, or to walk across the room.

None of these interruptions are prerequisite to mental review, however. Recapitulation can be accomplished in the few seconds most speakers occasionally insert between two sentences. Generally speaking, we will find it easiest and most profitable to make these mental summaries just a few seconds before a deductively built point is brought to a close, or just a few seconds after the introduction of a new point which is being developed inductively. At these instants we can recapitulate without running any chance of missing the statement of a generalization necessary to a full comprehension of the talk.

Returning to our analogy of the railroad track, we should think of recapitulation as a quick mental dash by the listener back down the track in the direction from which the speaker has been proceeding. The hearer quickly re-examines the ground which has been covered in order to remember it more easily and in order to anticipate more successfully the next point the speaker will probably discuss.

These mental excursions to the rear definitely improve our comprehension and retention of what we hear. They utilize profitably

**11713**

another portion of the differential between thought speed and speech speed, and contribute to our ability to stay "on track" — to avoid the mental tangents always luring us away from the path of the speaker.

Concentration is acquirable. All of us possess an innate capacity for a more conscious focusing of our own mental faculties. Giving sustained attention to a speaker may be difficult, but it is by no means impossible. Our greatest gains in ability to concentrate will result from understanding and continually practicing the four ingredient skills we have just discussed.

To strengthen this most important of all the components of effective listening, we need to develop it both inside and outside the classroom. It would help us tremendously if we would but try, for one minute of every hour, to give our fullest possible attention to a person talking. Be he infant or adult, friend or foe, leader or drone, if we tune him in we are the ones who gain. If there is no voice to hear, we might select a sound — an airplane overhead, a bird's song, a church bell, the hum of a machine. Whatever the source, we should put everything else out of our minds and concentrate on that one sound. Hard though such concentration may be at first, we will steadily increase our power to achieve it. Practice will not make us perfect, but it can make us strong. It will pay off in improved scholarship, closer friendships, better vocational prospects, less friction and irritation in all our day-to-day contacts with other people.

Speaking
and
Listening . . .

# . . . the organization
# and analysis

## Part A: The Organization of Speeches in General

For nearly twenty-five hundred years the pattern of speech organization proposed by Corax of Sicily (circa 470 B. C.) has been tested and found good. He was no armchair philosopher considering what ought to work in the speech situation; he was a successful speaker and teacher of speech who recorded those methods which worked. Down through the years others have tested these suggestions in the crucible of experience. We can profit from the practices of these many centuries. Throughout the years other speech teachers have proposed many variations and elaborations. Some have described speech organization in the terminology of modern psychology. All these "new and different" outlines, all these "magic formulae" are simply adaptations of what Corax proposed.

In addition to the over-all organizational pattern for the total speech from introduction to conclusion, we must be particularly concerned about the point development of the subject chosen. This process involves analysis of the possible divisions of the subject and the development of a final pattern or order of arrangement. This is a difficult art and one that cannot be accomplished with "a lick and a promise" a half hour before class. Furthermore, as listeners we must analyze the point development pattern of each speech we hear. We will have an additional learning experience in the art of organization and analysis each time we listen to a speech.

In this chapter we shall discuss the general organizational pattern applicable to all complete speeches, consider the principal type of point arrangement patterns which may develop from the analysis of the subject, and describe the process of listening as it deals with the various analysis patterns.

## Four Part Structure in Speeches

A speech is structured somewhat like a complicated machine or building in that a general pattern defines the parts in broad outline and a more defined pattern occurs within these several parts. Except for one-point speeches, which are usually only parts of a total speech, our general pattern should show an *introduction*, a statement of *contract*, a *body*, and a *conclusion*. One-point speeches are usually those which appear as a part of discussion programs, as committee reports, or in reports made during business conferences.

The general structure of the speech is tremendously important and deserves our attention in every speech we plan to give. Not only must all the parts be present in the outline but each must be developed for the particular purpose we have in mind. Beginning speakers frequently forget the introduction or conclusion entirely and often the statement of contract appears in fuzzy form. These oversights need not occur. Every speech we make should be visualized and planned in terms of the four essential parts and the development of the speech will depend upon the careful handling of these parts in relation to our purpose, the available material, and the interest of the audience. This is the simple plan to be followed:

   I. Introduction: (develop attention and good will of the audience and orient them to the subject)

  II. Contract: (state clearly what we are going to do, and in some cases indicate the number of points we will develop)

 III. Body: (develop the several main points or divisions of our talk)

 IV. Conclusion: (develop a lasting effect)

## The Introduction

First impressions are strong impressions. For each particular speech, our introduction is our first contact with the audience. Outside this classroom it is often the first chance our audience has to evaluate us and our speaking. Introductions, therefore, are extremely important. We should spend enough time in preparation to do the job well. As speakers we must be interesting and we must be interesting at the very beginning. The introduction gives us this opportunity to be interesting from the start.

We must remember that a speech, at best, is a transient interaction of speaker and audience, subject and occasion. It dies as quickly as it is born. Our audience must get our message as we speak, for they will have no chance to read our words at leisure, or hear us talk again tomorrow or the next day. We should plan the opening remarks of our speech to make our audience want to listen, to capture their involuntary (as opposed to voluntary, or forced) attention.

## *Capturing Attention*

How can we capture attention? Each speech, audience and occasion offers its separate opportunities, but certain general techniques can be described. There are four basic ways to get immediate attention: (a) by the use of narrative, (b) by the use of a stanza of poetry, short poem, or bit of quoted prose, (c) by the use of dramatization, and (d) by the use of the shock treatment.

Of these methods the narrative is most frequently used. The narrative used in the introduction may be in the form of a story, an illustration, a happening from history, or some anecdote. Such narratives gain immediate attention when told well and every speaker should learn how to use them for the introduction and also as supporting materials for the body of the speech. The narrative should, of course, point up the statement of the contract which is to follow immediately.

Many speeches are begun with a short stanza of poetry or a brief bit of prose. When this device is used in the introduction, it usually requires an amplification of what the author meant. Quoted material is more frequently used in conclusions for speeches but serves for getting attention when employed at the beginning of the speech.

Again, such materials should point up the statement of the contract which is to follow.

Dramatization as an opening for a speech can take many forms. Briefly, the speaker attempts to dramatize a situation or event with whatever tools can best be employed. He might use an analogy or a visual aid; he might use impersonation or a bit of acting. Whatever he uses is for the purpose of vivifying a real or imaginary situation. The shock treatment involves just what it says. By startling or unexpected statement we shock our listeners into immediate attention. As with other beginnings, the dramatization or shock statement must have a direct application to the contract upon which we expect to expand.

*Orienting
the Listener*

The introduction should also provide the audience with background information necessary for orienting the listener to the speech. Such basic information can be given in the form of definition and in historical treatment of previous events leading up to the particular subject to be discussed. Information of this type should be kept at a minimum; unnecessary explanation of any kind is a waste of time.

*Ethical Proof*

Unless the speaker has been adequately introduced, still a third thing should be done in the introduction of the speech. The speaker should provide some justification for speaking on the topic which he has selected. A listener has the right to know why he should listen to this speaker on the topic proposed. Does the speaker have more than common information? Is he an authority? Even in the classroom, such a justification is vital to the acceptance of the ideas presented and, since no lengthy introduction is provided there, the speaker must give such information. This information should be given in all modesty and should be brief. If our listeners know why we are justified in using a topic, then no statement of that nature is necessary.

*Faults in
Introductions*

The introduction may and often does go astray. In the first place, there is no need for apologies in our introduction for choice of subject, lack of adequate preparation, or any other reason. No good speaker is ever quite satisfied with his speech, but it is an insult to an audience to suggest, "I know you won't be interested in my subject today," or "I want first to apologize for my lack of preparation." This negative approach "will get us nowhere fast." The beginning speaker is frequently guilty of this apologizing type of introduction. We must remember that when we make such statements we are saying to the listeners "You need not listen to this talk because I haven't anything to say anyway." Second, our introduction will repel the audience if it is deadly dull. Ours must have sparkle and life, vigor and vitality. Third, the introduction may be out of keeping with the mood of the occasion. It often is a mistake to introduce a serious speech with a joke. If we start our audience on the verbal "dessert" of entertainment they may react unfavorably to the serious "meat and potatoes" of information later on. Emotional introductions for informative speeches must be handled with care — if used at all. A fourth fault is demonstrated in introductions which ramble on and on interminably, stealing time which should be given to the body of our speech. Finally, there is the unforgivable fault of omission. Under all circumstances with which we are likely to be familiar, the introduction has an important function or functions to perform. It should not be left out.

Many beginning speakers probably plan the introduction first because it appears first on the outline form. This is usually a mistake in procedure. The introduction should ordinarily be planned last, when we know what we have to introduce. The catchy illustration we think of first may really belong under point one or point two of the body of the speech rather than at the beginning of the speech.

## The Contract

Every speaker needs to know exactly what he proposes to do. There are no if's or and's about this matter. If the speaker doesn't know where he is going, it is fair to assume he won't get far and he will do little for his listener. The contract is a clear and concise statement of what we propose to do in the speech we are about to deliver. It is not a phrase or a long paragraph, but a single sentence or two which states exactly the ground we intend to cover in the time at our disposal. In informative speaking this contract may state a point of view: "There are three essential qualities every good teacher must possess." In a persuasive speech it may merely point out the ground the speaker intends to cover: "We will consider this matter of water fluoridation by pursuing the answer to three questions." No point of view has been stated in this latter contract and no ill-will immediately created.

<table>
<tr><td>*Importance of*<br>*Contract*</td><td>In either type of speech, however, the contract must not be left out because it is important to both speaker and listener. The statement binds the speaker to a set purpose with his listeners (a contract) and it serves</td></tr>
</table>

to keep him on the track as well as to orient the audience. Extraneous material tends to be kept out of the speech which has a clear contract statement. If it does creep in the listeners realize at once they are being bilked.

The contract should not be confused with the speech subject — what the speaker is to talk about in general. We may talk about "Athletic Policy" but if we do only that, we do not have a speech. We do not have a speech because we have made no obligation with ourselves or with our audience. The contract under the general subject field "Athletic Policy" might be "Athletic subsidies are important to a college participating in intercollegiate athletics for three reasons."

The contract must not be confused with the speech title any more than with the general subject field. The speech title is a catchy phrase used for advertising purposes. On the bulletin boards in front of churches we often see the sermon titles, but these would seldom be the contract to be used with the sermon. Such titles may not even describe the general subject field; they usually bear about the same relation to the speech as book titles do to the subject matter of books. Attractive titles for speeches on athletic policy might be "Dollars or Scholars," "The Tea Formation," "Getting our Quarterback," etc. These titles form no agreement between speaker and listener.

<table>
<tr><td>*Contract Errors*</td><td>The most common failure of amateur speakers is the failure to state an acceptable contract. The next most common failure is to get the statement in the wrong place in the</td></tr>
</table>

speech. It is frequently used as the introduction. A planned introduction for each talk will prevent this error of substituting the second essential part of the speech for the first.

<table>
<tr><td>**The Body**</td><td>The body, the main part of the speech, consists of the discussion and development of the contract statement. In this part of our speech we present the</td></tr>
</table>

divisional headings of the discussion, arrived at through careful analysis, together with the evidence necessary for their support.

This portion of speech organization has come to be called arrangement, the order of the parts within the body of the speech. In part two of this chapter we shall deal with analysis and arrangement.

| **The Conclusion** |
| --- |

The conclusion is our final impression upon our audience. If it is weak, that weakness will persist in the minds of our hearers. A strong conclusion leaves a good impression.

The basic purpose of the conclusion in an expository speech is to review what we have done. The listening audience is the forgetting audience, and we need to summarize at the end of our speech what we have covered. We should remember the admonition given playrights that any essential piece of information should be repeated three times. In our speeches we need to tell our audience what we are going to tell them, to tell them, and to tell them what we have told them. The conclusion fills this last function.

When we finish the last step in the development of our contract, (our last topical division), we may well begin our conclusion with a restatement of our obligation sentence. We may say "During my speech today I have. . ." or "For the last few minutes we have been considering together. . ." It is frequently possible for us to give this restatement as the concluding portion of a final summary sentence. "If you will plant and cultivate with care, if you are able to prevent disease and insect destruction, and if you are able to reach an early market, you have a good chance of making a neat profit from growing watermelons."

Frequently, when we finish the last step in the development of our contract (the last main point), we need to review briefly the main divisions of our speech. This summary should be short and simple with a phrase or sentence for each main point discussed. In long, complicated speeches the summary may be more complete. We should use our best judgment concerning length, but we must not fail to remind our audience what we have done. Poor listeners in our audience may have missed one of our points because of some temporary distraction and our summary may help complete for them the points we made.

Our summary need not be dull and routine. A student speaking about life-saving methods of nonswimmers might emphasize her words with a brief summary which has its own appeal: "If you can't swim, and see a person drowning, row (a boat to the victim) if you must, throw (a life preserver) if possible, tow (stretching out arm or leg to the victim) where you can."

| Application |

In addition to restatment of central idea and summary of points, we should make some application of what we have said for the future welfare of our listeners. Our classroom audience may listen to our informative speeches and at the end say: "Very well done, but just what does that have to do with me?" It is our duty to let our listeners know why we feel the speech is important for them.

| *Faults in Conclusion* |

Some speakers don't know that the audience forgets easily and they feel that because something has been said once, it should never be repeated. This is a serious mistake and will lead to abrupt endings and poor recall by the audience. Again, a conclusion may beat around the bush interminably until the audience wishes, silently or audibly, that the speaker would shut up and sit down.

Our conclusion has a job to do; once that job is done, we should quit. Sometimes we make the mistake of calling our last point a conclusion. Many speakers have the bad habit of saying when they reach the last of the analysis, "And in conclusion I would like to make this last point. . ." This is not a true conclusion and does not fulfll its functions. Finally, our speech can build up to an awful letdown. We must learn to stop when we are through, and not to add weaker and still weaker explanations or apologies or "just one thing more. . ."

| **Partition** |

An optional fifth element in speech composition is the partition, a preview or pre-summary coming immediately after the contract statement. It is a look ahead at the major divisions to be developed, and may, like the summary, be full and complete or rapid and sketchy. In long and complex informative speeches the partition is a useful device. In our short speeches a formal and elaborate petition will probably repel audience interest. The device should be used with caution because in short speeches it is a waste of time. It may also be a distinct liability in that we have robbed ourselves of some interest by revealing too much of our speech too soon.

| Transitions |

Because the minds of our listeners wander and forget, we need to build verbal bridges between each new part of our speech organization and the preceding part. This "verbal bridge" is the process of transition. In written communication we probably dismiss this task with such transitional words as nevertheless, however, therefore, moreover, in addition, on the other hand, besides. Because the listening audience can so easily miss these expressions altogether and forget what has gone before, the process is more important and more difficult in oral composition.

The first transition comes between introduction and contract. Some speakers pride themselves on a smooth blend of introduction and contract so that listeners never exactly get the central idea. This is a mistake. We should call attention to our contract statement, make our listeners perk up their ears and listen to this most important sentence. One way of doing this is to refer to the introduction by "therefore" or "because of its great significance to us," and then continue with "my subject is" or "I would like to discuss with you today. . ." (reference to speaker, audience, and occasion). Many similar expressions can be used. Variety in language usage is important but we must make sure that the audience cannot miss our purpose statement.

The second transition leads from the contract statement to the first main division of the speech. Other transitional elements will be needed between the main divisions as they are brought forward. Each of these should include a restatement of the contract and a reference to the preceding division or divisions. We must be sure the audience does not miss the "bones" or structure of our speech. We must not be afraid of being too mechanical. Writers underline, paragraph, print in italics or capitals or boldface letters. Speakers emphasize transitions through pause and voice change and movement, but need vital transitions in addition. A beginning speaker *can* be too mechanical, but is not likely to be.

# Part B: Types of Point Arrangement and Speech Outlining

Once the purpose of our speech has been determined we must analyze it so that the supporting materials can be gathered and organized. Analysis is the process of separating anything into its constituent parts or elements. Chemists analyze complex substances to find the elements of which they are composed. A speaker must analyze his subject to uncover those parts essential for its development. Practically, analysis in speech making is the process of discovering in our subject the two, three, or more topical divisions (otherwise known as "main heads" or just plain "points") which best develop the central idea.

*One Point Speeches*

Probably the simplest speech pattern is the one-point speech, a purpose sentence followed by as many illustrations and examples as time permits. All supporting materials in the one-point speech develop directly the purpose sentence. For instance, we might make a talk concerning school spirit at our college, developing our evaluation of its condition by citing specific occasions (homecoming, elections, graduation) upon which students showed either great or little loyalty to their institution. The one-point speech requires no subordinate generalization or topical divisions — just the one central idea plus whatever amount of evidence time permits.

*Purpose of Analysis*

Most of our speeches need further division, two or three subordinate statements, around which evidence can be grouped. Ideas and supporting material need careful arrangement. Order marks the skillful speaker. Informative speaking in particular aims at audience comprehension, and our clear and systematic analysis helps our audience understand and remember what we have to say.

In the field of industrial productivity a similar contribution is made through *job analysis.* This is the skilled art of the highly paid efficiency expert. His contribution is in breaking down a complex process into its component steps or elements. Only then can industrial personnel so understand the total operation that improvement can be made in the production method. Likewise the speech maker, if he is to justify taking the time of the audience, must prepare carefully and present his best analysis of the subject under discussion.

Two speeches may contain the same material — facts, examples, authorities, analogies. One may be a sound, strong, efficient bridge between the minds of speaker and audience. The other, with the same material, may be nothing better than a confused jumble of jackstraw girders leading nowhere and accomplishing nothing. The first is the result of a careful pattern of analysis; the second is the result of lack of patterned analysis.

**Analysis According to the Problem**

Many and varied are the patterns of analysis. No two speeches or audiences offer quite the same problem; each is a separate experience with particular and sometimes peculiar demands. Most topics can be analyzed in a number of different ways, each satisfactory, the choice among them depending upon that complex speaker-audience-subject-occasion interaction which characterizes oral communication.

All patterns of analysis are inductive or deductive in relation to the position of the *real* purpose appearing in the conclusion of the speech. When the contract following the introduction lets the audience know immediately the purpose of the speaker, the pattern will be deductive in nature. The pattern for most informative speaking will be deductive in nature. In speeches to persuade, the inductive pattern is the better method.

Another way of describing the pattern of analysis is according to the *position* of the main points as they appear in the speech. When the most telling points appear first in the development of the body outline, the order is an anticlimactic one; when the most important point is reserved to last, the order is climactic in development. The order of main points is more important in persuasive speaking than in expository speaking and most space should be given to the most important point.

**The Patterns for the Main Points**

The speech maker is primarily interested, however, in the type of division used in setting up the main points to develop the contract. The discussion of analysis which follows will concern itself with this most meaningful procedure for the beginning student in speech. Listed following are examples of several such patterns of analysis extremely useful to us as speakers. There are other patterns, of course, but these include the most common ones.

**Chronological, or Time Sequence**

A common pattern for many informative speeches is chronology, or time sequence. Lectures in history or literature are often arranged by year, decade, period or century. So are biographical or autobiographical narratives, whether in books, magazine articles, or speeches.

We frequently use this pattern in everday conversation. Narratives of various kinds are primarily chronological. When we describe an experience to our roommate or to a speech class, we probably use chronological narration. We may describe a day in the life of a waitress, how we learned to drive, or our first parachute jump. Perhaps our subject might be the assembly line at Ford's River Rouge plant, one flight for an airline stewardess, or making a ground controlled landing through heavy fog. All these are suitable topics for chronological analysis, though each can be analyzed in other ways.

One typical speech for which a chronological pattern is indicated is the "process" speech. At some time during the course you may choose to tell the class how to do something. You may discuss water skiing, underwater swimming, fishing, diving for or cleaning sponges, life saving, artificial respiration, hunting ducks, building a bird house, preparing rattlesnake meat, baking a cake, making fudge, cutting out a dress, selling tobacco at an auction, or one of many other skills. Here is an example of a process speech using a chronological sequence: Statement of contract: "Successful growing of shade tobacco requires four essential steps."

A. Shading the growing space.
B. Preparation of the soil.
C. Cultivation of the growing plants.
D. Spraying for insect control.

**Geographical, or Space Sequence**

Another common and useful pattern of analysis involves space instead of time. A course in geography may have conditioned us to consider such diverse subjects as farm productivity and election forecasts from the viewpoint of spatial or geographical units. Many descriptions — the Black Hills, Rock City, the Carlsbad Caverns, the University of Illinois, or even a new Ford or Chevrolet — use space relationships for their over-all pattern. When someone at home asks what the college campus or the new men's dormitory looks like, our answer will probably be organized according to spatial units.

Geographical analysis is useful for much more than simple descriptions. Consider its application to election forecasts, for example. In a national election the complete pattern would include fifty items, one for each state (and, incidentally, would illustrate a complete "enumeration" as well as a geographical pattern of analysis.)

The geographical analysis usually developed by radio or newspaper reporters for election forecasts or results will group the various states into contingent areas which make up the generally used and somewhat flexible units. Examples of such groupings might include: New England, the South, the Eastern Seaboard, the Middle West, the Southwest, the Mountain States, the Northeast, the Far West.

The description of a trip we have made usually combines chronological and geographical analysis. History courses often do the same. A description of the Revolutionary War, for instance, may be based upon geographical analysis: Contract: "The Revolutionary War was fought in four general areas. Let us review them."

A. The war in the New England states.
B. The war in the Middle Colonies.
C. The war in the South.
D. The war on the sea.

This outline roughly approximates the chronological sequence as well; except for point D, the war was fought in A, B, and C in that time order.

**Enumeration**

Many analyses, especially complete surveys, consist of an enumeration. When the census takers make their rounds, they and their colleagues are making a complete enumeration of the people in the United States. We might enumerate the thirteen original colonies, list the books by a famous author, tell where we get our names for the days of the week or the months of the year. Simple enumeration is not enough; each item must be described or defined or otherwise meaningfully treated. For instance, one way of demonstrating the weakness of the thirteen colonies at the time of the Revolution would be to discuss the economic and military potential of each colony in turn. From this composite picture valid conclusions could be drawn concerning the colonies as a whole.

Other examples will occur to us as we consider occasions like these. When CBS or NBC covers election night returns, the announcer frequently "reads the board" giving the latest available returns from each of the fifty states. His is a simple enumeration, usually arranged alphabetically. An athletic director might enumerate the members of a particular conference or discuss the football games his college will play at home this fall. (This last topic might or might not be treated chronologically as well.) Our history professor may use a simple enumeration pattern when he describes the difficult decisions made by eight border states at the time of the Civil War.

In our classroom speeches we will seldom have time for complete and lengthy enumerations like some of these, but we could probably list and describe briefly the three most important industries of our state, or her three most important natural resources. We might enumerate (and describe, compare, contrast or otherwise consider) the principal means of public transportation out of our home town: bus, train, air. Someone may be interested in naming and identifying the principal national forests in the United States. Local prospects in football may be interpreted by enumerating the positions on the team (ends, tackles, guards, center, quarterback, halfbacks, fullback) and describing leading candidates for each position.

All told, this is a useful pattern of analysis for many topics. Let us remember that a list is not a speech, and we will need to do much more than list or itemize; we must give illustrations, examples, descriptions, comparisons and finally make an application of this material for our audience.

**Topical Analysis**

Many subjects have within themselves divisions well known to us and our audience. When such possibilities are present, we will do well not to ignore such "stereotyped" divisions. Sometimes we will do best to give our audience the divisions it is looking for.

In many sports, such as football, baseball, and basketball, the common topics are (a) defense and (b) offense. In track there are (a) running events such as sprints, distance runs, hurdles, and relays and (b) field events such as discus, shot put, javelin, and pole vault. Our personal finance — or somebody's ideal college budget — can be examined in terms of (a) receipts and (b) expenditures. In a discussion of our federal government, an audience would expect to see divisions relating to the executive, legislative, and judicial functions thereof.

Occasionally the topical pattern of analysis is nothing more than a listing of the two or three most important ideas we can think of to develop a particular topic. For example, take the following: Contract: "A college education secures three advantages to the student. Let us consider them."

A. Skill enough to earn a living.
B. Ability to think clearly and without bias.
C. Poise in dealing with associates.

Other values might be listed, or our speech narrowed to one of these, or these same values stated or subdivided in other ways. The main points outlined make no pretense of being all-inclusive nor do they even assert that these are the most important advantages of a college education.

**Problem-Causes-Solutions**

Several patterns of analysis involve causation. This is a concept with which we deal constantly in nearly every class we take, and with which we are concerned every day of our lives. Why do things turn out as they do? Why does this — flunking out, election to Phi Beta Kappa, physical or nervous breakdown, selection for one of the athletic squads — happen to me?

Ours is an ordered world. Events do not happen by chance through the throw of some cosmic dice. Events are caused, and they in turn produce effects. This kind of relationship often provides a useful pattern of analysis for our speeches. We have heard it used many times: the coach discusses the reasons for last Saturday's victory (or defeat); the sociologist asks why lynchings and race riots occur; the political scientist interprets how a presidential election was won or lost; a faculty counselor suggests why our marks are not all they should be.

Often our contract sentence states what has happened and asks what the probable causes were. Why have federal taxes remained so high? What led to the decision to build the H-bomb? Why did the football team have such a poor season? Why have highway accidents continued to increase? Our causal analysis will usually not stop with the problem and causes but will continue with solutions. Thus we develop what is commonly described as the *problem-causes-solutions* pattern of analysis.

**Problem-Effect-Solution**

We should look at causal relation from the other direction. Here we start with a known cause and seek to explain what the probable effects may be. What changes would result from the university's decision to abandon intercollegiate sports? If the state legislature were changed to a unicameral body, what might the effect be? As our school grows,

what can be expected in the way of increased facilities? What have
been the effects of large dams built by the federal government?
What will be the effects of partial or total mobilization? What are or
will be the effects of the breakdown of the United Nations committee on atomic energy? If we wish to make a persuasive speech
on the *problem-effect* analysis, we will naturally add *solution* to it
and so produce what is commonly called the *problem-effect-solution*
pattern.

**Interrogative Pattern**

The speech to persuade often takes
an organizational pattern which, because of the sentences used as the divisions, has come to be called the in-
terrogative pattern. The outline of the body of the speech will appear in the form of questions.

    II.  Contract:
        "Before we decide on where we stand with respect to the
        use of pesticides, we shall need the answers to three
        questions."
   III.  Body:
       A.  Are pesticides harmful to humans?
       B.  Do pesticides kill large numbers of birds and other
          wild life?
       C.  What are the conditions where pesticides are not used?

This is particularly effective organization when the speaker knows
a great many of his audience favor a point of view which he would
like to change. By stating his contract in the form of a question
he does not take an immediate stand. He appears to be willing to
consider all the aspects of the problem and with his audience reach
the conclusion which seems most logical. Eventually, at the close
of the discussion, he does state his point of view but by that time
he can hope that a good portion of his audience have reached the
same decision on the basis of the "fair" consideration of all aspects
of the issue which he has brought to them.

This pattern of organization is automatically inductive in nature
and one of the best persuasive patterns available. In his handling
of the "questions," the speaker can appear at some points to be actually arguing for a conclusion the reverse of the one at which he
finally arrives. The number of divisions used in this type of pattern
will depend upon the time available and the amount of evidence
which can be gathered on each division.

| Narrative Pattern |
|---|

You will have observed that narrative serves many uses in speech making. It is probably the best kind of introduction possible. It is far better than definition as a means of clarifying word or point. Moreover, a whole speech can be built on a narrative pattern in which a single narrative is related and a conclusion or conclusions drawn from it or in which each point is carried to conclusion by a separate narrative.

The contract of a single narrative speech might be: "Today I wish to tell you the three ways in which Jim McNeeley used his master's degree in agriculture." Disarming as this statement of purpose may sound, it may well lead to one or more conclusions which would sway an audience of farmers to a new way of doing something which they had long resisted. The beautiful thing about the use of the narrative is that the speaker is hardly thought of as a persuader and therefore suffers very little ready-built audience resistance. For this reason, and for the reason that narrative is so easily remembered, this pattern of organization is at once the most subtle and the most effective form of persuasion.

| Cumulative Narrative |
|---|

The ninth pattern of speech organization is similar to the preceding except in the number of narratives used. Again it is all narrative but it springs from what appears to be a three prong development as it is announced in the contract. Such a contract might be stated in the following fashion: "I would like to tell you how three individuals looked at the same city zoning problem." Again, the listener does not know what the speaker proposes to do with these three points of view with respect to the specific problem.

It would be possible to use this type of development for an expository speech but the chances are good the purpose will be persuasion to a point of view. The skilled speaker will probably use the three narratives to point up a conclusion which he wishes his listeners to accept.

| Outlining the Speech |
|---|

Except for oral practices, our speech preparation ends with a full content outline derived from our analysis and organization. Notice in the sample following that the contract and all divisions are written as complete sentences, not abbreviated as subject or title phrases. Most transitions are omitted and no illustrative material included.

This outline brings to a focus our speech preparation, but it should not be used as "speech notes" before the class. If we must use notes, we should write a few key words on a 3 x 5 card. Complete sentences will do us more harm than good by interrupting our eye-contact with our audience.

Analysis and organization are skills of the process of thought. Our success at informative speaking, perhaps even more than at persuasion, depends a great deal upon our ability to break apart or analyze and to synthesize into a coherent, well-ordered whole. Since they are arts, we must practice them over and over. These skills will pay dividends in every task of communication, oral or written, we ever face.

*Sample Outline*
(Introduction, contract, and conclusion in full)

I. *Introduction*: When the old Romans tired of everything else in life, they retired to gardening to seek happiness. Most of us are planning for the day when we will be possessors of a nice home with beautiful surroundings. When we realize that aim we will at the same time have an opportunity to secure the happiness in the fashion of the Romans. Proper gardening about the home, however, is not a hit or miss matter. It requires careful planning.

II. *Contract and simple partition*: This morning I will discuss with you the planning for the three areas around the home which will make for attractive and comfortable living.

III. *Body*:
   A. The public area, called the front yard, is the portion we usually allow everyone to enjoy with us.
      1. It is the duty of the home owner to make this area attractive.
         a. An attractive front yard leaves the center of lawn relatively free of planting.
            (1) A few trees may be used.
            (2) Some specimen planting may be used.
         b. Foundation planting in borders about the house and yard may employ massed shrubbery.
            (1) Such planting makes possible a transition between grounds and house.
            (2) Such planting must consider form, color, and mass.

2. The public area must frame the house not hide it.

    a. The planting must supplement the architecture of the house.

    b. The planting must harmonize with rather than draw attention away from the house.

B. The private area is developed for the enjoyment of our family and our guests.

    1. The private area should serve the function of an outdoor living room.

        a. Easy chairs should be placed in good shade and for a good view.

        b. The planting must insure privacy.

            (1) Shrubs and trees along the edges will give a room like effect.

            (2) Walls or lattice fences help screen off the view from the street

        c. Flower borders and rose beds provide fragrance.

        d. Rock gardens and pools provide beauty.

    2. The private area is an extension of the house.

        a. The pleasing proportions with the house must be secured.

        b. Entrances and walks to this area must be carefully planned.

C. The service area is set aside and planned for utilitarian use.

    1. This area should be screened from other areas as well as from the street.

        a. The garage and workshop is a part of this area.

        b. The laundry yard must be carefully planned in this area.

        c. The vegetable garden is placed in this area.

    2. The service area should be kept in simple formality.

        a. Level land is best for this area.

        b. The vegetable garden must be kept small.

        c. Pathways and walks must be provided.

        d. Planting should be principally for screening.

IV. Conclusion:

Restatement, summary, and application: In discussing the planning for the three areas about the home, we have noted that the public area should be open to view so that the planting makes the house seem a part of the ground; that the private area should be attractive and secluded, really an extension of the house; and that the service area should be simple and hidden from the living area as well as from the public.

As we plan our future homes we should keep the things we have discussed in mind. A really beautiful home doesn't just happen that way. It has come about because of careful planning on the part of the owner and is well worth the thought and time that it takes.

### Speaker's Outline

The outline of the body of the speech used as speaker's notes should look more nearly like this:

A. Public area
   1. Attractive
   2. Frame for house
B. Private area
   1. Outdoor living room
   2. Extension of building
C. Service area
   1. Screening
   2. Simple formality

# Part C: Listening to Speech Organization and Arrangement Patterns

The speech organization and the pattern of arrangement of points are set up twice by the speaker. The first time he does it is during his thought processes as he proceeds to construct the speech prior to delivery. The second time it appears is during the actual delivery of the speech to the audience. On this latter occasion the listener completes the communication process if he follows successfully the ideas according to the design formulated by the speaker.

This following of the speech design is not always an easy thing. Sometimes the design has not been carefully drawn; sometimes the speaker has failed to erect the signposts which make for easy mental travel. Nevertheless, as a listener it is our duty to follow the trail whether it be easy or difficult. The first task is to grasp the four part division as these are presented and so sense where we are in the talk at all times. The second task, and one of greater importance than the first, is to recognize and follow the arrangement pattern or patterns being used so that the proper response can be made. The two jobs for the listener are intertwined because the arrangement of points appears as the speaker develops the third of the four sections of the over-all organization.

## Structure and Arrangement

Listening for speech structure and arrangement involves more than merely taking notice of these parts. The recognition of the speech parts is necessary but it constitutes only the first job for the listener. As we listen we must constantly analyze and evaluate the development of these parts. In other words our thought processes are just as involved with the ideas being presented as are those of the speaker. Unless we are completely involved, we are only half listening and we can never be listening critically.

## Listening to the Introduction

In a five-minute talk the introduction will usually run from twenty seconds to ninety seconds in length, averaging about sixty seconds. In a ten- or fifteen-minute speech, it will average between two and three minutes in length; it grows but little longer after that regardless of the increasing length of the whole discourse. The introduction to a fifty-minute lecture will not average more than three minutes in duration. *What is effective listener activity while the introduction to the typical organized talk is being presented?*

Contrary to the advice of many how-to-study manuals, this is no time to plunge in as they command us to do. The "plunging in" they refer to relates to the taking of notes and, as we shall see in the next chapter, immediate action of that kind is more disruptive than helpful. Instead, this is a time to tune in aurally, but with considerable detachment to proceed to identify and check off mentally the attention-getting technique of the communicator. We are wise to visualize mentally the four parts of the organized speech as Roman numerals I, II, III, and IV: to do this so persistently that the practice becomes purely automatic. As the speaker moves into his transitional sentences and approaches part II of his talk, we must focus every faculty sharply upon him. We are about to hear the most important single statement in his entire discourse.

## Listening to the Contract

The contract in the organized talk is a concise statement of the purpose of the speaker in developing his topic or proposition. No element in the talk is as vital to the listener in his attempt to understand the speaker's motives, ideas, and procedures. It should be noted that some speech texts include the contract element as a part of the introduction. From the standpoint of the assimilator it is certainly preferable to consider it as a separate and distinct unit. Occasionally a speaker puts his contract statement in interrogative form. Although this causes the listener no real difficulty, it might be well to look at a specimen so written. An example might read: "Who was Thomas Paine? What contributions did he make to early America? How should we regard him today? These questions are well worth our consideration."

*What is effective listener activity at the moment the speaker states his contract?* To listen as intently as we can for every possible visual and oral cue is the only answer to be made. No instant is more critical to our understanding of the entire presentation. Certainly this is no time for literal note-taking of any kind; rather, all our energies should be devoted to *mental* note-taking of the most intense character.

## Identifying the Speaker's Goal

It is extremely desirable to identify the real goal or aim of the speaker as quickly and as certainly as we possibly can. The earliest possible moment for such identification is when he states his contract. If we are fortunate enough to learn, for instance, that he seeks our understanding of a process whose explanation he proposes to cover by considering five separate aspects of it, our chances for improved comprehension are tremendously enhanced. It will then be much easier for us to follow his talk and check off mentally each phase of his exposition as it is developed. No trained speaker, of course, tries to conceal the pattern of organization within his talk. Just the reverse is true. The more effective he is, the more clearly and persistently he strives to reveal his plan. Despite the many clues he offers, without direct attention to this assimilative skill many of us may still confuse his intent and procedure.

## Listening to the Body of the Speech

The body of the speech is the longest of the four major divisions. In a five-minute talk it will consume from three to three and one-half minutes of the total time; in a fifty-minute talk it will consume from forty to forty-five minutes. The structural elements of the body of the talk constitute what is normally called "the point arrangement pattern of the speech." *What is the effective listener activity while the body of each oral discourse is being presented?*

Fortunately, the listener's primary goal is comprehension regardless of whether the address is instructive or persuasive. The time has not yet arrived for passing judgment upon the merits of the speaker's ideas. But the soundness of that eventual judgment is directly determined by how accurately the listener appraises the supporting material used to develop each main point in the body of the speech, and how accurately he appraises the success of the speaker in finally completing or establishing his contract.

Just as we should cultivate the mental attachment of a Roman numeral I to the introduction, II to the contract, and IV to the conclusion, we should always visualize a Roman numeral III beside "Body of the Speech." It is desirable to go still further and to visualize a capital letter standing before each of the main points fitted below our mental numeral III.

| Identifying the Points |

The expression "perceiving the structure" or "identifying the organizational plan" simply refers to our ability to detect the four major parts within each organized talk. By far the most important structural elements for us to perceive are the numeral III and its subordinate, or capital-letter, components. These items constitute what is normally called "the point arrangement pattern of the speech." To be able to visualize it, and to understand the reason for its internal order is prerequisite to full comprehension of the discourse. That the trained speaker never includes more than five main points in the body of his speech, and seldom deviates from the numbers two, three, or four simplifies considerably an acquirement of the understanding we should like to attain concerning his methods.

As discussed under part two of this chapter, there are nine systems of point arrangement frequently encountered in organized talks. They do not constitute an exhaustive list, but other systems are met so infrequently as to be insignificant. One complication is that within the same speech there will occasionally be combinations of these patterns. In a lengthy speech, for example, the development of each main point may in itself be quite similar to the development of the entire body of a short talk. Thus, point A might be developed chronologically and point B spatially. The listener's best adjustment to such a mixture is that of (a) recognizing that it is being done; (b) checking mentally the statement of each point with the speaker's statement of his thesis; (c) recapitulating mentally all the foregoing main points after the completion of each new and additional one.

Fortunately, few speakers complicate the comprehension problems of their listeners through this kind of compositional confusion.

| **Listening to the Chronological Pattern** | A very common pattern in informative speech is based upon time sequence. It is convenient for both conveyor and auditor because it is so easy to remember. Many a |

classroom lecture in history or literature has been constructed upon a purely chronological sequence; and many an exposition of a process has followed the same route. An example of the contract in an informative speech built upon this pattern might read: "Let us consider the three steps a man must take if he would build his wife a cedar chest." The skeletal outline of the body of this talk might then look as follows:

III. Body
   A. Acquiring the needed materials
   B. Constructing the chest
   C. Applying the exterior finish

As soon as we recognize the chronological character of a talk we are hearing, we would do well to check immediately, literally or mentally, the wording used by the speaker when he stated his contract. Almost without exception we will discover that he started with a generalization, that he openly declared his intention to support it, and that he is now proceeding to do so in strictly deductive fashion. In the rare instance when our backtracking fails to verify these anticipated conditions, we will probably then be satisfied that the talk being made is persuasive. In subsequent pages we shall learn how in that case we can best assimilate and evaluate the discourse.

| **Listening to the Spatial Pattern** | A space sequence (sometimes called topographical or geographical) is nearly as common as the chronological one in informative speech. It too is convenient for both conveyor and auditor to recall. If we set out |

to describe either our campus or the layout of the newest model car we will doubtless follow this arrangement of points. An example of a contract for an instructive speech built upon this pattern might read: "In the next election .......................................... will probably carry all four of the major geographical areas of our nation. I draw your attention to the facts leading to this conclusion." A skeletal outline of the body of this talk might look like this:

III. Body
   A. The outlook in the eastern states
   B. The outlook in the south
   C. The outlook in the north
   D. The outlook in the far west

As soon as we recognize the spatial character of the plan of organization, we can profit by checking it, too, against the wording of the speaker's stated aim.

Typically the contract will have included a generalization along with an openly declared intent to support it deductively. If our backtracking fails to verify these anticipated findings, we know that the talk being made is probably persuasive and that we shall need to assimilate and evaluate it in the light of that knowledge.

*Listening to the Enumerative Pattern*

A third pattern of point arrangement used almost exclusively in informative speech is enumerative in character. It normally is used when the speaker believes it impossible to achieve his ends without violating the taboo of including more than five points in his discourse. By straight vertical enumeration, often with a chronological, alliterative, or some other kind of mnemonic device to make it easier for both him and his auditors to remember them, he produces a rather extensive list of items for discussion in the body of his talk. Only brief treatment can be given each, of course. An example of a contract for an instructive speech built upon this pattern might read: "Our course in contemporary literature consists essentially of reading and discussing the twelve most important books of the past twenty years. Let us devote this first hour of the semester's work to a brief justification for the inclusion of each book in our list of twelve." Almost without exception lengthy enumerations are found in informative talks proceeding deductively from an initial generalization to the submitting of details that develop and support it.

*Listening to the Topical Pattern*

Many subjects discussed informatively seem to fall almost automatically into natural major divisions. For example, were we to discuss the topic "Chief Values of a College Education," many of us might decide, acting individually and independently, to discuss: (A) Social values; (B) Cultural values; (C) Vocational values. It is apparent that these three main points are not arranged according to any of the patterns for instructive speech so far discussed, and yet that their order is a reasonably logical one. Many times speakers follow a topical arrangement for purely personal reasons. For instance, in discussing the general subject of "Winter Sports," the speaker might well select the two sports he himself enjoys most or performs the best.

An example of a contract for a speech following a topical arrangement might read: "There are two aspects of our reciprocal trade agreements whose understanding will require considerable study on our part." The skeletal outline of the body of the ensuing speech might look like this:

III. Body
    A. Political aspects
    B. Economic aspects

Again, the professed aim of the speaker contains a generalization with its proposed support deductively developed. A real help to the hearer in identifying the topical pattern is to listen for these words: phases, aspects, considerations, angles, approaches. One or another of them almost always appears in the contract statement.

*Listening to the Problem-Causes-Solutions Pattern*

The fifth conventional pattern for point arrangement in an informative speech is a very common one, but we must be very careful to distinguish it from a very similarly worded one used with almost equal exclusiveness in persuasive discourse. The pattern is an extremely valuable and suitable arrangement for organizing many instructional topics and is delightfully easy for both conveyor and learner to remember. The three main points are suggested in its label. An example of a contract for an instructive speech built upon this pattern might read: "Our state is acknowledged by everyone to be in bad financial straits. Let us take a close look at the full dimensions of our problem, examine the forces causing it, and then investigate the various solutions being proposed." A skeletal outline of the body of this talk would of course look like this:

III. Body
    A. The problem
    B. The causes
    C. The proposed solutions

Among the clues that clearly identify this talk as informative in character are the following: the generalization appearing in the contract, the obviously deductive arrangement of the main points in the body, the plurality of the word "causes" and the word "solutions." The latter word is much more likely to be kept singular when a speaker uses a somewhat parallel pattern of point arrangement in composing a persuasive speech.

---

*Listening to the*
*Problem-Effect-*
*Solution Pattern*

Very similar to the problem-causes-solutions pattern used in informative speech is the problem-effect-solution pattern used in persuasion. We should note that the second main point of the latter pattern is concerned not with causes but with the effect of the problem on the audience; and that for his third main point the speaker has only one solution for which to urge adoption, not several to be analyzed and studied. We listeners, as soon as we identify this pattern, should recheck closely the manner in which the speaker stated his contract. Usually we find that only the procedure was clarified, and that the speaker's convictions were not revealed; also that we are led to believe that some kind of generalization or conclusion will be reached later on in the discourse. Typically the purpose statement preceding this point-arrangement system would read like this: "There are three phases of this matter which deserve our careful attention." The skeletal outline of the body of the ensuing speech would look like this:

III. Body
    A. The problem
    B. Its effect upon the members of this audience
    C. Our best course of action

We should note that while the contract may seem to imply something of the speaker's position, no open declaration will be forthcoming until the very late stages of the speech. The words "phases, considerations, and elements" commonly appear in the thesis statement. Knowing the inductive and persuasive character of the discourse, we should (a) listen intently to assure comprehension as complete as possible; (b) carefully weigh the speaker's appeal for listener response when it eventually comes, with the evidence submitted as a basis for that appeal; (c) schedule a later period for evaluation of the speaker's proposition and the making of a decision as to what our personal reaction to it should be.

*Listening to the
Interrogative Pattern*
The interrogative pattern is a common, persuasive and inductive system for point arrangement in a speech. It has the advantage to the speaker of making him sound quite judicious, learned, and restrained. The contract statement reveals procedure, conceals conviction, suggests inductive development, and capitalizes upon the word "issues" or "questions." An example might well read like this: "Before we can sensibly decide whether or not to vote for an expansion of our present student union facilities, we must carefully answer three questions." The skeletal outline of the body of the ensuing speech would look something like this:

III. Body
    A. Can we get along with our present facilities?
    B. Would the proposed expansion really do for us what is being claimed?
    C. Would the cost be exorbitant?

Effective listener activity while following the interrogative pattern is precisely the same as that prescribed for the preceeding one. Frequently the truly persuasive speaker will seem to lean one way in answering the first question, the opposite way on the second, and reveal his ultimate appeal only at the latest possible moment in his talk. In this fashion he capitalizes upon suspense as well as upon our increasing respect for his thoroughgoing analysis and reasoned judgment.

*Listening to the
Narrative Pattern*
The eighth conventional pattern of point arrangement in speeches is a strictly narrative one. It is inductive, and a highly effective persuasive technique when skillfully used for that purpose. It consists of the relating of a single and comparatively lengthy narrative, with either the speaker himself or a person known well by most of the auditors as a central character in the tale. Almost always the outcome of the story is tragic, with certain very dramatic elements of it leading inescapably to the two or three conclusions the speaker has intended to reach from the very first. When the outcome is not tragic, the speech has probably been given for purely entertainment purposes.

The very simply stated contract clarifies procedure but conceals convictions. It forecasts what is essentially a one-point speech, and usually has approximately this wording: "This evening I should like to tell you of an experience I had last December." Not till the summary stage of the conclusion has been reached does the speaker make any effort to generalize his tale and draw conclusions from it. His ensuing appeal for audience action is likely to be a highly emotional one, for his pattern permits persuasion to operate in its most subtle form. Effective listener adjustment to the narratively built speech should include the same three steps described under listening to the Problem-Effect-Solution Pattern.

*Listening to the Cumulative Narrative Pattern* — The cumulative narrative pattern consists of a series of narrative specific instances, or examples, with a common point made in each. It is sometimes used for entertainment speaking, but almost always for strictly persuasive purposes. The contract is inductively stated, revealing procedure but carefully concealing the speaker's convictions. Unlike the narrative pattern in which one story is told with perhaps two or three conclusions drawn from it, the cumulative narrative pattern calls for the telling of several shorter stories with a single conclusion to be drawn from the entire group.

An example of a purpose statement for a speech developed in this fashion might read: "This morning I wish to tell the stories of three criminals — three entirely factual case histories drawn directly from the F. B. I. files in Washington, D. C." The skeletal outline of the body of the ensuing speech would look like this:

III. Body
    A. The story of Rat Moore, pickpocket
    B. The story of Tookie Allen, holdup artist
    C. The story of Jake the Barber, assassin for hire

Not until the summary element of the conclusion has been reached does the speaker identify the central conclusion to be drawn from his narratives, or make any effort to generalize them.

To adjust to this most subtle and effective of all persuasive speech patterns, effective listener activity must again include (a) an effort to achieve fullest possible comprehension; (b) careful balancing of the speaker's emotional appeal against the evidence presented to support that appeal; (c) a postponement until a later period of reflection our evaluation of the speaker's proposition and the making of a decision as to what our personal reaction to it should be.

---
*Listening to the*
*Unorganized Speech*

---

It is unfortunate but true that during our lives we are likely to hear fewer carefully composed speeches than unorganized or very poorly organized ones. It is not very difficult to identify the unorganized discourse. The direction followed is largely controlled by free association, and free association alone. Our recognition of what is happening is inevitable once we discover that even in mid-sentence our speaker tends to turn off on verbal side-paths. The communicator so beguiled by his own language as to turn aside when motivated by only a simple word or phrase grows steadily more fascinated by his own allusions. By branching off from one allusion to another he may lead us through incredible mental jungles.

To verify how carefully a person has composed his talk we need but look for four clues. The unprepared speaker will (a) be tardy in getting under way; (b) elicit suggestions from the audience, and then debate the suggestions; (c) resort to "kidding" the audience -- presumably showing his cleverness and charm; (d) be oversolicitous concerning the listeners' comfort, thus delaying the discourse in the hope that some heaven-sent inspiration will meanwhile arrive.

What is effective listener activity? To achieve any real comprehension of the unorganized lecture or address we shall need to adopt immediately the one system of note-taking permitting adequate assimilation of such disjointed material. This system, number four in the following chapter, is described at that point in detail. We would do well, too, if we are students and the poorly organized speaker is our instructor, to secure an individual conference with the man. In this conference we should speak pointedly of three things: our difficulties, his strengths, and his weaknesses. This may require some courage on our part but it seldom, if ever, results in the feared failing grade. Unless we do follow the enlightened policy in this world of praising the good and refusing to tolerate the bad, we have no one but ourselves to blame for the unpleasant and painful elements of our culture.

---
**Listening to the Conclusion**

---

The conclusion of the organized speech normally contains two elements: a summary and a final appeal. There is considerable variation in the nature of these elements, depending upon whether the speech is informative or persuasive in character.

In the informative talk the summary is an orderly recapitulation of the main points developed in the body. Usually the speaker restates his main points in slightly different language; moreover, he usually reiterates his general purpose which presumably has now been established with the help of the main points he has built. The appeal element in the conclusion of the informative speech is really less of an appeal than it is a relating of the material to the audience, a pointing of the way in which the material can be utilized. The comparatively mild plea made by the speaker is one for the *application* of what may have been gained. It is dispassionate, objectively worded, coldly reasoned.

In the persuasive talk — and this is always true if the discourse has been carefully and inductively constructed — the summary element is far more than a restatement of main points. It is the long-delayed moment at which the speaker in weighing the evidence for and against a proposition finally reveals clearly his own convictions and point of view toward that proposition. Gathering together the examples or conditions discussed throughout the body of his talk, he finds them containing a common thread leading to an inescapable generalization. This generalization is now revealed to be the speaker's true conviction and one upon which he seeks active listener response. The appeal element immediately following is likely to be highly emotional in both content and delivery. It usually shows how the perfectly natural motives impelling the listeners to a certain course of action can only lead, in view of the material they have just heard, to act now in conformity with the proposition the speaker has unfolded.

What is effective listener activity while the conclusion is being heard? Again, the listener is interested primarily in comprehension regardless of whether the address is instructive or persuasive. Effective listening, however, requires attention to two items at this moment. First, the listener must appraise the fairness and reasonableness with which the speaker matches his appeal to the basis for that appeal — the content of the body of the speech. This is likely to have considerable influence upon the listener's eventual evaluation and possible action in response to the speaker's pleas. Second, the listener must schedule for himself an interval for later reflection upon the proposal he has just heard developed. He should plan during this later reflection interval to make his personal evaluation and decision on the proposition just propounded to him. The building of the habit of usually postponing decisions until more time for reflection can be had is fundamental to effective listening. It is the strongest, if indeed not the only, defense against the truly persuasive artist on the speech platform.

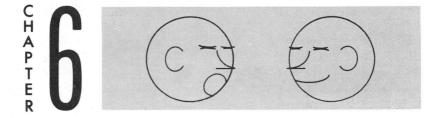

CHAPTER 6

Speaking
and
Listening . . .

# . . . the tools of sending and receiving

## Part A: The Symbol System of Speech

In the "Grapes of Wrath" John Steinbeck called attention to differences in pronunciation. " 'Evr'body says words different,' said Ivy. 'Arkansas folks says 'em different, and Oklahomy folks says 'em different. And we seen a lady from Massachusetts, an' she said 'em differentest of all. Couldn' hardly make out what she was saying.' " Obviously there is no standard pronunciation for the entire United States, nor should there be. Standardization in language is as deadly as standardization in tastes of any sort. At its worst, uniformity in language stifles expression and makes phraseology dull.

There are at least three general areas of the United States which present language characteristics different enough to be easily discernible. The General American pattern is spoken by about 70 percent of our population, the Southern type by about 20 percent, and the Eastern standard by approximately 10 percent. These differences are becoming less pronounced. Florida is thought of as a Southern state but the speech pattern is no longer distinctly Southern except in the tier of counties along the Georgia line. In Miami, St. Petersburg, and other resort cities the General American and Eastern patterns of speech are predominant. The chief difference between these regional patterns is that of vowel articulation, although the dropping or adding of the *r* sound is probably more spectacular.

Those who advocate a "correct" standard of pronunciation maintain that without such a standard a chaos in pronunciation will result — that oral language will become unintelligible. Such expected deterioration in language patterns has always been threatened and has never occurred. Such degeneration is impossible because the function of language is to communicate. If it does not, it would cease to exist altogether.

*Avoid the Substandard*

The point of this discussion is to emphasize that no single dialect needs to be taken as standard. This is not to say that all regard for articulation and pronunciation is a waste of time. Common sense dictates that substandard utterance of speech sounds and words should be avoided. Poor articulation of sounds either makes the communicator unintelligible or, at best, throws too much of a burden on the listener in trying to interpret what is being said. Pronunciation which varies in an unusual way from what is commonly heard may block communication. More often it sidetracks the listener from any ideas being presented to the mishandled word itself. An even worse condition results when a mispronunciation sidetracks the listener to reflections about its user.

We should relieve ourselves of any unnecessary embarrassment because of a word pronounced too far from the common usage. Although the spelling of English words is largely phonetic, there are many exceptions. In addition there is the problem of accent which is uncertain. We should look up in the dictionary the division of syllables, the individual sounds and the accent of any new word we contact.

*Get the Troublemakers*

It is an unusual individual who does not slip on the pronunciation of a word now and then. There is no need to feel unduly embarrassed on such infrequent occasions. The matter of becoming relatively sure of ourselves in oral usage is no minor accomplishment. The developing of accurate pronunciation will continue throughout our lives; no single speech course can completely satisfy the requirements on this score. The task, however, is not so hopeless that we should forget all about the attempt to improve. A relatively few words in common everyday usage cause most of the trouble. If we once learn to pronounce those few correctly, most of our problem of pronunciation will be solved.

If our difficulty is one of acceptable articulation, however, the solution may not be so easy. The sooner we make a direct attack on this kind of error, the better. There are approximately forty-seven distinctly different English sounds which we must learn to manipulate. They have been divided by phoneticians into three classifications: (a) consonant sounds (twenty-five), (b) vowel sounds (sixteen), and (c) dipthongs (six). Most of our difficulty with articulation does not come from our inability to produce correctly any one of these forty-seven sounds; it arises, instead, from our slovenly fabrication of sound sequence in connected speech. Sometimes we slight important speech sounds in such fashion that the listener has great difficulty in making out what we have said. Such handling of the oral language is inexcusable.

**Pronunciation**

It seems obvious that strict adherence to an absolute standard of pronunciation of words would soon become obnoxious and intolerable. Yet we have self-appointed authorities in English and speech classes and elsewhere who are constantly promoting a "right" way to speak words. This condition exists in spite of disagreement among these "authorities" themselves. Instead of a right way of saying a word a better standard to follow is that of acceptable usage. The acceptable way may involve one of several variants. The word *data* for example may be acceptably pronounced as dā'tȧ ('detə), dăt'ȧ ('dætə), or dä'tȧ ('datə); the word *piano* is "right" when it is called pĭ ă n' ō (pɪ'æno), pĭ än' ō (pɪ'ano), or pĭ ăn' ȧ (pɪ'æn ɔ), as in pianoforte.

We would never want a dictatorship by any single or group authority over the way words are uttered. Whatever is in reputable usage at any given time in a section of the country should be our guide. Al Smith's rădio, (rædɪo) failed to secure wide adoption but (ɪk'spɛrəmənt) might well become (ɛk'spɪrəmənt). We should keep in mind that the ability to pronounce words is not an end in itself. Effective usage avoids mistaken meaning, makes the speaker instantly intelligible, and avoids the criticism of the would-be purist.

**Acceptable Usage**

The pronunciation of a word is in reputable or acceptable usage when a large number of cultivated speakers say it in a certain way. What is a large number and who are the cultivated? We can depend upon the oral usage of the educated people in our community. Although educated people do not follow an absolute standard in pronunciation, we can depend upon what we hear them use. Whether they use one possible variant or another makes little difference. The dictionary makers do not claim that the first choice listed is any better than the second. We may say lē'vēr, or lĕv'ēr, as suits us; dĕ-tāl' or dē'tāl, whichever pleases us.

There are two ways in which we can learn the reputable usage in oral language. The first, and perhaps the best way, is to listen carefully to how words are sounded. Few of us actually do this. That is why oral language so quickly identifies us with a specific cnvironment. We learn to speak by mimicking others. Once the mimicry is satisfactory for an environmental situation, we do little to change that word pattern later. If we will ask a person to say ten o'clock when his habitual pattern has been "tin" o'clock, he fails to hear any difference. He has long since stopped hearing the individual sounds within that word. Careful listening is the first step in the process of relearning the word. The second way to know reputable usage is through the dictionary. We should make use of such books every time we find a strange word and even to check possibilities in usage for words with which we are relatively familiar.

**Spelling and Pronunciation**

One of the reasons why we have so much trouble with pronunciation is that spelling gives us a false clue in many instances. We have actually gotten to the point where approximately forty-seven English sounds are represented by more than 250 different spellings. Sporadic attempts to simplify the spellings have met with only a small measure of success, and the problem continues to grow.

Eventually, it would appear, the difficulties existing between spelling and pronunciation would become so chaotic that a revolution in spelling must occur. In the meantime we struggle to learn pronunciation in spite of the handicap. The present system of spelling allows, for example, the letter o to represent different sounds in woman, women, does, shoes, hoes, dog, and not. The sound called "short i" is represented by approximately twenty different spellings. The system of diacritical marks, never completely accurate, gives the various values to the vowels as they appear in specific words. Unfortunately our reading materials are seldom marked for us and so we rely upon the dictionary for help. The dictionary, however, doesn't give us the complete picture, for some words are sounded differently in connected discourse.

### Silent Letters — Variant Consonants — Accent

Silent and variant consonants, also the result of difference between oral and written representation, cause us still further trouble with pronunciation. Many letters in words are completely silent or have a very slight audible value given them. Instances such as subtle, knew, gnat, and palm are numerous. Moreover, in many cases the consonant sound is produced as though it were another; for example, the s in plurals is commonly z, the suffix ed is frequently t, and the initial s is sometimes sh (sure) (sugar).

In addition to these difficulties there is the matter of accent. When words are constructed so that the sounds are grouped together in syllables, proper pronunciation demands a knowledge of stress — the syllable or syllables accented. Since there are no good rules for learning accent, the only practical solution is to follow what is heard from educated people or to refer to the dictionary. Fortunately the reading of the dictionary with reference to accent is an easy matter.

### Levels of Usage

It would be well for us to recognize that pronunciation is more carefully attended by the speaker in some situations than in others. On informal occasions colloquial utterance of words might be perfectly acceptable whereas the same usage might not fit the needs of the formal speaking engagement. This is to say that cultivated speakers in the conversation situation are usually more concerned with what they are saying than how.

We should remember that it is an easy thing to go "informal" in our oral use of language; the real task for us is to acquire the socially acceptable which is good on any occasion with any group. Perhaps we have felt that the following of reputable usage will antagonize those who are careless in language habits. This constitutes a nice rationalization for our own poor speech patterns. It does not fit the facts. If people react adversely to us it is because of something other than our use of the language. A more serious reaction will be the belief that an education has not done much for us. Such a judgment may be based upon our oral language patterns.

| Faults of Pronunciation |
| --- |

Speech clinicians tell us that errors of pronunciation fall into five general classifications.

(a) *Accent error.* If we fail to place stress on the proper syllable within the word, we have made an error in location of accent. *Ce' ment, ci' gar, es' cape,* and *po' lice* are examples of such unacceptable usage. Sometimes the stress on a word is misplaced because we do not recognize the syllabication ordinarily followed: *sec' re tive, muni cip' al, pre' late,* and *pre fer'- able* are thus falsely produced.

(b) *Sound substitution.* If we use a vowel or consonant sound not ordinarily found in the oral production of a word we have an error of substitution. If we listen carefully we will hear *git* for *get,* *jist* for *just, sich* for *such, ketch* for *catch, pore* for *poor, aig* for *egg,* and *laig* for *leg.* Less acceptable substitutions occur in *wittle* for *little, wun* for *run, bedder* for *better,* or *dit* for *did.* We will hear all of these substitutions and many others in substandard speech.

(c) *Addition of sounds.* If extra sounds appear in our pronunciation of words we have also violated acceptable usage. We may hear rather frequently ath(a)lete, sta(s)tistics, col(y)umn, or umb(e)rella.

(d) *Omitting of sounds.* The reverse of adding sounds is, of course, omitting sounds where they should be presented. Such failures produce reco( )nize, he( )p, su( )prise, fi( )m , kep( ), or w( )ich. Sometimes the speaker tends so much toward brevity that whole syllables or even words are left out. This laziness in speech habits causes *smatter* for *what's the matter?, zatso* for *is that so?,* and *skwup* for *let's go up.*

(e) *Transposition of sounds.* Another variance from the speech of cultivated people occurs when all the sounds of the word are present but they are in improper sequence. This variance to common usage is particularly disturbing to many persons. Examples of transposition include: *modren* for *modern, calvary* for *cavalry, hunderd* for *hundred, preform* for *perform, larnyx* for *larynx,* and *pervent* for *prevent.* We should keep a list of those words which we vocalize in an unacceptable pattern and change every one thorough intensive practice.

## Articulation

The oral symbols used by the speaker must be *instantly intelligible* if communication is to be effectively completed, and the symbols should be *easily recognized* by the listener if the communication is to be satisfactorily executed. We can only assume that the person who takes the trouble to talk wishes to make something known. It would seem unlikely then that this person should deliberately hinder the clarity of his expression through faulty articulation. Since this is frequently done, however, we must believe that such a person is ignorant of the relationship between good articulation and good reception of the oral message by the listener. If we are frequently guilty of poor articulation to the extent that listeners have to ask us to repeat our words, we need to improve our vocalization processes. Our production of the oral symbols should be *easily* and *accurately* recognized by those listening to us.

## Production of the Individual Sounds

Articulation involves the production of the consonant and vowel sounds in our language. This process takes place within the oral cavity or closely related areas of the mouth. To produce and modify the sounds within this oral region, the movements of the tongue, jaw, lips, velum, and throat must be fairly accurate and consistent for good results. Many of the errors of symbol vocalization are relatively easy to correct once the individual knows what he is trying to do. Old habits embodying incorrect use of the articulating mechanism have to be broken and new habits of use established. Training of the ear to specific sounds is an important part of this process of retraining.

The remedial procedure in the case of an articulation problem is clear-cut. It may be to say *little* instead of *wittle* or *rabbit* instead of *wabbit*. It may be to say a sharp tongue tip *s* rather than a lateral over the sides of the tongue *s*. It may be to learn to push the tongue between the teeth a little to get (th) rather than f and thus say *with* rather than *wif*. Whatever the fault, the path of correction is that of breaking an old pattern of producing a sound and establishing a new pattern in its place. Once we are able to produce the proper sound, the correction of the fault involves practice and more practice to make the new tongue position habitual.

**Slurring of
Speech Sounds**

Another difficult problem, at least one stubborn of correction by those who have it, is called slighting or slurring. Many of us are guilty of some slighting errors because of long established habit or because we are too lazy to improve. Many of us are lazy in respect to full and adequate use of tongue, lip, and jaw movement as we speak. The resulting speech is not easy to understand. We are thus guilty of violating the first law of good communication — that we be understood. We have all seen the person who tries to speak with a stiff lower jaw and who as a consequence strains all the sounds through his teeth. Frequently we see those who try to speak the sounds without lip movement as well as without jaw movement. Our speech will improve if we quit trying to be ventriloquists without dummies.

**Artificial Utterance**

The stress upon clear articulation does not call for what has been termed over-precise articulation. Each syllable in a word need not be singled out in the speaking process. In connected discourse, we unstress many of the vowels. The pronunciation of *the* and *a* in discourse characterizes the problem. All the vowels — a, e, i, o, u — frequently appear in audible speech in the unstressed form as "uh." This same principle of reducing the value of certain sounds leads, in discourse, to the elimination of some sounds, both vowels and consonants, altogether. When we say "bread and butter" the "n" is all that is heard of the spelling *and*. To pronounce such words in discourse as they are pronounced in isolation is undesirable affectation.

**Speaking Rate
and Distinctness**

Speaking rate also affects clear articulation and understandability of speech. The rate of speech varies somewhat with the individual but can easily be too slow or too fast. The matter of rate is a function of the duration of syllables and the pauses between words. The average person will speak about 125 words per minute. We should consider carefully what others have to say about our speaking rate. When others complain that we speak too fast they probably have reference to the lack of pauses between a series of words and not the use of the pause as a device for emphasis. The speaker is still communicating during a pause through his eye contact and use of body. Nothing is quite so indicative that the speaker is in complete command of the audience as his effective use of the pause. With experience we will learn to time the pauses so they are neither too long nor too short. The listeners must be given just the right amount of time to think along with the speaker and react to his words.

**Excess Vocalization**

There is a considerable pressure on the speaker to keep the words coming, and except for the use of the pause this is a just demand on the part of the audience. No one wants a speaker to hem and haw, begin sentences over, unnecessarily repeat words or phrases. A speaker who for lack of preparation or for some other reason has many hesitations in his speech is apt to fall into the "and-uh" habit. This excess vocalization is undesirable and is not to be mistaken for the emphatic use of pauses.

Whatever the reason for "and-uh" or "uh-uh" habit, we must get rid of it as quickly as we can. We should ask our classmates to keep a count of the number of times excess vocalization appears in our speeches If the realization of the number of occurrences doesn't help us break the habit, we may need to resort to a shock treatment of some sort. Perhaps the raising of hands by classmates with each instance of vocalization without words will correct this bad habit.

# Part B: Use of Language and Visual Aids

Words and word combinations are the primary devices for transmitting meaning from one person to another. These words may be received aurally as in speech or visually as in reading. As explained earlier, roughly 75 percent of our communication time deals with transmitting or receiving these oral symbols. This fact points up the importance of developing skill in handling oral symbols whether as a speaker or listener.

In the oral situation, however, meaning is ordinarily carried through both sound and sight and sometimes through the other senses. Instances might be pointed out, of course, where the visual element may be completely absent. For example, if we speak to another person in absolute darkness, sound waves become the sole medium of communication. Nevertheless, the most efficient communication demands the use of both sight and hearing.

Abundant experimental evidence has demonstrated that listeners comprehend and retain a significantly greater quantity of information when they can see as well as hear the speaker. From this experimentation we can see that, although language is of primary importance in the oral process, we must not forget the importance of the visual reinforcement. This visual reinforcement enters the speaking situation in two ways: (a) through the use of graphic or visual aids, and (b) through signals initiated by the speaker through bodily action. The discussion of the latter will be reserved for the following chapter.

## Choice of Language

In business contacts, in the professional pursuits, and in the social world the knowledge of words and how to use them is of extreme importance. In fact, one of the most important elements in the whole communication process is the choice and use of language. Without language man can neither think effectively nor communicate adequately his ideas to others. In the oral communication process, therefore, we must be much concerned with the individual words we use and the manner in which we combine these words into phrases, clauses, and sentences.

There is a direct relationship between vocabulary and vocational success. Some studies have indicated that exact and extensive knowledge of English word meanings is the oustanding single characteristic of successful persons. Since the choice of language is so important, the skill we demonstrate in the use of these audible symbols may largely determine whether our communication succeeds or fails.

## Develop a Large Vocabulary

The extent of our vocabulary will affect any of the methods of communication which use such symbolism — speaking, listening, writing, and reading. We are limited more by poor vocabulary in speaking and listening than in writing and reading. This is true because of the nature of the processes. In speaking and listening we must be able to use the words we need without much time for reflection or consultation of sources. A broad vocabulary for ready reference is thus imperative to us as speakers or listeners. The building of this permanent supply of words is a long time process and will continue as long as we remain active thinkers.

*Some Effort Needed* In order for this word-building operation to be effective, we must constantly be using the eye and ear in discovering new words and determining their meaning. When we hear or see a new word and cannot determine its meaning from the context, the proper step is to look up the word in a dictionary and then to use the word until it has become a part of the permanent supply. Each college course offers a whole new vocabulary, and general reading of books, magazines, and newspapers will help increase our knowledge of words. Unless these new words are consciously used, however, they may never become a part of our speech.

The point we must remember is that the extent of our vocabulary makes a tremendous difference in our ability to give or get ideas. A meager vocabulary restricts us to crude ideas and makes us seem more barren in thought than we actually are. On the other hand, a wide vocabulary contributes to our fluency and makes it easier for us to make our ideas clear in easy, rapid, and efficient fashion.

**Use of Simple Words** We do not broaden our stock of words so that we can *impress* our listeners. In talking with other persons it is better to use simple words rather than strange, unusual ones. The reaction on the part of an audience to the excessive use of big words is usually detrimental to the clarity and force of the ideas presented. We should speak easily and naturally about ideas which we understand. A thorough understanding of the ideas about which we speak is the best guarantee that our style will be clear, forceful, and direct. Perhaps some of the pretensions in word choice come from our failure to be original.

We should realize that we cannot talk like a book and successfully communicate our ideas. Such language draws attention to itself and away from the ideas being presented. We should stay away from obscure language because we know that the oral communication process is a transitory experience and, hence, that our words must be instantly intelligible. We should remember that short words hit hard and help make communication clear. The advice of 2,000 years ago is still applicable today. "So likewise ye, except ye utter by the tongue words easy to be understood, how shall it be known what is spoken? for ye shall speak into the air." — I Corinthians, XIV, 9.

*Don't Parade
the Vocabulary*

Our classmates know when we are trying to show off by using big words where small ones would be better. They will probably titter in embarrassment for us and they will grin and glance at the instructor. All this detracts from the communication of thought. We should not refuse to use a large word, however, when it serves best to carry the meaning we have in mind. These students to whom we speak are high school graduates and all have a large listening vocabulary. We need not speak down to them in either ideas or words.

**The Problem of General
Fluency**

Many of us put too high a premium on keeping the words rolling. In fact, we are so afraid of having unvocalized pauses in our speech that we fill in all such gaps with *uh* or *and-uh* or even with words which do not carry the meaning we want to express. Such excess vocalization or misuse of language often becomes far more distracting than the pauses. Let us remember that few speakers can talk extemporaneously without hesitation of some type. Let us also remember that a few such hesitancies will be accepted by an audience. This is not to say that we need not pay any attention to the matter, for most good speakers hold these breaks in fluency to a minimum.

Good preparation encourages fluency, and with practice in speaking we realize when we are falling into a stumbling pattern and thus we are stimulated to move along with fewer breaks. As we become more accustomed to the speaking situation, we will probably smooth out the delivery of our language. A broad vocabulary is an essential requirement for easy expression, since with wide choice the possibility of a wise selection of words becomes easier. The extent of the vocabulary is thus used to get exact meanings rather than to show off.

**Exactness in Words
for Meaning and
Correct Idiom**

Words must precisely fit the ideas for which they stand before we can be assured the communication will be good. There is no reason to be less exact in our speaking than in our mathematics and biology; yet many persons who pride themselves on being scientifically correct use *infer* for *imply*, *practical* for *practicable*, *pseudo* for *quasi*, *majority* for *plurality,* for *creditable, reckon* for *suppose, can* for *may, hygienic* for *sanitary, learn* for *teach,* and *leave* for *let.* The disturbance in communication occurs in two ways: (a) the use of the wrong word conveys a meaning we did not wish to give, and (b) the listener gets the meaning in spite of our error, but then begins to think about the mistake and so does not continue to follow our ideas.

Muddy language is the result of poor thinking. When we think through our ideas carefully, we usually will have little trouble finding words to say exactly what we mean to say. The difficulty in expression arises when the student has a nebulous idea of what he wishes to say and tries to "bull" his way through a perfomance.

*Write It Out Sometimes*

It is good practice for us to write out the speech or portions of the speech we plan to use. This process will demonstrate to us vividly the difficulty of getting the exact words we want for clear expression. When the speech is presented to the class, we throw away the manuscript which we have prepared and speak with or without notes, with the language being that of the moment. Memorization is time-wasting and stultifying.

When words are combined in a manner contrary to general usage, we have a faulty idiom. Here again we attempt correct usage more because of the indirect effect on communication than on a real inability of the listener to get the meaning. Let us say "She is angry *with* me" rather than *"at"* for correctness in idiom. "They chose several boys *from* (rather than *among*) the group" and "you are wrong *in regard* (rather than *as* regards) to the time of the meeting" are other examples of idiomatic choice.

**Use of Concrete and Specific Words**

Effective language is that which is concrete rather than abstract and specific rather than general. If we say, "He went across the street and into the building," we have couched our sentence in general terms. We have only the vaguest idea of the action and things described. The verb *went,* for example, conveys only the impression of the movement from place to place. We have no inkling of the *kind* of movement that took place. The person might have staggered, shuffled, skipped, or even crawled on his hands and knees. But we would never know — all we have is *went.* Building is another general term. A *building* conveys only the idea of some kind of structure. A building might be a cathedral, a department store, a museum, a bank, a theater, a school, a prison or any of a dozen others. When we use general terms like *went* and *building* we give our listeners only a blurred and hazy picture of the events we are talking about. We must learn to use specific terms. We could say, "The ragged bum shuffled unsteadily across the street and into Flannery's flophouse."

In our speaking we must learn to name persons, places, and objects and thus be concrete. The verbs, adjectives, and adverbs which talk about these things must be specific. When we talk about concrete things in specific language, we will get immediate consideration for our ideas. A speech criticism which says "I thought it was a good performance" is next to useless as a comment. *What* was good about it and *how* those things were good will mean something. We must be specific.

## Use of Appropriate Language

The standards of appropriateness vary somewhat with the formality of the speech occasion. In friendly conversation we use many colloquial expressions and a certain amount of slang. This is as it should be; it is "easy" speech. *"He hasn't got any"* is colloquial usage; in formal speech we should say, *"He has none."*

Sometimes, however, we use localisms and provincialisms the meaning of which may be misunderstood. This should be avoided. For example, localisms such as *plumb* for *completely, crazy* for *eager,* and *to lift* for *to steal* probably should be avoided along with such provincialisms as *poke* for *bag, creepie* for *three-legged stool,* and *zany* for *simpleton.* The use of such words might confuse the communication completely. Slang often gives a loose expression also. "I felt like I'd croak if I didn't take a grab at that invite" and "That line you are blurbing around is a lot of hooey" do not convey exactness in meaning. We also should learn to avoid trite expressions. They lack originality and are loose in meaning. We know these expressions and should be able to avoid them. Examples of the common ones would include "at one fell swoop," "as luck would have it," "nipped in the bud," and "at the crack of dawn."

We will improve our language in the formal speaking situations only through improving our language in everyday conversation situations. Using slang and localistic expressions bordering on the unacceptable for most of the day will not lessen the chances of our using them in our formal presentations. The fact of the matter is that we talk worse than we need to much of the time. As a consequence, we have difficulty avoiding poor expression on occasions when we really care.

| **Use of Vivid and Colorful Words** |

Many words really carry two meanings — what they denote and what they connote. The denotation or literal meaning can be found in the dictionary while the connotation has suggestive powers that reach beyond the definition of the word. A *house* and a *home* are similarly defined by a dictionary but the connotations vary considerably. The word propaganda denotes the spreading of the truth, but it now implies (connotes) spreading of falsehood or at least unreliable information. A *hat, fez, sombrero,* or *wimple* are all coverings for the head; the first word is far less vivid, stimulating, and imaginative than the others. We should deliberately try to use words that will connote vivid sensory images.

Vividness in one's language is also obtained by the use of apt figures of speech. The use of a simile or metaphor is one of the surest ways of adding spark and color to our speaking. Originality in such use is naturally at a premium; trite figures are not as successful as fresh ones. When the poet said "The thirsty soil drank up the rain," the figurative language gave a suggestive value not found in "The soil soaked up the rain." Henry Canby said well with figurative language what many of us know, "Writing is like pulling the trigger of a gun; if you are not loaded, nothing happens." It will perhaps take real effort on our part to use irony, hyperbole, personification, metaphor, or simile but the effect will certainly be worth the struggle.

| **Use of Contact Language** |

Speaking differs from written style largely in its directness. Such a style allows for more informality and hence a closer contact between speaker and audience. The directness so desirable in the speaking situation can be obtained partially through the choice of words and sentence construction.

With respect to word choice, contact language requires the use of many personal pronouns. *I, you,* and *we* appear frequently in informal address. In addition the direct speaker makes free use of contractions. He says, "I don't" rather than "I do not"; "I'm going" rather than "I am going." By wide use of personal pronouns and contractions he gets away from a "literary" style. He also uses action verbs as much as possible.

In the matter of sentences the direct speaker may do several things. First, he makes frequent use of the interrogative, exclamatory, and the imperative sentences; he uses the question form particularly. We must learn to phrase and use contact sentences such as "This is an important point," "I will repeat that," "Don't you agree?" and "You see the implication." The good speaker keeps his sentences short; the simple sentence, like the simple word, hits harder and is more easily comprehended. All sentences, however, cannot be short because such a style is choppy and tiresome. For the sake of variety some complex sentences must be used, but the important ideas can be kept in the briefer ones. It is also probably effective to use periodic sentences now and then to vary from the usual structure. Parallel structure, too, is usually very effective.

**Avoid Grammatical Errors in Speech**

There are a few grammatical errors so common with students that attention should be called to them in this chapter. Most of them could be eliminated with a minimum of effort. Most of the errors are avoided by students when their communication is written and show up only in the spoken communication.

The first of these errors, shift in tense, is not too common but is considered childish when it does occur in an unacceptable shift. "After things *quiet* down I *begin* reading again" or "The man *opened* the door and then *comes* stalking through the hall," shows an undesirable shift of tense. Moreover, some students use adjectives when they should use adverbs and, less frequently, adverbs when they should use adjectives. The careful student will have little trouble except perhaps with the following pairs: good-well, real-very, some-somewhat, and most-almost. He ran *well* (not good). Write *very* soon (not real). I was *somewhat* tired (not some). They ate almost everything (not most). A third difficulty is with the case of pronouns. It is *he* (not him). Still more bothersome seems to be the choice of case for the first person pronoun when used as a part of a compound predicate. That secret is between you and *me* (not I).

Many students demonstrate inability to distinguish between transitive and intransitive verbs. Three pairs of such verbs cause a great deal of difficulty. These pairs are: set-sit, raise-rise, and lay-lie. Students should notice the meaning of these verbs, whether they are transitive or intransitive, and the principal parts of each. Sit (sat, sat), for example, means *to be in a position* and it is an intransitive verb and so will not take an object. With such knowledge, "I sat the bucket on the table" might be avoided. Knowing that set (set, set) means *to put in place* and is a transitive verb might avoid "I set on the table to talk." Likewise lie (lay, lain) is intransitive and means *to recline;* lay (laid, laid) is transitive and means *to put in place*. And rise (rose, risen) means *to get up* or *go up* and is intransitive; raise (raised, raised) is transitive and means *to lift, to bring up,* or *to cause to get up*. It is also essential that a speaker know the parts of the irregular verbs which he uses. Most of us know and would not use Dizzy Dean's "slud" as the past tense of slide; would we refuse "drug" as the past tense of drag? It might not be amiss to point out also that *come* has a past tense form.

Two other errors deserve mention in this section. College students are usually able to get subject and verb to agree in person. Few would say "They knew where he were" or "There is three mistakes in this paragraph." They do have difficulty once in a while with agreement in number because of words coming between the subject and verb. "The prices of practically all qualities of nylon *has* increased a great deal" may occur because the subject *prices* got separated so far from the verb. The same thing happened to produce "One of my opinions *are* that you work too hard." Or, a mistaken subject might produce "There *is* Wayne and Mary." The final error to be pointed out is that of the old double negative bugaboo. "He couldn't find it nowhere" or "you can't do nothing right" illustrates this type of mistake. We should recognize this error and make a real attempt to avoid it. There are many other difficulties with grammar in oral communication but those named probably cause the most difficulty.

## Visual Aids

How many of us have seen an aircraft carrier? A few, perhaps! More than likely we are familiar with one through magazine or newspaper illustrations, movies, or models. Suppose we had never seen a picture or a model: what would the words aircraft carrier mean to us then? We would have a general idea of a craft transporting airplanes but there would be no specific visual image. Suppose we were shown a picture. The hazy image of the carrier takes a clearer shape in our mind. When someone points out to us in the picture the flight deck, the bridge, and the other parts of the carrier, our conception becomes even clearer. This explanation, together with the visual aid, is the nearest substitute a speaker can give us for seeing the aircraft carrier itself.

**The General Purpose
of Visual Aids**

Since early times man has realized the value of visual aids in trying to explain a real life experience or to describe a real object. Primitive man used drawings in the sand or on walls of a cave to help get ideas across. Since that day diagrams have been a fundamental device to aid in the communication of ideas. We learn by seeing as well as by hearing.

Abstract words and ideas which mean little to the ears of the students often make sense when supported by a picture, diagram, or model. Ideas are clarified not only through the sense of sight, but through other senses too. We understand a thing better if we hear its sound, feel its texture, or taste its flavor. We gain experience through our senses. The more experience we have the better we understand. The use of a visual aid, or the use of any other sensory aid, is a means by which the speaker can give his listener "experience" with the object being described or the process being explained. A teacher often uses visual aids to provide for his students the background of experience which they lack.

The Army and the Navy have made us aware of the power which lies in the use of visual aids. We all know how the armed forces were confronted during World War II with the problem of teaching highly technical skills to millions of men. Unparalleled use was made of visual, auditory, and tactile aids in a multitude of forms. Such aids as charts, maps, cartoons, schematic drawings, mockups, and models were skillfully designed and ingeniously used. Although we are not concerned with training our listeners to highly specific tasks, we are interested in a technique which will promote clarity and interest in our speaking.

The purpose for which we use visual aids will be to make what we have to say seem like a "real" experience to our listeners. If a picture of cotton or corn will help our listeners who have never lived on a farm to better attention and understanding of the plan we are describing, we should use a picture. If our speeches deal with geographic relationships, there is no better way of making ourselves clear than with a map.

| | Visual aids serve specific purposes. |
|---|---|
| **The Specific Purposes for Visual Aids** | The most important use of a visual aid is to *save time*. In many speaking situations a diagram, model, or map becomes a short cut to clarity. One such instru- |

ment may shorten a speaker's talk by many words. It may save him from the criticism of being too wordy.

We can use a visual aid to help clarify what we are explaining or describing. Suppose we are describing an underwater fish gun to our audience. We want to go further and explain just how the missile is ejected. Would not a model or a good diagram help to make our listeners "see" and understand more clearly just what we are talking about?

We can use a visual aid to secure *attention* and *interest*. A good visual aid is often an attention getter. We can use one effectively in our introduction where getting the attention and securing the interest of the audience are the main purposes. Even as simple a use as holding up the book for the audience to see when we begin a book review gets attention. Skillful use may be made of an appropriate visual aid when we reach the climax of our talk.

We can use a visual aid for *emphasis*. Capitalized or underscored words on the blackboard, enlarged portions on a diagram or cartoon will give prominence to those ideas we consider most important. Again, in building to a climax in our talk, we may use a visual aid to good effect in developing step by step to the peak we wish to reach.

| | As we prepare the visual aids for our |
|---|---|
| *Don't Overdo Visual Aids* | talk, we must remember these cautions. All talks do not require the use of visual materials. In some instances such materials would be strikingly inappropriate. On the |

other hand, there are visual materials that can be used without the aid of verbal support. When these particular materials are used, the center of attention is directed toward the demonstrations of displays or skills. The interest of the audience is focused on the aid rather than on the speaker. A listener may become absorbed in watching the dextrous hand movements and forget the toymaker himself, or he may become fascinated by the workings of a complicated household gadget and lose all thought of the speaker who is manipulating it.

In this class we shall be interested in talks where visual materials can be used as a purposeful aid rather than an end in themselves. At all times we should keep the audience aware of us, the speakers.

**Types of Visual Aids**

Some subjects lend themselves more readily to visual helps than others. The following topics have been developed successfully by students for talks supported by visual aids: The process of sewing, hanging, and firing tobacco; The way your palm is read; A way to make your own iced-tea glasses; The sport of skeet shooting; My hobby — scrapbook making; Traffic signals; The making of an underwater fish gun; Linoleum block printing; Points to consider in selecting books for children; Making a weather map; One process in sculpturing; Colors and their combinations applied to clothing and house furnishings; The structure of the United Nations and the functions of its various parts; The process of chromium electroplating.

After we have selected our topic and organized our speech, we should select the visual aids that will carry out the purpose of our speech. The types of visual aids that are suitable for use in the classroom situation can be classified in the following groups:

1. Objects taken from their natural settings such as models, samples, specimens.
2. Printed pictures, photographs.
3. Graphic materials such as diagrams, graphs, charts, maps, cartoons, posters.

Visual aids that we cannot control, such as animals, reptiles, chemicals, weapons, should not be used. Aids like movies, filmstrips, slides, opaque projections can be employed effectively but they are not easily available for general student use.

**The Preparation for Use of a Visual Aid**

We should prepare our visual aids carefully and plan for their use ahead of time. We should be sure that we know the exact purpose for which we are going to use our pictures, graphs, or models. We should know also in just what manner we are going to use them. If we are not thoroughly familiar with our materials we may distract or confuse our listeners by clumsy handling. If diagrams are to be made on the board during our talk, we should practice drawing our figures beforehand so that we will not be continually erasing and redrawing our lines. Color can be used for comparison. By all means, we must erase the board of other materials before we begin our speech. As soon as we finish with the aid we should remove it from sight.

When selecting our model or pictures, we should be sure that our material is large enough for all the members of the audience to see well. Students frequently choose visual aids that are too small and as a result are practically useless or even positive distractions. We should not have to apologize to the audience for the smallness of our model or diagram. Also, the exhibit should be planned so that it contains only the elements which are necessary for us to use; the presence of unexplained details is distracting to the observers.

We should make careful note of the place where we are to give our talk. The setting for our visual aids should be one that will enable the members of our audience to see clearly and to pay attention. When visual aids play a very important part in a talk, we should plan to introduce them properly; thus the meaning of our materials, as used, will be instantly intelligible to our listeners.

*Hide the Aid Until Proper Time*

Since a visual aid always attracts too much attention before the talk or during the time we are not using it, we should keep it covered up when not in use. We must make sure that the light is right on our model or on the blackboard if we draw a diagram. Pictures or samples should be passed out to the audience *only* if they are all alike and if we have enough for all members. The entire audience should focus its attention on a single visual aid at the same time and when the speaker wants that focus on the aid. The passing of things to an audience is always dangerous because we have then lost control of attention. The point of our explanation will be lost if the audience is looking at various pictures and samples while we are talking.

**The Effective Use of Visual Aids**

As we begin our talk, we must remember to face our audience at all times. We should not talk to our model or materials. If we need to refer specifically to our visual aid, we should point out the detail we wish to call attention to and then turn back to our listeners as we continue our explanation. We must be sure to stand clear of our visual aid. Often beginning speakers "forget" and stand between their exhibit and the audience. We may stand back of or to one side of a chart. In pointing out details we should use our nearest hand as a pointer. If we are right-handed, we should stand to the audience's right of our drawing or model, if left-handed, to the left. If using the blackboard, we should draw a larger figure with heavier lines than ordinarily necessary rather than risk having the figure invisible to our listeners. If pictures or samples are passed out, the passing out ought to be timed so that it does not distract from our words. In most instances, the passing out of material should wait until the end of the talk.

## Part C: Four Systems of Note-taking

It is often necessary for us to take notes upon things we read and hear. Many a treatise is available on how best to list the essential elements from the documents we read. Much less guidance has been supplied on how best to extract and record the significant facts and ideas presented in lectures and informative speech. It is this kind of note-taking, therefore, with which we shall be chiefly concerned.

Expository lectures and discussions are ever-present factors in our continuous growth — in our acquirement of knowledge and our power to put it to work. The trained note-taker may not grasp the things he hears any better than the person untrained in this skill, but the former has a tremendous advantage on the occasion of a later review of what was said. Effective note-taking is just as important in listening to propositional as to instructive discourse.

Taking notes without previous training in *how* to take them is of debatable value. It is true that good students and notebooks always seem to appear together. Almost every study made of this matter reports just that phenomenon. But which is the cause and which is the effect? Do the notebooks make the good students? Or do good students — because of some prodding of conscience — build notebooks just because they feel they ought to be doing so? Actually, this pivotal question of which is the cause and which is the effect is still unanswered. We simply do not know. It is entirely probable that in the past the business of taking notes without careful guidance has been vastly overdone. Apparently most students tend to sense their own inadequacies in respect to note-taking ability.

*Values in
Note-taking*

Despite the confused character of the issue, certain residual values make the acquirement of note-taking skill highly desirable. First, note-taking tends to sustain the attention of the listener, at least to some degree. If we are conscientiously following the thread of the discourse in order to make a written record of its highlights, we are much less likely to turn off in pursuit of some mental tangent. Second, the accumulating of written notes carries the implicit assumption that a later period will be scheduled for their review and for reflection upon their meaning. Since as much learning is likely to take place during that later period as during the immediate one, the assumption itself serves to increase the chances that the reflection hour will materialize. Third, concise digests of the material heard help us to get acquainted with ourselves as listeners and prove invaluable as a basis for later review. To receive full dividends for the time we shall later want to invest in reflection and review, we must make careful advance preparation for these activities. A notebook simplifies our task; it tends to reveal to us the gaps and weaknesses in our own learning. Most important of all, it sometimes becomes a veritable wellspring of ideas whose flow might never have originated had we not tackled the problem of translating the thoughts of others into words of our own. This process of translation serves to "prime the pump" and make our personal growth and maturation more certain.

This part of the chapter describes in detail four workable systems of taking notes. It explains the strengths and the weaknesses of each, and suggests ways to insure that each method will be used to fullest advantage. Before we examine the several systems, however, we may well profit by considering carefully six guiding principles to be followed regardless of which method we elect to use. They deserve careful attention.

*Type of Speech
Determines System*

Our choice of note-taking system must always be based upon the organizational pattern (or the absence of one) being followed by the speaker. No one system will serve all purposes; we must adapt our procedure to each presentation we hear. Until we are able to make our selection, it is best to take no written notes. Obviously, however, the earlier in the presentation we can make our choice, the better.

*System Selected
Should Be Followed*

Effective listening to speech of any kind demands the following of a definite and specific system of note-taking. This system may well be one of taking no literal notes but of making mental notes only; or it may be the use of one of the four systems we shall examine in detail. Bad note-taking, by contrast, is a random, nondiscriminating jotting down of whatever catches the attention;it lacks consistent adherence to a definite plan of procedure and usually fails to recognize the relative importance or unimportance of the items recorded.

*Notes Should Be
Clear for Review*

Regardless of the system used, all notes should be written so clearly and meaningfully as to give no confusion to the writer when he rereads them after a long lapse of time. If we jot down words or phrases which we ourselves will have difficulty in interpreting later, the note-taking process immediately turns from asset to liability.

Regardles of the system used, the note-taker should at the time of taking either literal or mental notes always schedule a later time for their review. If the notes are not worth subsequent reflection, they are not worth keeping and should be cast aside.

*Notes Should
Be Brief*

The function of written notes is merely to complement and improve the recall of material acquired through straight aural assimilation. Because any and all writing tends to disrupt communication between speaker and listener, the less of it done the better.

*Kind of Speech
Must Be
Identified Quickly*

Choosing the best system to use is greatly expedited by a quick decision on whether the presentation is basically informative or persuasive. Fortunately, most informative talks and discussions are deductively planned and developed, and all four systems of note-taking we shall discuss are applicable. On the other hand, only systems three and four are really contributory when the presentation is an unorganized speech or discussion, or when the speech is inductively organized and developed. In these latter instances the listener needs special guidance as we shall see in the following pages.

**Outlining the Speech or Discussion**

The most commonly used of all systems of note-taking is that of making a written outline of the discourse as it is being presented. Indeed, as one study reported, poor listeners tend to regard note-taking and outlining as strictly synonymous terms. Outlines vary tremendously in their effectiveness and, despite the fact that the method is frequently very badly abused, outlining possesses a number of distinct advantages.

*Strengths of Outlining*

Notes so taken are usually neat, reasonably brief, and easily filed. When the method has been adapted to the compositional scheme of the speaker, the product is exceedingly useful for purposes of review and reflection. The method also tends to develop the listener's power to coordinate items of equal rank and to subordinate materials of less importance. Since a great portion of our waking day is devoted to deciding the relative importance of all kinds of tasks, problems and issues, any contribution to our skill in this respect is a decidedly valuable by-product of this method of note-taking. Finally, making effective outlines improves our knowledge of the symbols we use for that purpose. These symbols have scores of uses. To learn to use them deftly and accurately is to capitalize on another worthwhile by-product of this note-taking system.

*Weaknesses of Outlining*

The chief weakness of the outline method of taking notes lies in its limited usefulness. It is an impractical system unless the speech we are hearing was prepared from an outline. What proportion of all the formal talks and discussions we hear have been carefully outlined in advance? An exact answer is of course impossible. It is being very conservative to estimate, however, that fewer than half the discourses we hear possess an inherent organization lending itself to the outline method of taking notes. When the discourse heard is unorganized, system one is inapplicable; when the discourse is inductively organized and developed, system one is so poorly applicable that we are ill-advised to attempt its use. It is almost impossible to spot in advance the significant supporting items for a generalization whose identity we cannot discover before the conclusion of the talk.

Another weakness of the outline method is that there are vast subject-matter areas in which the system tends to work very badly. The natural sciences area is an excellent example. The student who has tried to outline a typical lecture in chemistry soon abandons the technique and either concocts an original system of his own or turns to textbook annotation.

A third weakness of outlining is that it frequently tends to confuse symbols and knowledge in the mind of the user. We often seem to feel that if all the symbols are in perfect order and all the indentations are symmetrical and neat, the outline must therefore contain meaningful and useful content. Such an inference does not necessarily follow.

**Increasing Outlining Effectiveness**

To outline effectively we must listen intently for contextual clues. The greater our skill in detecting the structure of the discourse the easier it is outline it. Every effective speaker is at pains to make clear his organizational plan. He may even talk from a distributed outline, or from one placed on the blackboard. In any case he realizes the need for maximum clarity and hence by means of preliminary announcements, by carefully worded transitional phrases and periodic summaries, by slowly stated enumerations and by many other contextual clues, he gives the listener every bit of help possible. These clues are invaluable to those who would use the outline system.

*Use Four Part Outline*

We construct our outlines most clearly if we are careful not to start taking notes too soon. In the outline we will do well to record the conventional elements of the introduction by word or phrase only. When we come to the contract, unless the speaker allows us adequate time for writing his statement in complete-sentence form, we will do well to leave abundant blank space for this purpose once we are certain of its wording. Often it is best to write in the thesis statement *after* the talk when, having heard it reiterated two or three times, we are much more likely to record it accurately.

To avoid any possibility of later confusion of their meaning, we should put in complete sentences at least the main points in the body of the speech. We should also put in complete-sentence form the exact action or application the speaker requests us, as listeners, to make of his material. This is a highly critical statement, and one to be recorded with utmost care.

**Evaluation of the Method**

All in all it is fair to say that the outline system of taking notes has in the past been overworked and greatly overrated. It is strictly limited in its usefulness and applicability. Because it requires the most writing of all, it disrupts the communicative process more than any of the other three systems. It is most useful when the listener is well acquainted with a speaker's techniques and can depend upon him to give a series of highly organized and deductively developed informative speeches.

**Annotating of Book or Manuscript**

Many of the new textbooks and workbooks used in certain courses, particularly those in the natural sciences, are arranged with text material on each left-hand page with the opposite right-hand page left entirely blank. As text material is explained or elaborated by the instructor, the student can conveniently record important notes immediately opposite the corresponding printed discussion. This system of note-taking is known as annotation, and is of course much expedited by the alternate blank pages devised to encourage and facilitate its use. Students soon develop various kinds of lines, arrows, or other symbols to suggest the relationships between the notes they write and the related items being supplemented in the text.

Annotation, however, has been in use for many centuries — long before the alternate blank-page scheme was to make its appearance. In books and manuscripts with wide margins it is always possible to write in considerable supplementary material. Even with narrow margins it requires but little imagination to devise a workable code of symbols which are more or less readily interpreted by their creator to suggest varying degrees of emphasis and significance. For example, let us examine the following liberally marked passage.

> *Rattlesnake*
> "The rattlesnake is a venomous reptile with a rattle of horny rings at the end of the tail. *A long fang is borne on each maxilla,* and is perforated by a canal down which the venomous secretion of a modified salivary gland flows when the rattler strikes. **The poison is deadly to snakes as well as**

**men.** Behind each fang are several reserve fangs which replace it after breakage — a not infrequent result of the bite. There are about fifteen species, exclusively American.

*Fang Replacement*

∗∗
∗∗∗∗∗
The Southern states have a species known as the **diamond rattlesnake** (Crotalus adamanteus) on account of the **rhomboidal black blotches,** each perfect in all its angles and edged with yellow, which ornament its yellowish body. This snake sometimes reaches, on the Mangrove Islands of Western Florida, a length of 8 feet. The young are brought forth alive."

*Southern Name*

*Size*

*"Viviparous"*

---

| Strengths and Weaknesses of System Two |
| --- |

The annotating system for taking notes possesses certain definite strengths. It tends to result in very few errors or misconstructions and to speed the locating, during review, of items of interest to the learner. It is particularly valuable in many science courses and in those situations in which a discourse containing technical content is supplemented by manuscripts placed beforehand in the hands of the listeners. Finally, it tremendously enhances the value of the book annotated to the owner, and possibly to someone who might otherwise be interested in purchasing it.

The weaknesses of annotation are conspicuous. It is cumbersome, complicates any plan for filing the notes taken, and makes review sessions extraordinarily long. It is of very limited usefulness, since it is highly ineffective or completely inapplicable to unorganized speeches and discussions as well as to any talk which is inductively organized and developed. Finally, annotation fails to contribute significantly to two very important educational skills: the power to write clear, complete sentences and the power to discriminate between ideas of coordinate and subordinate rank in importance.

**Increasing Effectiveness of Method**

All of us will profit if we very carefully devise a definite and coded system of symbols for emphasizing certain elements by underlining them or by writing in the adjacent margins of the text. We should carefully graduate, by using different symbols, the degree of significance we attach to various passages. We will profit by placing our code in the front of each text in which we plan to use it, and then by closely adhering to its sequences. Soon it will become an automatic part of our note-taking methods.

When we write comments in margins or blank areas we will find it distinctly advantageous to write as clearly and neatly as possible. If there is any probability of later misinterpretation of our own jottings, these jottings should be written in complete-sentence form.

**Evaluation of Annotating Method**

Of our four general systems of note-taking, annotation is probably the least disruptive of the flow of communication. Little writing is required. Annotation is also, however, the least generally useful of the four systems. The number of situations in which it would work effectively for most of us is very severely limited. Actually many of us will find it a more frequently useful concomitant of silent reading and study than effective activity while listening to oral presentations.

**Précis Writing**

The third system of note-taking, précis writing, involves the accumulating of a series of very carefully written short paragraphs of material. Each paragraph is a very brief abstract, written in complete sentences, of a lengthy passage of the discourse being heard. In preparing these paragraphs the listener writes nothing at all for perhaps three or four minutes; during this interval, although he is listening as intently as he can to the discourse, he is at the same time planning how best to summarize the content he is assimilating. Thus the actual writing he does is at widely-spaced intervals which are themselves of comparatively short duration. Perhaps the following brief example will help clarify the system.

The actual excerpt from the speech being given might be as follows:

> These seem to be the statistics on the matter. In the year 1900, life expectancy in this country was 47 years. In the year 1950, life expectancy was 67 years. Between the years 1930 and 1940 alone, the median age in America went up 2 1/2 years. Soon, it is predicted by Dr. Edward Stieglitz, the median age in America will probably be about 40 years. In those few years between 1930 and 1940, the general population in the country increased 7 percent. The population of our old people, those 65 years of age or more, increased in that decade 35 percent, or five times the rate of the over-all population increase.
>
> Today we have in America, past the age of 60, about 15,000,000 people or about 10 percent of our population. Soon,

if predictions come true, about 20 percent, or possibly even 25 percent, of our population will be 60 years of age or more.

One writer (I think he is quite extreme on it) actually predicts that by the year 2,000, the life expectancy for men in this country will be 95 years, and the life expectancy for women will be 150 years.

The précis covering the foregoing passage might be: "There is abundant evidence that we are becoming a nation of old people."

**Strengths and Weaknesses of System Three**

Précis writing results in notes that are brief, easily filed, and extremely useful for later review and reflection. There is very little chance that the notes thus taken will cause their author confusion later, for they tend to be quickly and fully meaningful. This third note-taking system is workable regardless of whether the discourse is inductively or deductively developed, organized or unorganized in character. Finally, it contributes significantly to the important educational skills of learning to think and write in complete sentences and in discriminating between ideas of subordinate and coordinate importance.

System three, however, despite all that can be done to lessen the drawback, results in too much writing. There is a consequent almost complete loss of comprehension during the interval when the writing is being done. To avoid this weakness, some students have tried to write their abstracts *after* the lecture on the basis of simple jottings of facts during its presentation. Unless a vacant period is available immediately following the talk, this method soon proves unworkable. Usually the recording of significant facts under this system, unless it is being operated with exceptional skill, is slighted or completely omitted. There is also a tendency for the speaker's over-all organizational plan to be lost sight of, with consequent loss of the listener's ability to evaluate the whole effort fairly. Finally, the system is not suitable for certain subject matter areas, particularly those of the natural and biological sciences.

**Suggestions for Increasing Effectiveness**

Most speakers tend to indicate the unusual significance of some item by emphasizing it through transitional words or phrases which suggest its importance to the listener. We should make every effort to recognize these clues and to capitalize on them in composing our written abstracts.

It will pay us to avoid taking notes too early in the discourse, and particularly to delay our attempt to state the central purpose of the discourse until after the presentation has been completed. Moreover we always profit by writing down exactly what the speaker urges us to do when he makes his final appeal or states the application he would have us make of the material he has presented.

*Keep the Abstracts Brief*

In general, the shorter we make our abtracts the greater will be our comprehension of the discourse. A single sentence may well summarize an entire passage of the speech. We should try hard to include no more than two or three sentences in each written paragraph.

**Evaluation of the Method**

Précis writing is valuable primarily because of its general usefulness. It is applicable to both persuasive and informative speech or discussion; to both deductively and inductively developed discourse; and to both the organized and unorganized presentation. Its chief drawback lies in its excessive interruption of the flow of communication. This interruption is serious at times, for when it occurs it results in an almost complete loss of comprehension during the short intervals devoted to composing the written abstracts.

**Recording Fact Versus Principle**

The fourth general system of note-taking requires listing vertically, in parallel columns, the important facts and principles derived from the discourse. Two pages opposite one another, with the word "Facts" written on the top line of one and "Principles" written on the top line of the other, are made ready before the discourse starts. Three bits of information, the name of the speaker, his subject, and the date, should also be recorded at the top of each page. The only writing the listener does to supplement his listening is to jot down a significant fact or principle whenever he hears and recognizes one. If he should get a sudden idea of his own which he would like to think more about later, he can easily label it and jot it down at the bottom of the "Principles" page. In this way he avoids losing either his idea or the ensuing content of the speaker. Such suddenly acquired ideas may prove invaluable. Thomas Paine once wrote of them:

"There are two distinct classes of what are called thoughts — those that we produce in ourselves by reflection and the act of thinking, and those that bolt into the mind of their own accord. I have always made it a rule to treat those voluntary visitors with civility, taking care to examine, as well as I was able, if they were worth entertaining, and it is from them I have acquired almost all the knowledge that I have."

One obvious demand of this note-taking method is that the listener be able to distinguish between fact and principle. This actually is more difficult than it sounds. To be sure, a fact is "some deed, or act, or condition said and accepted to be true; some reality that exists." To be sure, a principle is a "law, doctrine, rule, broad truth, generalization; something controlling or giving system to a large number of facts." But facts are closely related to time; what is accepted as truth in one generation or century is often labeled false by the next. And when a principle is said to be "broad truth," it becomes evident that in some instances the decision on where to catalogue an item must rest upon the hearer's estimate of its dimension. Despite occasional confusion and difficulty in classifying the items to be recorded, however, the method suffers but little from this characteristic.

It should be noted in the accompanying illustration that Arabic numerals are used in the "Facts" column and Roman numerals in the "Principles" column. This greatly simplifies the task at a later period of assembling between parentheses signs placed immediately beneath each principle — in a space intentionally left there for the purpose — the numbers identifying those facts believed to support each principle. Some students prefer to indicate relationships between the two columns through some coding system such as this simple one. Others prefer the commonly used alternative of completely transcribing all such notes by making a single outline synthesizing the contents of the two columns.

The sample of recording fact versus principle on the top of the next page may help to clarify.

**Strengths and Weaknesses of System Four**

Vertical recording of fact and principle has many advantages as a note-taking system. Without excessive writing, it results in notes that are brief, easily filed, and excellent for review and reflection. It tends to be accurate; to develop the important educational skills of subordination and coordination and of differentiating fact and idea. One of its finest values is that it quickly exposes

Dr. Connor
"Gifted Children"
2/22/64

## FACTS

1. The proportion of great men is limited by nature.
2. The number can be foretold.
3. There are differing degrees of eminence.
4. Very few can become really illustrious.
5. Only one per cent of the population have I.Q.'s over 130.
6. Hollingsworth says that to be creative one must have an I.Q. over 165.
7. Intellect and stature are positively correlated.
8. Many greatly gifted individuals of the past have been either persecuted or deified.
9. Galton himself had an I.Q. of 200.
10. Adopted sons of the Popes were not as eminent as true sons.

Dr. Connor
"Gifted Children"
2/22/64

## PRINCIPLES

I. One does not become eminent unless he is gifted; one may not become eminent just because he is gifted. (1, 2, 3, 4, 5, 6, 7)

II. Eminence tends to run in families.

(1, 4, 6, 8, 9, 10)

## IDEAS AND QUESTIONS

°Ought we to establish a super-university to educate for leadership only the greatly gifted among us?

the superficial speaker. For example, if an instructor continues day after day to produce from twenty to thirty significant facts and from one to three important principles during each class hour, he is a gem indeed. If another is addicted to indefiniteness, indirection, non-preparation, and emotional harangue, his daily contribution will be meager by contrast, some days dropping to zero in both columns. His incompetence and his inadequacies cannot be long concealed from students employing this fourth system of note-taking. Finally, the system is workable regardless of whether the discourse is informative or persuasive, organized or unorganized.

System four has certain weaknesses. While it works well in some subject matter areas — psychology, education, philosophy, literature, the humanities, for example — it is much less suitable in others, such as the natural sciences. Occasionally the system seems to result in a loss of understanding of the basic structure of the speech. Finally, the fact that the line separating fact and idea is never an entirely clear-cut one offers some difficulty.

**Ways to Increased Effectiveness**

As soon as possible after hearing the discourse we should transcribe our notes, or at least recode them, so that those basic facts secured to support each principle listed are shown in their proper relation to it. If several principles seem to support a still greater generalization, we should give the latter the label of concept, and tabulate these occasional concepts separately. They deserve and must receive considerable time for additional reflection and discussion.

In periods of later review or reflection, we ought to spend most of our time thinking about and discussing the implications of the principles we have tabulated. Almost automatically the facts supporting these principles will tend somehow to become associated with them in our minds.

**Evaluation of the Method**

The fourth system of note-taking, all things considered, may very well be the most utilitarian of all. It necessitates a minimum amount of writing while listening, thus the least interruption of the flow of communication. In subject matter areas suitable to its use, it is applicable to both persuasive and informative speech or discussion; to both deductive and inductive development; and to both the organized and unorganized presentation.

**Note-taking and the Unorganized Speech**

As soon as the listener becomes aware that the discourse he is hearing is either unprepared or very poorly prepared, he knows that trying to make an outline of it is an exceedingly bad investment of time. He therefore will immediately reject outlining, the first system of note-taking. Unless the discourse is one of elaborating and expanding a text or manuscript placed by the speaker in the hands of the listener, annotation, the second system, should also be quickly rejected. Thus, a quick decision should be made to use either system three or system four, précis writing or the recording-of-fact-versus-principle method. For reasons already pointed out most of us will usually find the latter procedure more useful.

|  |
| --- |
| **Note-taking and the Inductively-Developed Persuasive Speech** |

As soon as we discover that we are listening to an inductively developed persuasive speech, we should recognize the real challenge afforded by the experience ahead. The earliest point at which we can verify the characteristics of the talk is when the speaker makes his contract statement. If it indicates procedure only, concealing the conveyor's convictions and personal position with respect to his topic, and obviously suggests that the presentation will proceed from specific instances to an ultimate generalization, we can be sure that we are now to hear the most exciting of all speech developments. The highly trained speakers employing this method usually are persons of tremendous skill. Unless we are very alert, we shall soon find ourselves committed to some belief or action without knowing how we ever came to take the step or make the agreement.

The possible note-taking systems useful in this situation are immediately narrowed to two: précis writing or recording fact versus principle. Either will work reasonably well if the point arrangement plan is either the interrogative pattern or the problem-effect-solution pattern. Both will need some modification of normal procedure if the point arrangement pattern is either narrative or cumulative-narrative in character.

The latter two patterns are extremely subtle and are developed through the use of a single long narrative or a series of narrative specific instances of a point never fully revealed until all the stories are told.

What can audience members profitably do while listening to narration? Obviously, note-taking should come nearly to a standstill. At the end of each narrative specific instance related by the speaker, however, the listener will profit by getting down a single written sentence, either in précis form or in the "Facts" column, in approximately this form: The case of ........................... (name of central character in the story told) ...................... suggests that ...................... (whatever conclusion is suggested to the mind of the hearer) ........................... When all the stories are finished, we should have three or four such sentences. If the point or points brought to our minds differ from those now declared by the speaker to be logical inferences, we shall want to compare his conclusions very carefully with our own. In any case, full proof of the speaker's central proposition demands more than the citation of examples.

As the stories are concluded and the discourse draws to a close we shall want to listen with all of our alertness to see if, and how, the examples can be factually, statistically, or authoritatively generalized. We should anticipate a statement somewhat on the order of the following:

"The three stories you have just heard are not isolated cases. They are typical of 72.2 percent of all the workers employed by the Achilles Pump Corporation if last year's report of the Federal Mediation Service is to be believed."

Perhaps the final generalization will be based upon the testimony of some accepted and acceptable authority. In that case it might well sound about like this:

"The governor of our state, certainly the one man in the best position to understand the seriousness of this problem after hearing the report of his special commission appointed to study it last year, indicated that these cases are merely typical of thousands of others when he ringingly declared in his Fourth of July address last summer: 'The working conditions in one of our largest industries, the Achilles Pump Corporation, are atrocious — incredible to anyone interested in health, safety, and sanitation.'"

We shall, of course, want as much of this final generalization in our notes as we can possibly get down. In addition, before making a final decision as to whether or not to respond in accordance with the speaker's pleas, we shall want to reflect at length upon the discourse we have just heard. One of the wisest decisions we can make, and quite probably one we will never regret, is to postpone our final decision for a day or so until we have had more adequate time for reflection.

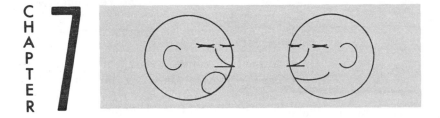

## CHAPTER 7

## Speaking
## and
## Listening . . .

# . . . the personal
# elements

## Part A: Emotional Control in Speaking and Listening

Emotional control is essential to an effective speaking or oral reading performance. Much has been written about causes, effects, and methods of cure for stage fright, but it is doubtful that the primary problem of the present generation of college students with emotional control is that of stage fright.

The authors of this book believe the real problem in emotional control for most college students is the failure to secure the heightened emotions which will make them, as personalities, seem vigorous and alive. The average college student appears to practice an inhibition of his emotional reactions to ideas. Such speakers seldom achieve success in their speech purpose. Informative and persuasive speaking, although directed primarily to the understanding, does not prevent the speaker from revealing enthusiasm for his ideas. In fact, it is imperative that enthusiasm be shown, in physical and vocal directness, which will demonstrate concern for the subject and the audience. In other words, the listeners must be made to feel without question that the speaker is mentally alert and earnestly seeking their attention.

*Concern Begets Concern*

As speakers we must remember that enthusiasm is a highly contagious thing. We cannot, therefore, avoid that display of emotion which is necessary to win interest in our subject and concern for our ideas. Too often, however, the speaker is more like a semianimated fence post than like a live human being with real blood coursing through his veins. This lack of animation may well be a pseudo-sophisticated attitude under purposeful cultivation but, whatever it is, it does not help the speaker or the listener with the communication of ideas. This take-it-or-leave-it attitude can only make the oral performance, speaking or reading, lifeless and unimportant. Somehow, we must break out of our shells and show our audience our emotions, our strength of feeling, and our personalities.

The foregoing is not to say we should become raging dynamos in wild use of body and voice when we appear on the platform. Although expressed, our emotions are always kept under proper control. We need not weep, nor shout, nor gesticulate widely, nor pound on the desk with fist, but we must let the audience know we believe what we say.

**Some Tension Is Normal**

Nearly everyone experiences an emotional arousal before an important speaking performance. This stimulation of the emotions, fear to some minds, is a common reaction and not a real fear in the usual sense of the word. A good athlete feels a similar emotion just before an important game. Baseball, basketball, and football players have undergone this heightening of the emotions many times over. They found that when the game is under way and when the mind is occupied with the progress of the plays, the before-game tension lessens and does not prevent a skillful performance. So, too, with speaking. After the speech is under way and we are concerned with the unfolding of our ideas, the emotional arousal usually diminishes and does not keep us from saying what we have in mind.

*Stage-fright Lessens with Participation*

After several speech performances we will probably find that stage fright has lost much of its force and no longer keeps us from making an acceptable or even superior speech. As a matter of fact, the person who feels little or no tension in an important speaking situation probably has too much confidence for good quality work.

The extent to which we are affected by this emotional arousal varies considerably from individual to individual but the pattern can be easily described. We have a hollow feeling in the stomach, our heart is beating rapidly, our hands and forehead break out in sweat, our mouth feels dry and our knees shake. In addition, we may find that our voice quivers, we do not see clearly, and our normal mental processes fail to function. This type of reaction has been felt by some to such a degree that they refuse to face an audience again. They make no attempt to analyze the cause, they feel it is an abnormal experience peculiar to them, and they succumb completely to their "fears." Others have much the same reaction before the audience but resolve manfully to do battle with their "weaknesses."

This heightened emotion is essentially an extra supply of energy. We should understand that certain organs of the body respond to emotional stimulation by pouring an extra supply of chemicals into the blood stream for specific purposes. Nature tries to tone us up and to provide us with sufficient energy for an exciting experience. In an athletic contest we make use of these preparations but in the speaking situation we cannot burn up this energy immediately. So we shake or prance about in an attempt to get rid of our abundant energy.

| |
|---|
| **Some Tension Is an Asset** |

We should come to treasure this emotional stimulation as a priceless asset to our speaking. We should learn techniques for harnessing it and we will then cash in on this muscle tonicity and this extra shot of energy in increased animation and improved projection. Without such emotional arousal we will never become good speakers; with it unharnessed we will always be handicapped; but with it under control we have every chance of success.

How can we harness this emotional stimulation? We can lessen our personal tensions by freeing our feelings about our subject matter. We should go about the business of making a speech with enthusiasm and real concern. We should act confident; the mere acting will often give us confidence. Moreover, our tenseness will reduce in direct proportion to our ability to think about things other than ourselves. Our real job in speaking or reading is to think about our subject and our audience. We might ask ourselves such questions as these: Am I stating this matter in such a way that my audience understands it? Am I making this idea seem really important? Am I extracting the full meaning from these written symbols? If we will keep our minds engaged with these questions we will not have time to fret about ourselves.

| *Keep Your Goals Realistic* |
|---|

Perhaps we are tense because we are making a false evaluation of ourselves and our abilities. We must remember that we are speaking to an audience of our peers. They, too, are students learning the business of oral communication. Actually with adequate preparation, we can know more about our subject than anyone else in the room. We are then the authority; we are then in the driver's seat. When our message is important. we can control the audience rather than letting it control us.

The only "cure" for hard-to-control tensions is familiarity with the situations which cause them. The more speeches we make the better we should be able to capitalize on this bodily readiness. We should, therefore, never evade a speaking situation. Also, the substitution of a pleasant emotion for an unpleasant one will help release us from the dread of performing before a group. How about substituting the pleasant emotion of work well done and a job accomplished for the unpleasant emotion of failure to achieve? Finally, it is well to remember that physical activity will help remove tensions. We should move about while speaking or reading. We should use the blackboard, if feasible, and gesture often. The tense feeling will usually disappear a few seconds after we begin our speech and start occupying the mind with the job of transmitting ideas to the audience. The *best progress* in this course will probably be made by those individuals who have feared and avoided speech experiences. By learning that an audience will not hurt them, they will have opened the gates to a social experience which will be stimulating, satisfying, and profitable.

# Part B: The Body and Voice in Speaking

The fundamental concept concerning the use of bodily activity in speech is that all of its form — eye contact, facial expression, gestures, posture, and walking — must promote the communication of ideas between speaker and listener. The use of the body as a visual aid to the sounds uttered deserves considerable attention from students of speech because such visual helps are important implementations. No one can speak before an audience without using the body in some way but the activity may be so minimized that the action is of small value. Conversely, the use to which the body is put actually may be distracting and, therefore, a hindrance to the oral performance.

**Use the Body in Speaking**

Effective bodily activity, however, promotes the communication process in several ways. It serves to attract the attention of the listeners and to maintain an interest in the speaker. In this way the oral performance becomes attractive, animated, and interesting. The meaning of the words and ideas is aided and promoted by the visual cues given by the speaker and the memory is actually facilitated through the additional associations. This has been demonstrated by several controlled studies. The visual cues also provide the audience with a measure of judgment concerning the personality of the speaker and his attitude and intention toward them. In addition, a relaxed speaker who makes free and easy platform movements will be more likely to secure a relaxed audience.

Movements of the body also serve as transition aids within the speech and help in the integration of the total speech performance. It should certainly be emphasized that utilizing the body in speaking facilitates other speech processes such as the use of the voice and releases tensions. As previously mentioned, persons who are nervous in the speaking situation soon learn that some body movement reduces the nervousness. It can also be observed how quickly the voice responds to an alert and vigorous use of gesture; a monotonous voice cannot coexist with a live and vigorous body. If good use of head, body, arms and legs served no other purpose, its importance in promoting vivacious voice usage alone would warrant the study and development of effective bodily activity.

**Eye Contact and Speech**

By far and away the most important single element of bodily action on the part of the speaker is direct eye contact with the listeners. The whole matter of effective bodily action hinges on the single element of looking the audience in the eye. Why is this true? A speech situation is a reciprocal social interaction between speaker and listener. This is true whether the speech situation be that of conversation, discussion, formal speaking, or oral reading.

The speaker is attempting to understand what his listeners are thinking as he speaks, whether the audience be large or small. The listeners are trying to know what the speaker is thinking over and above what his words say. This interaction between speaker and listener is a constant one during the entire communication situation. The speaker who neglects the matter of eye contact is not engaged in oral communication at all. He is, instead, sending a kind of oral letter in which the immediate audience reaction is considered unimportant.

*Look at Your Audience*

Eye contact means exactly what it says; it means that the speaker is looking his listeners in the eye. He must actually see his hearers. It does not mean looking just over the heads of the audience; it does not mean seeing the audience as a blurred group; it does not mean picking out a friendly face or two in the audience and looking at them; in the classroom, it does not mean looking at the instructor. After a speech to a small group of twenty-five or thirty persons, everyone in the group should feel he has been the center of the speaker's attention for some short period, perhaps several times.

*Shift Contact Frequently*

In conversation with one person it is easy enough to establish eye contact while we speak and to hold it while we listen. The short breaks between our speeches and those of our companion give an opportunity for shifting the eyes to other scenes. In the formal speech situation we, as speakers, must learn to shift the direction of our attention frequently from one individual to another.

We should not give the impression of staring at any individual and to avoid it we look at as many different listeners as we can — but only one at a time. This shifting of attention must not become mechanical, so we must not establish a sequence of attention in an unvaried pattern from one section of the audience to another. The problem of eye contact while reading from a manuscript becomes difficult for us; however, the same rule applies. We must have as much eye contact as we can get.

*The Speaker Should See While He Speaks*

Most important, we who have some directness know something about what is happening in the minds of our audience. We are thereby able to respond to what we see, if we feel it desirable. We may see that a point of information is still unclear, or that an argument is still unestablished. Sometimes we may see that further elaboration on a point would be time wasting — the listeners in great part have understood it.

Second, we may perceive certain general reaction in our listeners. Are they bored? Are any sound asleep? Are they alert? Are they enjoying what we have to say? The speaking situation involves a circular response important to both listener and speaker. After a performance, many inexperienced speakers report they do not know how well they have done. If we cannot tell how we have done, we have not seen our audience. They are telling us all the time how we are doing.

Finally, looking at our listeners serves as a means of holding attention. Good eye contact invites good eye contact. Listeners do not go to sleep, literally or figuratively, while we are speaking directly to them. We must strive for good physical directness from our first speaking appearances in this course. It is tremendously important.

**Facial Expression and Speech**

Since the face of the speaker is the center of attention, it is the most revealing means of physical expression. The speaker's facial expression, then, will have a great deal to do with the communication process. The face, for example, tells us whether the speaker is an individual who reacts to life in an alert and vigorous fashion.

*Appear Pleasant*

In most speech situations, the performer should have a pleasant facial expression. He should not scowl or frown except when some emotion calls such expression into being. On the other hand, he should not possess a continuous silly grin. The expression of the face should conform to the words being spoken either as reinforcement or as complete denial. The twinkle in the eye or the curl of the lip may carry as much meaning to an observer as the words themselves. We should let the face express the message which is to be delivered and thus secure an added power for the oral language.

**Gestures and Speech**

When beginning speakers think about gestures in relation to speech, they seem to feel that such bodily movements are unnatural. On the contrary, gesturing is a very natural method of reinforcing our sound language. We have only to watch people in conversation to verify this. If a speaker hesitates to use bodily signals, it is because he refuses to do the natural thing.

In a speech the gestures will certainly attract and help hold attention. The attention gained may be good or bad according to its focus. If the attention is attracted to the movements themselves (their beauty or awkwardness), then they are not good. If the attention is attracted to the speaker and his words, then that attention is desirable. The best bodily actions are not obvious ones; that is, they are not noticed directly by the listeners. Sometimes gestures may help bridge the periods of nonfluency and thus serve to smooth out the whole pattern of the performance.

*Best Movement*
*Not Perceived*
*as Movement*

The best visual cues are so unified with the thought, so spontaneous with the emotion of the speaker that they implement the important element in any speech — the thought. Every gesture, then, should be meaningful and direct in purpose. Actually, those movements of the speaker which are not adapted to the thought processes are really not gestures; such random activity is merely physical movement. Playing with pencils, picking at clothing, rubbing the desk top, picking up papers or books and putting them down again, and pulling the fingers or ears are not gestures at all and should be minimized, if not completely eliminated.

*Practice Gestures,*
*Don't Plan Them*

Effective movements of arms and hands should be vigorous, timed correctly, definite, and varied. Half-hearted and indefinite movements contribute little to the speech; the poorly timed gesture is laugh provoking and thus detracts; the frequently repeated gesture becomes monotonous. The size and kind of audience will govern somewhat the kind of movement made. The most common visual cues are those which are suggestive, descriptive, and emphatic. All speakers can cultivate their use so that they become an important adjunct to the speech. Although gestures should "come from the heart," there is nothing wrong in practicing them. Since the lack of gesture in speech is due to inhibition of some kind, the forced use will help eliminate the inhibition.

**Head and Body Gestures**

Head movements serve as important gestures and may identify persons or objects. The movements are slight but positive and serve to energize the oral statements. A young lady may use rather vigorous head movements where vigorous arm and hand movements might not be quite appropriate. The only danger in head movements is that they may be overused and thus become monotonous. Body gestures are commonly a part of the head and arm movement and make their contribution in that way. In addition, such movements as the shrugging of the shoulders reinforce the communication process.

**Hand and Arm Gestures**

Hand and arm movements, such as waving and pointing, serve to communicate without audible symbols; but their primary use is, of course, to implement words spoken. These movements are best when they proceed from a relaxed body, but the motion once started must be strong and purposive — sometimes vigorous, sometimes smooth and graceful. Certainly the speaker should use these movements freely and with wide variation, but never aimlessly. Gesturing should never become such an art that a listener becomes engrossed in it rather than in the oral symbols.

When gesturing with the hand and arm, the speaker should rarely follow his gesture with his own eyes. Bodily action should be kept under control — pounding of the table or rostrum is too strong. Moreover, when gesturing the hands should be brought up high enough that the physical action will be seen, and when a gesture is started it should be completed. Also, a speaker must watch the timing, for an ill-timed gesture is far worse than none at all.

*Do What Comes Naturally*

Students frequently want to know what they should do with their hands. The answer is that nothing in particular should be done with them unless the speaker has some need for them. If the hands are left alone, they will probably rest rather inconspicuously at the sides. Every movement cannot be kept purposive and some movements without purpose will not detract from the speech. So to put a hand in the pocket while making a speech is not bad, whereas cramming the hands in the pockets to hide them is not good. Without question, hands jammed in pockets or clasped behind the back are inappropriate as far as gesturing is concerned.

Above all we should remember that true art is not obvious — that the best gestures are those not really seen. In practicing gestures, then, we should work for coordination of ideas expressed orally with spontaneous movement of the body. We should never plan a gesture in complete detail, for it will then be obvious and ineffective.

**Posture and Speech**

Posture is important in speaking because it may be such as to detract from the performance. Good carriage of the body is a powerful suggestion of self-confidence and should be practiced by the beginning speaker for that reason. What is good posture? One should stand relaxed but not too relaxed. The speaker should not resemble a wooden Indian nor should he resemble the feeble form of the sick person. "To stand tall with the chin and chest up" is fair advice but it must not be taken too literally. The chin should not be up in the air nor should the chest be puffed out in a gesture of great strength.

Perhaps we should pay some attention to the way we stand and the way we use the rostrum. The spread eagle stance calls attention to itself and is therefore undesirable and the hip-out-of-joint stance is awkward and unattractive. When the rostrum is used by the speaker it should not be for the purpose of resting weary bones — for something to sprawl upon. Common sense should tell us what posture is good and what is undesirable. We should cultivate the good and eliminate the faulty.

**Personal Appearance and Speech**

The personal appearance of the speaker is important to the speaker himself and to the audience. The audience sees the speaker before they hear him and that first impression should be a good one. If the speaker knows he is acceptable in appearance, his own self-confidence is aided considerably.

No long discussion is needed on this topic of appearance. Cleanliness and neatness are the watchwords. The patterns of dress are fairly well established for college-age students. The speaking performance is formal enough and the individual performing is conspicuous enough to demand personal care for appearance. A young lady in bobby pins does not make a suitable appearance, a young man in bare feet or hip boots would not enhance his chances of success. Distractions in appearance should be avoided for the fundamental reason that such distractions subtract from rather than implement the speech. Sorority or fraternity initiation garb certainly detracts from a performance before a student audience or any other audience, for it diverts the minds of the listeners to other events.

**Walking and Speech** During our speaking performance we do three jobs of walking — from a seat to the position for the performance, from one position to another during the performance, and from the performance to the seat again. In walking to the position in front of the audience, the speaker should walk with an alert and elastic step. Certainly he should not drag his feet along the floor, nor should he clump his way forward. This same direction should be applied to the regaining of the seat after the talk or reading is finished. Certainly the approach should not be one of timidness or overaggressiveness, and the leaving of the platform should not resemble a run. The speaking should not begin during the approach to the front and the speaking shouldn't close while the speaker is returning to his seat.

Some walking during the performance may be desirable. When such walking is done, it should be done gracefully and easily. Sound advice dictates that the walking not be overdone nor at a pace like that of a wild animal in a cage, nor should it be done in studied steps — three this way and three that. Some inexperienced speakers walk in one spot while speaking. The shifting of the weight in spot walking is distracting and accompanying banging of heels and scraping of the shoe soles on the floor make the audience restless and inattentive. Too much walking or aimless walking attracts attention to itself and away from the words spoken. When he walks, the speaker should keep his eyes on the audience and not on his feet.

**Developing Effective Bodily Action** The technique for developing effective use of the body in speaking is much like the technique for developing any skill. The initial move involves the individual decision that attention to bodily activity has real importance in oral presentations. The steps to improve can only follow that initial decision.

We should observe the effect of good use of body in actual speaking situations. By watching others, we can see why some activity is helpful in promoting communication and why some either helps little or actually hinders. Our second step involves the elimination of habitual personal mannerisms. Some of these may be easy for us to break and others rather difficult.

Our final step is to establish through practice those patterns of bodily activity which reinforce the spoken words. As inexperienced speakers we have to learn not to inhibit the feeling for physical activity and to respond freely to the impulses for such activity. With practice, our former arm jerks will become full blown gestures. In practice sessions in private, there may be some virtue in our overemphasizing the number and the sweep or power of the physical movements. It is a relatively easy job to restrict gesturing — much easier than to get the activity started.

## Control the Voice

Without voice a person is seriously handicapped in communicating ideas. Although most of us do have voices, they are not alike. It would be a mistake to attempt to make them alike, or even the use of them alike. The voice does more than carry ideas from the speaker to the listener through a set of oral symbols. The tones and inflections of the voice describe the speaker and reflect his emotions and feelings. Someone has said that the voice is the mirror of the personality. To a great extent it is; for example, angry people have harsh voices and excited people have high pitched and strained voices. Not all unpleasant voices originate with unpleasant people, but certainly the person who wishes a pleasant voice must first have a pleasant personality.

In addition to carrying messages and describing the speaker the voice identifies the individual. One need not see a person to know the ownership of the voice; if we are well acquainted with a voice, our ear tells us when that person is speaking. In most cases that identification is possible even over a telephone transmitter, which is far from a perfect method of reproducing the tonal quality of sounds. The one voice we have difficulty in identifying is our own. The first time we hear such a reproduction on a tape or disc recording we may not wish to claim ownership to that vocal effect. Our friends recognize the reproduction, however, so we are forced to accept their identification.

Most persons agree that not only is a voice necessary, but that a good one is important to an individual. What is a good voice?

Without question the good one is that which calls the least attention to itself and best promotes the communication of ideas. A disagreeable phonation, for whatever reason, will certainly attract attention to itself. The degree of distraction will depend upon the degree of unpleasantness and upon the interest of the audience in the subject matter. It is rather remarkable how the ear will adjust to unpleasant oral sounds if those symbols are carrying a message of extreme interest. Obvious artistic display in vocal effort will distract from the ideas being presented in the same way that an unpleasant production distracts. The attention of the listener focuses on the voice itself and not on the message it carries. Few students in this beginning course will need worry about the latter type of distraction.

**Essentials of Voice Control**

There are at least three essentials of voice control for effective use of the voice. Most of these matters can be profitably studied and practiced by every student of speech. The sounds of speech should be *audible* to the listener and whether they will be depends upon the loudness or force of utterance and the rate of utterance. The quality should be *pleasant* to the listener and whether it is or not depends upon the average pitch level and resonance. The tone production should be *varied* enough to be interesting and that variation can be secured through changes in rate, pitch, quality and loudness.

Of these three essentials, *variety* is by far the most important. To gain flexibility we produce changes in rate, pitch, and loudness according to the mood and meaning of our message. We have little immediate control over the fundamental quality of our voices but over rate, pitch, and loudness we have absolute control. Variety in our speech pattern will do two important things for our communication effort. First, a varied tone is an interesting tone and will help hold attention of our listeners. More important, variety in speech production is the only possible way to complete meaning in the words the speaker uses. A monotonous voice delivers the words only without mood or emphasis.

*Use the Conversational Pattern*

In addition to the three essentials mentioned, the speaker should follow a conversational pattern of speech and the vocal tone should carry confidence and sincerity. The conversational pattern is secured through the controls we have learned to exercise in conversation over audibility, quality, variety, and fluency. The sincerity in the vocal effort is gained through the inflections and vocal quality used, since these elements carry the feelings of the speaker. Needless to say, the speaker should be sincere at heart in order to sound sincere.

*Poor Use of Voice*

A poor voice, by contrast, is one which is inaudible, unpleasant, monotonous, unconversational, and insincere. One poorly used may be too audible or too varied.

The speaker must learn to adjust his vocal level to the size of the room and audience. For a small audience in a small room, the speaker needs to use little force; for a small audience in a large room, if the audience is seated close to the speaker, little force is needed, but for a large audience in a large room, much force is needed. Only through practice can a speaker know what intensity level to use. Class criticism on loudness level should help the student speaker make this adjustment. For the average classroom situation, the same force as used in conversation will probably be sufficient.

The voice can be too varied if the rate, pitch, and loudness are being changed rapidly and for no communication purpose. Extensive variations in vocal controls which are out of tune with any real effort to carry the message call attention to the use of voice rather than to the ideas, and so must be condemned.

**Factors in Voice Analysis**

If we believe that a voice and the use of it can be improved, we must also believe there are separate factors which can be improved. Four of these factors can be controlled by the individual. They have already been mentioned in the description of good and poor voices but deserve a more complete discussion.

*Pitch*

Pitch in speech, as in singing, is the place on the musical scale at which sound is uttered. Every sound has some pitch and the difference between pitch in music and pitch in speech is that the pitch in music is absolute while pitch in speech is only relative. The individual's voice is his own guide in speech; in music the pitch is fixed by the scale. In speech we glide from one pitch to another; in music we go from one pitch to another in steps. Fortunately for most of us, we need not be able to sing the simplest tune in order to be a good speaker. In speaking, the individual uses whatever pitch is best suited to him.

The point to be emphasized about pitch is the necessity for conscious control over it. Without such control, the speaker cannot have a natural, pleasing, and impressive phonation. Often the tone rises to a high, unnatural level of pitch which is unpleasant; this is particularly true if the tone has a nasal quality. Many voices secure so little variation in pitch that even the low pitches become monotonous. What is low pitch for one speaker, however, may not be low pitch for another. The best use of pitch demands a variation in upward and downward movement. Such movement not only relieves the monotony but serves also to express different thoughts and emotions.

This upward and downward movement in pitch is called inflection. In prose the inflection of the voice helps with the intelligibility of the thoughts and in poetry it prevents montony and chanting. Variations in pitch then not only avoid monotony but aid in expression of thought and emotion. A good speaker should learn to use all of the means for communicating an idea.

| *Quality* |
|-----------|

No two voices sound alike; each has a timbre all its own due to the pitch and resonance used. A pleasant tone production secures resonance in such fashion that the sound is acceptable to the human ear. The unpleasant types are easier to define, and take several forms. Poor voices are usually classified as harsh, hoarse, breathy, and nasal in quality.

The harsh quality as far as present research has determined is probably due to faulty balance in resonance. Excessive resonance in the throat combined with muscle tensions in the same area serve to produce the unpleasant quality called harshness. Any person can simulate the harsh quality by tensing the throat muscles and giving an expression of hate, malice, or scorn.

The hoarse tone sounds as if the person has a cold which has settled in the larynx. Such a voice may be a result of prolonged misuse, postnasal drip, a growth on the vocal bands, or some other organic disorder. Anyone with severe hoarseness should have a doctor examine the throat and larynx.

The breathy or aspirate voice is a result of faulty breathing. The bit of breath which can be heard over and above the tone being produced probably is due to an emotional condition of the speaker. If a gasp for breath is heard between phrases spoken, the individual is failing to take in enough air to sustain normal speech. The breathy production is usually poor in audibility.

The nasal voice is so called because too much resonance takes place in the nasal cavities. Unless there exists some organic difficulty, an individual can with practice learn to get more oral resonance. Denasality results from an organic condition such as a nose infection, deviated septum, or excessive adenoid tissue. Correction of the organic difficulty will usually allow for rapid improvement in vocal quality.

When any student presents resonance deviations sufficient to produce a distinctly unpleasant voice quality, the instructor will recommend improvement procedures. The student should consider such recommendations as a service and not as a criticism. If our voices are poor, now is the time to do something about them.

## Loudness

Everyone has more or less control over volume, but few use this control to advantage. Changes in vocal force are used to relieve monotony and to secure interest and emphasis in speech. Too many persons associate loud volume with emphasis and fail to see that a subdued voice will serve the same purpose. In fact, a long continued high level of intensity loses its power of emphasis and becomes mere ranting or vociferation.

When uttering pathetic, solemn, or tranquil thoughts, we speak in the subdued tones of ordinary conversation. Narration, description, and unimpassioned thought demand no more than moderate loudness. Strong passion, whether of fear, anger, or scorn, usually calls for more forceful tones. Most of our speaking and reading exercises call for considerable variation within sentences and phrases; even the syllables of the same word vary in force (stress).

It should be understood that an increase in volume does not mean a higher pitch also. With more force we usually raise the pitch but that does not have to be so. The requirements for loudness, then, mean more than an easily audible voice because the variation avoids monotony and, if properly controlled, aids in carrying emotion and thought. We must adjust and vary the loudness according to the size of the room, the size of the audience, the occasion, and the emotional state of the speaker. We must get variation.

## Rate

Rate of speech involves the length of time occupied in saying individual words and the length of the pauses between words and sentences. Researchers have found that most speakers produce on the average between 125 and 150 words per minute. If we go too high above or too far below this average, we may well question our rate of speaking. Most of our difficulty, however, will not be with speech which is too slow or too fast, but with speech which is too much the same in rate. We dislike hearing the drawling speech or the awkward pausing, and we dislike speech so rapid that emphasis is impossible. Rate is the easiest of all factors of voice to define and talk about but the hardest of all to control.

With this factor, as with the preceding ones, we must attempt to break up rate patterns which create monotony in speech. Variety of emotion demands variety in rate. The pause is an important element in securing emphasis and the beginning speaker should practice its use. The length and frequency of pauses are determined by the sentiment being expressed. The marks of punctuation do not necessarily indicate the pauses or their length. Unless we present the problem of speaking too slow or too fast, our efforts should be turned to using pauses and to changing the rate of speech to suit our intellectual and emotional moods. Here as with the other factors of voice we are concerned with better communication of ideas, and rate is definitely a part of the communication process. A defect in rate wearies the audience and kills the effect of the speech.

*Conversational Pattern*

The proper control of pitch, quality, loudness, and rate will provide us with the conversational pattern which carries confidence and sincerity. The use of these factors gives emphasis to our speech; the kind and degree are determined by the speaker in relation to the sentiments he expresses.

In conversation with one or more persons, the speaker is usually able to get a synthesis and variation of pitch, loudness, rate, and quality in a combination both pleasant and impressive to the listener. On the platform, as a speaker or reader, this combination seems much more difficult to attain. This may be due partially to a false belief that the performer before a group must do something different from that done in conversation. As far as possible, we should achieve the same use of voice in speaking and reading that we do in conversation.

It is well to point out that this synthesis should be one's own. We should not try to copy the use of voice which we hear from someone else. We must rely on the development of our own talent, taste, and originality. The suggestions given in this chapter have been indicative rather than absolute. Speaking or reading is an art which must be developed by each individual according to his own personality.

---
**Improvement of the Voice**
---

Any student with serious deviations in voice or use of voice should secure advice and direction from a qualified speech clinician. Students who present minor defects may follow procedures for self-improvement as outlined by the instructor. Tape recorders, if available for practice periods, are wonderful devices for work upon flexibility and emphasis. There is nothing quite so useful as a method for improvement as the hearing of our own voices. Even those students with adequate and superior voices should work toward more skillful use of this tool.

As other skills for the student improve, this one will tend to keep abreast. Gesturing, for example, helps us improve the use of our vocal mechanism. The person with good use of body in the speaking situation can scarcely have poor use of voice. Enthusiasm and interest in one's topic and in one's audience will have similar effects. Also, we will develop better control over our voices as we gain control over our emotions.

## Part C:  Self-control in Listening

The first section of this chapter was concerned with the matter of control on the part of the speaker. It is doubtful that many of us have given much if any thought to the adjustments that need to be made by the listener. There are, however, at least three reaction points which call for conscious listener control if he wishes to be highly effective in his task. We must make adjustments to the speaker, to the ideas he expresses, and to the words he uses.

---
**Adjustment to the Speaker**
---

Every speaker has his peculiarities. It is entirely natural for the auditor to note them, to become preoccupied by them and, in time, to use them as a rationalization for choosing to follow some mental tangent rather than the thread of the oral discourse. Which one of us has not said, at some time or other, something like this? "I just didn't get a thing out of it. Who could? That speaker's ghastly, droning voice and barking cough every half minute made it impossible to listen to him."

Of course, some speakers are handicapped by more eccentricities than others, and it is more difficult to give them our sustained attention. Some have poor eye contact, odd pronunciations, distracting bodily activity. Unfortunate, too, in one sense, is the fact that the more speech training we get the easier it is to find flaws in the conveyor's manner of expression. Yet to throw the entire responsibility for communication upon the speaker is a serious listening fault — one of the worst. At most, no more than half such responsibility can logically be placed upon the conveyor. To improve our own aural assimilation we must continually battle the notion that we are the helpless victims of speakers with intolerable shortcomings.

One study of factors influencing the efficiency of oral communication found objective evidence that several of these factors are definitely related to the listener's attitude toward the speaking characteristics of the conveyor. Communicative efficiency is strongly affected by the audibility of the speakers and by the listener's estimate of propriety of the language being used. Communication is less strongly, but still consistently, affected by four other such factors: admiration for the speaker, estimate of his over-all effectiveness, amount of high school speech training received by the listener, and the listener's personal susceptibility to distraction.

The essential difference between a written essay and a speech is that if the latter is to be effective there must always be a vital, circular, and "living" relationship between speaker and listener. When effective oral communication is achieved, it is always the result of equally shared responsibility by the conveyor and the assimilator.

Our primary concern at this point is to consider what procedure is available to the listener when the speaker really seems pretty inadequate, when, as conveyor, he seems unwilling to assume his share of responsibility for communication. Is this sufficient justification for the listener to tune out the poorly projecting speaker and embark upon some mental tangent? The answer is "no." Two better recourses are available to him.

**The Listener's Responsibility in Learning**

The listener should ponder the basic nature of learning. Perhaps the best definition of learning is the simplest. Essentially, it is the refinement or expansion of one's apperceptive mass. What is an apperceptive mass? It is the sum total of all the thoughts, feeling, emotions, experiences, facts, and ideas that an individual possesses. When this mass is modified, altered, rearranged, refined, or expanded, learning is taking place.

*Learning for the listener is "inside" action on the part of the listener.* The speaker has comparatively little to do with it. He cannot learn for the listener. It is the listener's apperceptive mass which is to be modified. "Telling" is not necessarily teaching. And "getting told" is not necessarily learning. Learning is cortical activity within the listener resulting from something perceived.

Who is primarily at fault when we fail to understand, or perhaps even receive, the message sent our way? Essentially we "listen with our experience." Is the conveyor to be held responsible because we are poorly equipped to decode his message? We cannot understand everything that we hear, but one sure way we can raise the level of our understanding is to assume the responsibility which is inherently ours. One sure way to *lower* it is to blame the speaker for all breakdowns.

**The Listener's Responsibility to the Speaker**

The listener should try to stimulate the speaker. Anything said by a speaker and interpreted by us as listeners immediately influences us, and often in such a visible way as to affect the speaker at once. If he notes cynicism, open signs of disinterest, disapproval or disbelief, he usually becomes discouraged, tense, and less and less effective. He may "go to pieces" entirely. On the other hand, if we seem interested and responsive, he is likely to become encouraged, to lose many of his objectionable mannerisms or other initial handicaps, and to become more and more effective.

The point is that for selfish reasons alone one of the best investments we can make when afflicted with a weak speaker is to give him our conscious and overt attention. We should establish eye contact and maintain it; we should indicate by posture and facial expression that the occasion and the speaker's efforts are a matter of real concern to us; and we should give our applause at any point where it is at all deserved. When we do these things we help the speaker to improve himself, and in turn we profit by better understanding of the improved communication largely resultant from our own efforts. None of this implies, necessarily, acceptance of his point of view or favorable action upon some appeal which the speaker may make. It is, rather, an expression of interest.

It is a truth worth repeating that good listeners know that speaker and audience share responsibility for the success or failure of a speech. They assume their half of the obligation. Poor listeners slight their fair share of the task, and hold the conveyor singly responsible for holding their attention.

**Reconciliation of Thought Speed and Speech Speed**

One of the core problems of effective listening is the development of the utmost possible concentration in the immediate listening situation. Concentration by the learner, however, is inseparably intertwined with two variables largely beyond his control: his own speed of thought and the rate of speech of the communicator. A most significant component of effective listening requires reconciliation of thought speed and speech speed.

On the average in America we talk at about 125 words per minute. Informative speakers, however — or at any rate school classroom lecturers — average only 100 words per minute. This figure has been reported by several investigators working in widely separated localities. By contrast, how fast do we listen? Or, to put it more accurately, if thought could be measured in words per minute, how many words per minute do we think on the average when we are participating in a listening situation? Ten or fifteen years ago an answer to this question would have been pure guesswork. True, most psychologists have been in agreement for some time now that most of our thinking actually is done in language. But how can its speed be estimated? In recent years three kinds of evidence have been published, which in the composite give us a reasonably good answer.

This evidence has included (a) training speakers to talk at more than three times normal speed without significant loss in listening comprehension by the subjects hearing this rapid speech; (b) recording connected discourse on tape, piecing together the residual fragments after snipping out a large percentage of the total strip of tape, and playing back the deleted version without significant loss in listening comprehension by the subjects being tested; and (c) training numbers of students to read at an average pace of anywhere from 300 to 800 words per minute, and concurrently training them to think at this pace well enough to pass with high comprehension scores the tests then taken over the content of the materials read.

*Thinking Is Faster Than Talking*

Our best estimate after studying the available objective reports on the matter would be that an easy, average cruising speed of thought for most college classes would be at least four hundred words per minute. With some highly selected groups the average figure may be nearly twice as large. Now our problem and needed listening skill come sharply into focus. As learners we cruise along mentally at four hundred words per minute while the poor bumbling professor up front plods laboriously along at one hundred. It is beyond our power to force his rate up to ours; and it would be still more impractical to slow our thought speed to match his pace, even if we knew how to do it. Presently, although many of us can voluntarily control the *direction* of our thoughts, we have no evidence at all to suggest that we can voluntarily control their pace. *By reconciliation of thought speed and speech speed is meant the utilization of the differential between them to expedite comprehension and learning.* No attempt should be made to synchronize their rates.

How does the vast differential between thought speed and speech speed affect listening comprehension? The truth is that the differential serves as a tremendous handicap to the untrained learner. Although the disparity of rate can with training be made to expedite learning, it presently operates for the vast majority of us as a snare, a pitfall, and a delusion. It gives us a distinctly false sense of security during aural assimilation and encourages us to embark upon risky and unprofitable mental tangents.

Let us see how the disparity actually works. Let us consider a class of engineering students whose instructor has just walked in with a slide rule in his hands. He starts off his hour-long lecture with the declaration that as engineers the slide rule is certain to play an important role in the lives of every one of us. Then he proceeds to show how to use it. In a flash the typical student says to himself, "What a bore. I learned all about that as a junior in high school . . . Now what should I do about that soft tire on my Ford?" For the next sixty seconds he worries about the tire. During the following two seconds he tunes in the lecture, catches the word "subtraction," and turns again to his personal worry. At the end of each one- or two-minute interval he tunes in the lecture, establishes his feeling of familiarity and security, and then reverts to his next mental tangent. Then the catastrophic happens. Embarked upon the fascinating problem of which girl to call for a date that night, our mentally wandering engineer completely misses the difficult, the unknown, and the really substantial part of the lecture. The next thing he hears is the bell at the end of the hour and the instructor's final words having something to do with "square root." Panic may well set in; and perhaps a whole evening will be spent in trying to make up lost ground.

*Stay on the Listening Track*

Aural communication is truly a pathway beset with many perils. Worries may steal our attention. "How will I explain the F in chemistry to my father? Why did I waste so much money last night? . . ." Our thoughts may be about ourselves, about our families, about our latest love affair. To be diverted when reading does little harm, for we can come back to the point where we left the author when we are ready. Not so in listening; the speaker does not wait for us and, unless we keep up, we will lose those items covered while we were away. It is better to make a note, mental or otherwise, to pursue the stimulating thought after the speech is over; but to get back *now* on the listening track. All kinds of stimuli leading to mental tangents operate in every socialized listening situation. The rate differential between thought and speech encourages embarking upon these mental tangents, whereas efficient listening demands continuous attention — a staying "on track" with the speaker. The poor listener is the chap traveling the byways without even conscious recognition most of the time that he is doing so.

Efficient listening is a full-time job. Good listeners know this and usually apply all kinds of self-made little devices to stay "on track." Some incorporate danger signals to themselves in their note-taking; some set up whole systems of little personal rewards and penalties to stimulate concentration; and some employ eye contact as the main method of sustaining attention. All of these devices are of some benefit. Eye contact is particularly helpful. There seems to be no doubt at all that visually we catch and interpret many a helpful symbol or cue adding directly to understanding, and that in addition these visual symbols stimulate aural ones, actually causing us "to hear more."

**Adjustment to Emotion-Laden Words**

Parallel to the blind spots which afflict human beings are certain psychological deaf spots which far more significantly impair our ability to perceive and understand. These deaf spots are areas of tremendous sensitivity, and are the dwelling place of our most cherished notions, convictions, mores, and complexes. When a speaker invades one of these areas with a word, phrase, or argument which seems to violate our dearest belief, often we figuratively "freeze up" with respect to the remainder of his talk. We tune out the ensuing part of his discourse, and turn our mind to retraveling familiar mental pathways crisscrossing our invaded area of sensitivity; or, if the speaker has made an argument we can successfully challenge, we shrewdly plot a devastating rebuttal during all the remaining time of his discourse.

An important component of effective listening is that of adjustment to emotion-laden words. It is hard to believe in moments of detachment and cold analysis that just a word or phrase could possibly arouse one emotionally to a point of even momentary mental paralysis or impliability. Yet such is the case; and when such emotional deafness transpires, communicative efficiency drops rapidly toward the zero point.

Some words and phrases have emerged as more frequent troublemakers than others. Conceivably, almost any image-creating word or phrase could precipitate a psychological deaf spot in some auditor, at some time, and at some place. Among those known to have aroused and handicapped various college students the following must certainly be included: kike, hick, landlord, landlady, evolution, Jew, damn-Yankee, red-neck, wool-hat, field hand, sharecropper, sissy, sex pervert, venereal disease, income tax chiseler, Democrat, Republican, socialistic, communistic, Red, dumb farmer, Swamp Angel, peckerwood, mother-in-law, pink, fellow-traveler, red-tape, "Greetings," antivivisectionist, nigger, crooked politician, yokel, hick town. square, toady, flunky, cop, gangster, thug, bully, welsher, sadist.

One of the most conceivably helpful pieces of graduate research in education would be for some one to identify "the one hundred greatest word barriers to learning." Perhaps the troublemakers could be classified by grade levels. Such a study has not been made but should be undertaken, for we know that words alone can seriously impede learning. Good listeners are objective-minded and analytic enough to be but little affected; poor listeners are frequently aroused emotionally and seriously handicapped.

It is not enough to recognize that most deaf-spot creating words are epithet or invective although one may still be aroused by them. Rather, each of us will profit by doing three things:

1. Identifying the words or phrases which most upset us emotionally, and making a list of them.
2. Analyzing the reasons why each word influences us as it does; locating the original basis for our reaction to see if it still has a logical application to our current status.

3. Rationalizing the impact of each word upon us by discussing it freely with classmate, instructor, parent, or pastor.

A thorough examination will reveal that such words really should not bother us at all. Some of them are improper or are actually vulgar enough to weigh heavily against the one who uses them. Others carry purely personal connotation. Are we to let such feeble things impair our learning and growth? To dispose of them can give us only pleasure.

## Adjustment to Emotion-Rousing Points

Psychological deaf spots may be caused by quick and violent disagreement with the main points or arguments of the speaker rather than by reaction to just words or phrases. They are more serious in this case, largely because of their greater duration. In either instance the damage is done through *overstimulation*, which at times rivals the twin evil of understimulation in its detrimental influence on comprehension. Occasionally the overstimulation is roused in support of the speaker's point; usually it is exactly the reverse.

Good listeners tend to wait until they fully understand a point before attempting to judge it. Poor listeners have less emotional control. They frequently acquire an intense dislike for a speaker because of some point he makes, perhaps even a minor one introduced in a comparatively offhand manner. Their resulting overeagerness to debate or somehow to annoy the communicator is a common corollary of faulty comprehension. They consistently prepare an answer to a point, or questions about it, before the point itself is fully comprehended.

The overstimulated auditor usually becomes preoccupied by trying to do three things simultaneously: calculate what hurt is being done to his own pet ideas; plot an embarrassing question or refutation to hurl at the speaker at the earliest opportunity; enjoy mentally, prior to its realization, all the discomfiture visualized for the speaker once the devastating reply to him is launched. With all these things going on it is little wonder that subsequent passages of the discourse are tuned out, with comprehension of them sinking to a near zero level.

Three suggestions can be made to the person who would attempt to eliminate his personal problem of overstimulation with its corollary of decreased comprehension.

| *Withhold Evaluation* |
|---|

One of the most important principles governing all learning is at stake here. *We must withhold evaluation of a point until our comprehension of that point is complete.* At first this will require a good deal of self-control, but with persistence — and some classroom attention — it can be built into a regular habit. After the speech is over, and not until then, we need to review its main ideas and make our own assessment of them.

| *Hunt for Negative Evidence* |
|---|

To achieve real maturity all of us need to develop the practice, when one of our deep-seated opinions or prejudices is challenged, of hunting more diligently for evidence that we were originally wrong than for evidence that we were originally right. This is not easy. It requires a generous spirit and real breadth of outlook. It has frequently been said that to just such effort the world now owes every significant improvement in its standard of living. Every new fact or idea we assimilate requires some reorganization of what we previously believed. As psychologists frequently put it "The primary function of education is to teach us how to change our minds."

| *Make a Realistic Self-Analysis* |
|---|

Many of us need to face up to the fact that to our associates we seem veritable hedgehogs of prejudice, with spines extended and quiveringly pointing in every direction. Are people always stepping verbally on our mental toes? Do we often fret over society's apparent pursuit of false principle? Do we frequently find ourselves debating some point which its maker later modified just as we would have had him do, but which we somehow missed? If the answers to these questions are yes, the time has come for self-reform. Let us determine henceforth to "hear the man out," to withhold evaluation until comprehension is complete.

# 8

# Speaking
# and
# Listening . . .

# . . . the substratum
# elements

## Part A: The Analysis of Audience and Speaker

Early Greek and Roman rhetoricians had already recognized that oral-aural communications involved more than words spoken and listened to. These underlying elements involve the total consideration that a speaker must take into account in addition to the ideas to be presented and the forms and manner of expression to be used. From the standpoint of the listener these supporting attributes involve all those elements which help him comprehend the words being spoken.

In brief, the substratum elements of communication are those which concern a speaker with respect to his particular audience and the specific occasion and those which concern the listener in relation to the speaker, to the ideas being presented, and to the specific listening situation. Although on-the-spot adjustments may take place, these concerns of speaker and listener are largely preparations made prior to the oncoming event of actual communication.

**Concerns of the Speaker**

The immediate purpose of the speaker in any speech he makes is to arouse some fairly definite response in his listeners. These hoped-for responses vary from one speech occasion to another. On one occasion the speaker may hope to increase the general knowledge of his audience, on another to change attitudes or beliefs, on still another to secure some definite action. In many speeches the purpose of the speaker will be to do all these things. In any case the speaker can best secure his purpose or purposes if he knows something about his audience. It is then that he can decide what his best approach might be.

**The Audience in General**

The classroom audience for this speech course will be fairly stable with regard to these problems of analysis. We will, however, continue to study and learn more about our classmates as we proceed through the course. Our future audiences, of course, will present wide variations in age, sex, educational achievement, occupational interests and a host of other ways. One of the most important variations will involve social background and the consequent range of interests.

It may be clear enough to a beginning speaker that he would not make the same presentation to a group of young children as to a group of mature adults. It is not so obvious that presentations to mature audiences may vary considerably. A speaker who is concerned with audience response must be concerned with audience differences. The illustrations we use, the methods of expression we devise, and the points we emphasize are carefully chosen with regard to the particular audience we face.

The analysis of the audience is usually not as difficult as the foregoing might make it appear. If our speech is to be made to an organizational group or, as is frequently the case, to a division of that group, we can know a lot about the general interests without too much research. Since our audience adaptations must be made in terms of the greatest numbers of individuals, we can frequently establish the majority interests through simple inquiry. Sometimes the structure of the organization will give us the leads we need. The difficult job of audience analysis comes when the group organization does not reveal a mutuality of interests.

**Identification with the Audience**

The necessity for audience analysis is of extreme importance when we wish to speak in the hope of changing attitudes and fostering some definite action. If we hope to persuade, we can do it only by winning the listeners to our point of view. We cannot drive nor push them into a change. For this reason, the good persuader tries to identify himself with his audience in as many ways as possible. This identification is the starting point for the acceptance of change. The attitudes of the audience at the moment the talk begins therefore are of extreme importance to the speaker.

*Feedback*

As the speaker progresses, if he is effective the attitudes of the audience will be in some stage of change. The feedback which the persuader receives from his listeners helps him effect a new analysis of his audience as he proceeds from point to point in the progress of the talk. If the attitudes of the audience are perceived correctly, the speaker can then make the adjustments in the presentation which will best advance the purpose of the speech. Probably we have all observed on occasion how a speaker has completely misread his audience, either prior to the beginning of the speech or during the course of it, and has gone down to ignominious defeat.

**Range of Attitudes**

The attitudes of the audience on an occasion of a persuasive speech will range all the way from extremely favorable to the speaker's points of view to extremely unfavorable. The speaker has little problem with the favorable except in the instance where he hopes to push for positive action of some sort. Those who favor his line of argument may not be ready for any committal to action or more particularly for the specific action the speaker wants from them.

The chances are good that the group that is extremely unfavorable will be affected little by the speaker. The best he can hope for with this portion of his audience is that they swing ever so little away from the completely unfavorable attitude with respect to his views.

It is with the middle or neutral group that a persuader must hope for change. This group exists either because of little prior thought about the proposition being discussed or because they lack interest in any particular point of view. With this neutral group, the approach of the speaker is clear. He must stir up an interest in his proposition and at the same time build the support for his point of view which will convince for belief and action.

If we go about our job of speaking as we should, we will hold the interest of the favorable, secure interest, belief, and possible action with the neutral, and be tactful with the unfavorable. If the approach is interesting and the reasoning sound, there is a good chance that some minds will accept the point of view we prescribe.

| **Noncontroversial Speeches** |
| --- |

Many speeches are noncontroversial in nature and could be more accurately described as informational. Our audiences on such an occasion will range from vitally interested to fairly disinterested. Every classroom lecturer faces audiences of this type. The procedure for the speaker is obvious. He must get the interest of the audience and must hold it if he is to secure comprehension of the subject matter presented.

The audience analysis on such an occasion is largely in terms of educational maturity and experience. The materials presented must be within the understanding of the audience. In order to hold interest the materials will be presented best when they involve the use of the eyes as well as the ears of the listener.

| **Concerns of the Listener** |
| --- |

As members of the audience we will reverse the foregoing processes and attempt an analysis of the speaker. This analysis may seem simple on first thought, but if anything it is more difficult than that of analyzing an audience. It involves two important things for the listener to do; one of these involves a study made prior to the speech occasion and the other a study during the speech.

The study which involves a prior knowledge of the speaker involves a consideration for the speaker with respect to what Aristotle termed ethical elements of proof. This great Greek rhetorician was interested in informing speakers how they might use substratum elements in the presentation of their cases. He realized that what the audience thought of the speaker as a man would have a great deal to do with how they would listen to what he had to say. How true that is. To protect ourselves, as listeners, we must know the whole truth about the speaker and not just what he wants us to believe. To know the whole truth about a speaker, we must study his background and previous interests and experience.

| *Ability* |
| --- |

Is he an able man? Every person, if well known, has made some sort of a reputation for himself. Is this a reputation for wisdom or a reputation for always being on the other side of what we in our experience believe to be the proper point of view? Does he know what he is talking about? Is he dogmatic in his views?

| Goodness |

We want to know whether the speaker is a good man. Is he working for some private gain or does he have the interest of all as he tries to get us to believe and to do? We can only look at his past record to get any information along this line. If his motives are in doubt, we must look at what he has to say very carefully. If his past record is one of supporting those things we believe to be virtuous and just, we can more easily believe that his support of a present proposition is of the same mold.

| Knowledge |

If the speaker meets our qualifications of ability and character, we still want to know about his knowledge with reference to the matter under consideration. This is the study we make as we listen to what he has to say.

We will watch for his mastery over the subject being discussed. We will note this mastery in the clarity of his organization, in the sources of his supporting materials, and in the conclusions he draws from the facts in the light of the social considerations involved.

| Sincerity |

Our interest in a specific speaker with respect to a particular subject must add one additional element to those of ability, goodness and knowledge. This element will be recognized as present or absent as the speech progresses. How strongly does the speaker feel about what he proposes to have us believe and do? This is an extremely subtle bit of analysis on the part of the listener but a most important bit. We can make this judgment more upon the physical and vocal elements of the speaker's presentation than upon the words he uses.

| **Informative Speech Occasions** |

The analysis of the speaker on the occasion of speeches to inform is far less exacting for the listener. On these occasions our interest in the speaker is primarily one of ability and knowledge rather than motive. We are concerned with an understanding of the subject matter for ourselves and although this understanding may influence eventual belief and action, that is not the goal at the moment. We listen because the speaker knows his subject and is trying to share his knowledge with us.

# Part B:  Speaker Preparation in General

In view of the speaker analysis by the audience, as certain as death, those who would speak should take every precaution possible to insure their successful performance. It can be only brazen effrontery that enables some speakers to face an audience so ill-prepared and with so little chance of success. Perhaps audiences are too polite to express their real reactions to such performances, but whether or not the criticism is expressed verbally to us, we face that criticism anyway. We cannot avoid what occurs in other men's minds and we should try to make that reaction favorable to our efforts.

**Subjects of Speeches**

The subject choice of the speaker is of primary importance in his success or failure. When the speaker accepts without thought a subject allotted to him by some person or group, he is headed for real trouble. It may be that some particular subject is not a good one because of scanty knowledge or experience. On the other hand, it may be a poor choice because the proposed speaker has little interest in it. The latter may be generated with a little study but the former cannot be easily overcome.

We can overlook these objections for classroom speeches because these are learning experiences in close connection with the total school experience. In achieving the objective of common subject material, some members of the class will have had little in the way of knowledge, experience, or interest in the group topic. We are in a different experience with classroom work, however, than when we face an audience as a responsible citizen.

**Topics of Importance**

In order to meet the criticism that the speaker should have broad knowledge and experience with his subject, some speech classes fall into the terrible trap of allowing classroom speeches on inconsequential matters. This is an unforgivable course of action. This is the thing that has brought more criticism to speech courses than any other procedure, as well it might. Teachers and students of speech courses ought to condemn trivial subject matter to the point of its elimination.

The subject matter of classroom speeches must be on topics of extreme importance. These topics may be of current interest or those which are always of considerable interest. The topics listed in the second part of this book are always important to us although they may not be current in magazines and newspapers. From a wide selection of such possible subjects, a speech class will be able to find topics which will be of interest and importance for most of the members.

**Preparation Time**

Perhaps the chief trouble spot in most speech performances lies in the lack of preparation time allotted. It takes time to construct and prepare a really good speech for delivery. Most good speeches have had years of preparation, in a sense. The reading and thinking about a topic has been going on long before the speaker knows he will use that subject matter in a speech.

Frequently, classroom speakers put off the preparation of their speeches until too little time remains for the development of a good talk. Separate work periods scattered over a time span of several days will be required to develop a good classroom speech. The advantage of more than one work period lies in the rethinking possibility. The sooner we begin some preparation on our classroom topic after the assignment has been made the better.

What is said of poor preparation for classroom speeches can be said with added emphasis about nonclassroom speaking. We all lead busy lives and our speaking engagements are usually an added work load to our normal routine. There is a real danger that we will try to get by with inadequate survey of our subject matter. We cannot get by our listeners. At least many will know when we are shy on information, when our information is out of date, when, in fact, our preparation has been incomplete. To the responsible speaker such an assessment of prepartion can only be extremely embarrassing.

**Practice for Presentation**

In addition to seeking speech materials and organizing them into an effective pattern, we must allow time for sufficient practice in delivery. Many speeches suffer severely either for lack of delivery practice or for incorrect practice. Let us face the situation head-on. A speech that is read is not a speech; it is oral reading. The next chapter in our text will discuss oral reading as a type of performance. A speech that is memorized and delivered word for word is not a speech but declamation. Our times do not warrant the use of the memorized speech.

**Extemporaneous Speaking** | The type of formal speech making we will do inside and outside the classroom is called extemporaneous speaking. In this type of speaking we will have the ideas clearly in mind but we will not have the words to express them memorized in set sentences. We have the pattern of our thoughts so carefully constructed that we can supply the wording to carry out this outline at the moment.

Beginning speakers will assert that too much practice brings about memorization whether it is desirable or not. This will not happen, however, when the delivery practice is properly carried out. There is nothing wrong in writing a sample speech from the outline that has been constructed; in fact, it is a good way to get one's thoughts carefully expressed. The difficulty arises when the delivery practice consists of reading and rereading the written speech.

There is some reading to be done in the delivery practice, namely the reading and rereading of the carefully drawn outline. This outline has more than the main points and subpoints of the proposed talk. It contains also the supporting materials which put life and substance into the performance. The reading of the outline is followed by an attempt to go through the designed pattern without looking at the written materials. When this can be done, the speaker is ready for the complete rehearsal.

*Rehearsal* | In the rehearsal periods we must practice in a manner which approaches that of the real situation we will face. This means that we will stand up and pay attention to our posture and use of body while we go through the speech. It is well to practice in an unused classroom. Most campuses have such classrooms available after five o'clock in the afternoon or on weekends. If possible, it is well to have a buddy go to these practices with you to listen and to criticize.

The number of times needed in such rehearsals will vary from speech to speech and among individuals. You should practice until you have the speech well "in hand." If this take ten rehearsals, then that is what you should give it; if five will suffice, give it five. The guiding principle in how much practice is needed lies with the speaker's respect for himself and his ideas.

In spite of the criticism of memorized speeches offered in an earlier paragraph, it is not unwise for the beginning speaker to have the first few sentences of his talk committed to memory. This enables him to get off to a running start when he is tense. After a few speeches even this memory work is unnecessary and undesirable.

*Speaker's Notes*

All speakers are permitted to take notes to the platform with them. These are used best when they can be placed on the rostrum and referred to only when needed. If the notes must be held, they should be handled so as to call little attention to them. For short classroom speeches notes should probably be eliminated.

## Speaker Attitudes

Whether the speaker is trying to give information, change attitudes and beliefs, or to secure action, his degree of success depends on how the audience reacts toward him as a person as well as to the ideas he presents. Knowing this should make the speaker behave himself. Favorable reaction by the audience toward the speaker depends upon the speaker's respect for himself and his respect for his audience. These substratum elements of speech making are of tremendous importance.

*Humility*

As a speaker you must be humble about what you know and what you are. Modesty about personal achievements is difficult to attain but one of the most desirable and appreciated virtues an individual can possess. The listening audience has little respect for the conceited individual who "knows it all." The truly humble man has regard for others and their points of view and indicates in his presentation of ideas that he has such respect. For his own knowledge he is willing to concede imperfectness in quantity and quality.

*Enthusiasm*

The person who has little enthusiasm for the causes he espouses will do little to convince others. Enthusiasm is the telltale quality of any speech that is really effective. A listener's attention cannot be held long by one who hasn't enough physical and vocal vigor to make it seem he means what he says and he thinks what he says is important.

*Sense of Humor*

The ability to tell a joke or funny story or to laugh at one is not what is meant by possessing a sense of humor. The very dull can poke fun in a story or laugh at the right spot if the joke is clearly pointed. Too few have a true sense of humor. This quality requires a rare sense of perception and implies a kindly trait as well. Humor is the ability to see the incongruities in life as they arise from deep introspection into human character and conduct.

The possession of a sense of humor enables us to laugh at ourselves when absurdities in our personal conduct come to our attention. Moreover, it allows us to be tolerant of others because we have an understanding of the possible incongruities which permit what seems to us impractical or even irrational points of view. It is a kind of intellectual sympathy which fosters an understanding of positions differing from our own. Such a virtue will keep us from being too serious about ourselves; we are able to smile at life even when it portends serious consequences. The wise man usually has a sense of humor; the dull man usually does not.

*Intellectual Integrity*

A speaker's sense of responsibility for what he says is of tremendous importance in the eyes of the audience. With this in mind, we must be careful of making reckless statements which cannot be backed up with the facts. We must never be guilty of dealing in half-truths, reaching conclusions on the basis of partial evidence. When we do, we reveal ourselves as shallow thinkers who are willing to jump to conclusions which are clearly unwarranted in face of the full evidence.

It is our responsibiilty to know what we are talking about. We never should pretend to be an authority in an area where we have little competence. It is far better to admit a weakness in information than to "bull" our way through as though we know. The speaker who pretends to know when he doesn't is certain to fail with the discerning audience.

*Respect the Audience*

In addition to the attitudes which show a respect for ourselves as individuals, there is the important one of respect for the audience which should be demonstrated. It never will pay to tell the audience they are ignorant. It is true that their information may not be the same as ours, but that is not to say they are devoid of knowledge. We should not tell them that their beliefs are wrong. A direct approach to persuasion of this sort will only antagonize and never convince. The approach must be that of accepting the beliefs and knowledge of the listeners and building from there to the point of view we wish to reach. In other words, the process of persuasion involves a certain amount of restraint which recognizes that a change in thinking must have some time for development. If we try to do the job too quickly we will only close the communication channels completely and therefore fail in our purpose.

*Keep Time Limits* | A final respect for the audience involves our dealing with their patience and powers of concentration. Many speakers show little respect for time limits in their speaking. Every speaker ought to stay within the time period set for him. If the speech has been set for fifteen minutes, then the speaker should finish in that period of time.

# Part C: Preparation for Listening

Everyone knows that the speaker must make extensive preparation for his speaking assignment but few, apparently, feel that the listener needs to make any preparation for his task. How false this belief is! Listening also is a difficult task if it is done effectively. Perhaps the real reason why so little is done effectively arises from the lack of preparation for the job in either long range or immediate procedures.

**Previous Experience** | The poorest listeners of all are inexperienced listeners — inexperienced, that is, in hearing difficult, expository material. In one objective study, an unpublished doctoral dissertation by Ralph G. Nichols at the State University of Iowa in 1948, the one hundred poorest listeners in a university freshman population were identified. Their habits and characteristics were given close study through personal interviews, questionnaires and inventories, and measured performance on a number of standardized tests. Fewer than five per cent of them had ever heard of important educational radio programs of that period such as Invitation to Learning, America's Town Meeting of the Air, The Chicago Round Table, Meet the Press, and American Forum of the Air. Many were unacquainted with either the title or nature of these programs. Few ever attended occasional educational lectures occurring in their respective communities. Yet with scarcely an exception they knew all about and listened consistently to the then current light radio programs such as those of Bob Hope, Fibber Magee and Molly, Red Skelton, and The Lone Ranger!

By contrast, the one hundred best listeners in this same freshman population had heard the more difficult and expository radio programs many times. It appeared from a study of their daily activity programs that many apparently had developed an appetite for hearing a variety of expository presentations difficult enough to challenge their mental capacities. Many regularly attended occasional lectures coming to their respective communities.

To what conclusion must we come? Evidently one of the best adjectives to describe the ineffective listener to informative speech is *inexperienced*. No doubt in many instances inexperience with difficult material was less a matter of choice than a matter of less opportunity, poor home environment, dearth of parental interest and encouragement.

Perhaps even unenlightened instruction by teachers at lower grade levels pyramided the learners' problems. Certainly secondary school teachers could be of help by stressing that students who painstakingly avoid "tough" listening situations all their lives are pitifully unequipped to listen adequately when difficult expository presentations are encountered following graduation. To insure that every learner acquires experience in listening, challenging aural presentations of graduated difficulty ought to be made an integral part of every speech and English course. Motivated, intensive practice of this kind is invaluable to those who plan to enter college. If such motivated practice does *not* become a part of secondary school training, the youngster who has developed an appetite for easy listening experiences will be entirely out of his depth when suddenly plunged into his first college lecture in physics or chemistry.

*Can Amends Be Made?*

It is not too helpful to say to those handicapped by inexperience, "hurry up and gain some." In college, to be sure, manifold opportunities to repair the gap are available. Such an admonition has its drawbacks, however: the learner may well find himself thoroughly repelled by both the content and difficulty level of the presentations he is advised to hear.

What, then, should he do? Cancel his registration and leave school? Perhaps that will not be necessary. There are at least four expedients to try first.

First, the handicapped student should go directly to his speech, communication, or language arts instructor and seek help. A frank and objective discussion of the problem with the person most expert in the area and best acquainted with facilities available for a solution can do no harm and may do much good.

A second thing that might be done would be to talk with the instructor or instructors of the courses causing the chief difficulty. One purpose of this call would be to make the instructor aware of the problem. A second purpose would be to secure, if possible, such technical vocabulary helps as the instructor might be able to provide. This step is extremely important because each discipline has its peculiar vocabulary which must be learned. A third purpose would be to secure if possible a prescribed schedule of supplementary reading couched in simple language and designed to provide background in the content area of the course involved.

The third step for the handicapped one would be to strike up a friendship, if at all possible, with a classmate whose proficiency in assimilating certain lecture material is at a considerably higher level. A frank and objective discussion of the problem, with an appeal for help, will seldom fail to result in some benefit for the student in trouble. Lest he become guilty of pure "brain-picking," however, he ought to make every effort to repay his newly-made friend as best he can with intellectual efforts of his own.

A fourth step would be for the out-of-depth listener to engage a tutor. In almost all colleges graduate students can be found who, for a reasonable fee, will help an undergraduate to repair his weaknesses in specified content areas.

In some instances all four of the foregoing suggestions may be needed if the problem of the "inexperienced" listener is to be solved; in others, less drastic moves may be necessary. In any case, it would be unethical to pretend that inexperience is a problem easily solved or quickly overcome. Many of the great obstacles to a smooth and easy transition from high school to college are closely related to this first basis for effective listening — that of previous experience with difficult, expository material. Any person who in earlier years has developed the bad habit of avoiding difficult presentations simply because of their difficulty would do well to eliminate this handicap to his personal growth at once.

| **Energy Expenditure in Listening** | We must recognize that important components of listening are the physical condition and energy level of the learner. Efficient listening is hard work. There is no use in quibbling about it. |

Although efficient listening is the easiest way known to acquire ideas and information, it is still hard work. It is characterized by increased heart action, faster circulation of the blood, and even slightly increased body temperature. One of the most outstanding characteristics of poor listeners is the fact that they are disinclined to expend energy in a listening situation and are unchallenged by the physical demands made upon them.

| *Listening Fitness* | Inasmuch as learning through listening is something of a bodily strain, it behooves the learner to make some effort to ready himself physically as he enters each difficult situation. |

An appreciation of the true meaning of the word *attention* is of some help in this regard. The word is best conceived as a collection of mental tensions within the learner, tensions which can be resolved only by getting satisfactory messages related to them from the speaker. The learner entering an aurally assimilative situation should have these tensions; he should recognize that they put an actual physical strain upon him; and he should be willing to expend physical energy to resolve them.

Very few of us appreciate the significance of all the foregoing. One research reports that even in the instance of college students, by their own testimony, it is common occurrence for them to enter classes worn out physically; to assume postures which only overtly seem to give attention to the speaker; and then to proceed to catch up on needed rest or to reflect upon purely personal matters. This *faking* of attention is now known to be one of the surest of all indices to low-level comprehension. It is one of the worst habits afflicting us as a people; and in addition it may well be one of the worst parasites upon our entire industrial economy.

How can we as learners stir up tensions when we feel none? How can we invest energy when our supply is all too low to begin with? Four specific suggestions may be worth considering.

*We Must Get
More Sleep*

If we lack energy enough to assimilate well, we literally need more rest. A bad place to get it is in a classroom or auditorium. The speaker is likely to make our sleep so fitful! Let us get it at home, on a regular schedule.

*We Must Quit
Storing Up Problems*

We now know that the attention faker often behaves the way he does because he has stored up personal problems to solve during listening situations. Some of us apparently feel that in this way we gain time for brooding over purely personal affairs. If we must accumulate lists of decisions to be made, let us schedule the period for their resolution at some other time of day.

*We Must Give Prior
Thought to the Topic*

One of the best known ways to stir up interest in a topic is to discuss it with our friends before hearing its formal presentation. Prior exploration of the possible significance of a topic through talking it over with friends, parents, or classmates almost invariably leads to the development of real self-interest in it. The process creates tensions and readies us for energy expenditure.

*We Must Behave
Like Listeners*

If we would improve as listeners, we must behave like listeners. We already know enough about how a good listener performs to enable us to emulate him if we wish. It may well be more than empty gesture for us to make the effort. Eminent psychologists tell us that one of the ways to achieve a habit is to behave as if we had that habit.

**Improving the Listening
Situation**

Beyond the types of problems discussed in the foregoing pages are three others which are encountered frequently enough to deserve our attention. They probably should be regarded as aspects of abnormal situations; nevertheless, they should be considered. What should be the listener's behavior when physical conditions for oral communication are so bad that efficiency is impossible? What should he do when his fellow auditors are so noisy, inconsiderate, and discourteous as to drown out the presentation? Is there anything he can do to improve the climate for learning in a formal classroom atmosphere?

Good and poor listeners definitely react differently in these three situations. The good listeners tend to make quick adjustments for poor room ventilation or temperature, inaudibility of the speaker, personal hearing disabilities, unnecessary room noises which distract attention, and noisy neighbors or seat mates in the audience. Poor listeners, by contrast, tend to tolerate all of the foregoing conditions and, in some instances, even to create distractions themselves which needlessly impair comprehension. Let us investigate each issue as a specific problem in an abnormal situation; and, as we look at each one, see what routes can be followed to alleviate the difficulties it causes.

**Poor Physical Conditions**

Occasionally we find ourselves in a room or auditorium so overheated or poorly ventilated that most members of the audience are obviously very uncomfortable. Rather than sit and wonder why the speaker or chairman has not corrected the condition, the first one becoming conscious of it ought immediately to assume personally the assignment of making the majority comfortable. Occasionally, easier than doing the job ourselves, we can signal to a person close to a window to open it. We should be as unobtrusive as possible in any course we pursue, but we owe it to ourselves and to our mates to make the room comfortable.

We should always as a matter of routine seat ourselves where we can hear the words of the speaker easily. Also, it is much better to be able to see the speaker clearly in order to perceive any visual cues given. Front seats are better than back ones; seats in front of the speaker are better than those to the side.

If the speaker's voice is so subdued that it obviously cannot be heard by those toward the rear, the first auditor seated in the rear one-third of the audience to notice the problem should immediately attack it. He should wave a hand vigorously at the speaker and simultaneously sing out in a loud voice, "Sorry, sir. But we can't hear you back here. Would you like us to show a hand whenever you become inaudible?" This is not being rude to the speaker; it is being kind to him. If a speaker has any obligation at all in his work, it is that of being audible. In helping him to assume his obligation, the auditor should be careful to word his interruption as explained. If he fails to provide for a subsequent signaling at periods of inaudibility, he may find his speaker increasing vocal intensity for two or three sentences only. Unless our auditor has prepared the way for later interruptions he may be too embarrassed to make a second effort.

**Noisy Neighbors or Seat Mates**

Occasionally, too, we find ourselves in an audience containing certain noisy elements which make effective communication impossible. Such an element, be it either clique or claque, is of course inexcusably rude. The activities of its members may include all kinds of disruptive things: whispering or talking aloud, writing and exchanging notes, scuffling of feet, intentional coughing spells, hand signals across the room, open reading of paper or magazine, ostentatious display of pictures or other objects. Offenses of this kind are inexcusable.

There really is little debate on whether or not the problem should be attacked. It should be. Otherwise a great deal of time may be lost and an important message may go unheard. Emerson's statement, " 'Tis the good reader makes the good book" has a parallel in "It's a good audience which makes a good speech."

The discourtesy of the noisy group soon becomes intolerable to one who sincerely wants to hear the speaker's message. What can he do? Should he make himself terribly conspicuous, and perhaps badly embarrassed by openly reproving his neighbors? The problem is more difficult than the first one, but it is not insoluble. One possibility is to look around a complete circle of auditors quite conspicuously and then say as good humoredly as possible, "Quiet!" This should be followed by the remonstrator's immediate turning of his attention to the speaker. A second possibility is to arise from the seat first taken and move with a bit of ostentation down much closer to the speaker, with all actions indicating a real desire to hear the speaker. Still a third possibility, somewhat less satisfactory, is to confer with the speaker (or chairman) after the presentation and urge him to demand and secure better conditions for his next effort.

**Poor Rapport in the Classroom**

In a very important sense a college class — any college class — constitutes an abnormal or atypical kind of audience. Its homogeneity is seldom paralleled in other speaking situations. Here, particularly, there should be a very deep concern on the part of both instructor and the student group that all verbal communication within the class hour be as productive and contributory as possible. Despite this logical mutual aim, all too often a college group has distinctly low morale.

Granting that the chief fault usually lies with the instructor, are there any specific things the students themselves can do to improve conditions? Perhaps there are. Classroom communication is at its best when the mode of presentation has a distinctly conversational quality. Most instructors — all the carefully trained ones — know this and strive for a natural, friendly, and conversational classroom atmosphere.

Two parties are required for conversation. When we are cast in the student's role, how well do we converse with the instructor? What are our attitudes saying to him? Verbally, are we inclined to say anything at all? Instructors tend to appreciate deeply any kind of sincere expression by their students. Those students who take the trouble to praise the strong elements and criticize the weak elements in each course they take can serve to improve the efforts of every instructor they encounter. True, in some instances the dividends may not be attained till the following semester, and then by an entirely different group of students; however someone must initiate this chain reaction if all are eventually to profit. Years ago the old maxim that "Dead men tell no tales" was altered by someone to read "Lifeless speakers transmit no ideas." Perhaps a third version should read "Dead-pan listeners reap no inspiration."

# 9

Speaking
and
Listening . . .

# . . . the refined
# skills

## Part A: Transferring the Thoughts of Others

Some forty years ago educational theorists in their search for reasons for the inadequacy in silent reading ability decided that oral reading being practiced in the schools, particularly at the elementary level, hindered progress in silent reading skills. This theory has never been established. Nevertheless, as a result of the theory advanced, training in oral reading has practically disappeared from any of the courses in elementary and secondary schools. The results of the lack of such training are widely evident and sad to view. Very few of our college freshmen are able to read orally with even a modicum of effectiveness.

If reading aloud were not used as a method of oral communication, the situation would not be so bad. Reading aloud is however widely used in the home, in business meetings of all kinds, by teachers in the classroom, by ministers and by political leaders and legislators. Many of us believe that we will actually read aloud so seldom that any attempt to learn the technique will be largely wasted effort. This is a mistaken idea. Sooner than we think we will be reading aloud to our family at the breakfast table part of an interesting article from the newspaper, to our small son or daughter a bedtime story, to our neighbor a recipe, to our husband the directions for reassembling the vacuum cleaner, to our club a report from a committee.

Many speeches made before radio and television audiences are read rather than spoken. Even when speeches are primarily extemporaneous there comes the frequent need for a quotation and these are usually read to assure exactness. Moreover, certain of the speech skills such as those which involve voice and articulation are perhaps best practiced through reading from the printed page.

A former United States senator declared recently that training in oral reading is as important as training in extemporaneous speaking. He noted that few men in public life can read effectively from a manuscript and pointed out that former President Franklin D. Roosevelt was an exceptionally good oral reader and had used this skill to tremendous advantage.

Speakers read from manuscripts rather than speak extemporaneously from notes in the mistaken belief that they are doing a better job of communicating with that method. This is not even close to the truth for ninety-nine out of one hundred readers. It is much more difficult to be a good oral reader than a good extemporaneous speaker. The principles of good oral reading are easy enough to explain, but putting these in performance requires many long hours of practice.

**Oral Reading Is Communication**

Reading aloud from the printed page is every bit as much a process in oral communication as speaking. The purpose — transfer of ideas — is exactly the same in the two methods of communication; only the mechanics differ. Our business as an oral reader is to get an impression from the printed materials we read silently and then to express orally what we have gotten for our listeners. This re-creating of thought involves the assimilation of both the intellectual and emotional qualities or values of a piece of material and the reproduction of these for a group of listeners. Some aspects of oral reading are more simple than those for speaking but the important aspect of getting the full meaning of the ideas involved to the listener is more difficult.

**What to Read**

Since the purpose of oral reading is to share ideas, it is well to keep this in mind when selecting material. We should choose something in which we are interested, which we understand and which we believe our audience will also be interested in and understand. Before the material is chosen it is necessary we know several things about the audience. Most of these have been listed elsewhere in this book but briefly they are age, sex, occupation, nationality, economic status, education and interests. Our failure to recognize the importance of considering the audience may result in an unsuccessful reading experience.

If we are unskilled oral readers, there is one bit of important advice to heed. We should choose something simple. For most people poetry is harder to read than prose. We should, by all means, begin our practice of reading aloud with a prose selection. It is better not to select something we have once memorized for we will be apt to "recite" it without letting the ideas "come alive" and thus it will have little meaning for our listeners. If we are reading poetry we must be sure to get the mood and rhythm. Poetry must delight the ear as well as the mind, and thus cannot be read as prose. We should not let the mood and rhythm get us, however, and carry us away in a singsong pattern of accented meter and rhyme which means little to anyone and may lull our audience to sleep.

From whatever we choose, prose or poetry, we must convey the author's meaning to our audience. We should study our selection carefully to insure our comprehension of the main ideas and then practice to obtain their correct phrasing. If the material is prose, we should achieve a conversational manner so that the correct meaning is better communicated.

**Finding Reading Materials** American and English literature textbooks contain many selections which would adapt to the oral reading situation. Selections from such sources have the recommendations of authorities in the field of literature and most of them have "stood the test of time." Many of the past and present novels will offer selections worth reading to an audience. Perhaps an excerpt from our favorite novelist will make an excellent selection for the classroom audience. Books of informal essays offer still another source of oral reading material. We should also find textbooks in interpretation of literature a good source; most authors of such texts provide sample selections for student use. There are other sources such as magazines and newspapers. Whatever the source, the quality and the readability of the material are the two important things to consider in making the selection.

## Preparation for Performance

Part of the preparation for our reading performance is the arrangement of the material. If our book is large and our selection long we should plan to use a reading stand. We never should attempt to read from a single page of paper held in the hand; we may not be able to control its flexibility and our listeners' attention may be attracted to the movement of the paper instead of the ideas being expressed. If we have several pages of manuscript we should be sure they are plainly numbered and in proper sequence before we begin.

When the copy is held, it should be held high enough to be seen easily by the reader and not so high that the face of the performer is hidden. The eyes of the reader, not the whole head, should drop to the manuscript to read the wording. It will take quite a lot of practice before we can find our place in the manuscript unerringly; general practice improves this skill but familiarity with the specific material is important also. The eyes must be trained to read ahead, range beyond the voice, so that the whole of the idea is grasped before any part of it is spoken.

After we have chosen our material it is well to plan a brief introduction so our audience will know what we are going to read. Our information about the material to be read should not be detailed. We can rob our performance if we reveal too much. A bit of interesting information about the author or the selection acts as a good attention-getting device and arouses the interest of our listeners for the material to follow. Unless we put a little thought and originality into our introduction it is, however, better to omit it. There is no more trite or uninteresting way to begin than by using the customary phrase, "I should like to read."

## Getting the Ideas

An oral reading selection is good in proportion to the value of the ideas involved and the clearness and force with which these ideas are presented in language. An oral reading performance is good in proportion to the ability of the conveyor to receive and re-create these ideas for the audience. It is necessary, then, for us to understand fully the meaning and motive of the author. It is easy to detect the difference between the person who is getting an impression from the printed symbols and one who is reading a series of words without reaction to the ideas expressed. The silent reader can progress rapidly because he does only half the job of the oral communicator. He does not have to share with anyone else his reaction to the materials read.

This sharing process makes heavy demands on the oral reader but is not an overpowering task. It merely requires a thoughtful consideration of the use of voice in the re-creating process. Since the words are not those of the performer, voice usage is more difficult than in speaking. One who reads orally must certainly understand the vocabulary involved and, when dealing with emotional content, must have had experience with the ideas presented.

## Giving the Ideas

The reader must not only know the meanings and motives of the author but must get them across to the audience. All the qualities of good conversational speaking come into full play in oral reading. As in good speaking, the person reading aloud must reveal a sincere desire to communicate. To project the meaning of the author the reader must phrase the ideas properly. To project the force of the ideas he must use proper emphasis.

A knowledge of the meaning of the words and a grouping of the words into meaningful patterns are necessary. Unless the communicator is able to phrase for the meaning the author intended, he cannot carry the full meaning to the listener in a clear and easy fashion. If he is genuinely thinking the thought of the author, he should be able to phrase the words in such fashion as to re-create the same thought for others. In this process he will keep the phrases short and spaced with enough pause to allow the listener to react to the thought. Some of these pauses, according to the thought, will be longer than others. Another practical consideration in the use of pauses is that the reader must have an opportunity to breathe, and it is during these meaningful pauses that he does so.

The good performer will watch his listeners carefully for their reaction to the ideas being presented. If the members of the audience are interested and show that they are keeping up, the reading speed can be increased. In order to get the meaning of the author the punctuation marks may be used as a guide, but only as a guide. The author's punctuation will help us get his meaning, but we must put in the punctuation which our audience will hear. We punctuate by phrasing to show our thorough understanding of the material and by varying the length of pauses between phrases to show their relationships. Sometimes the audible punctuation which we put in as we read aloud coincides with the visible punctuation the author has in his script, but frequently it does not. We sometimes pause where there are no punctuation marks and often we disregard the punctuation marks we see. We might phrase the following sentence in this fashion: "Many a one — who peeped in his mirror last evening — and found a sprinkling of grey in his beard — despaired of making a home in the remote future, — and cast a package of faded letters in the fire — that he might enjoy the dismal pleasure — of beholding his hopes and his romances — die out in ashes." With this phrasing we have made seven distinct pauses although the sentence contains only one comma.

The feeling of the author towards his ideas can be partially conveyed to the audience through emphasis. One of the great faults in reading lies in emphasizing too many words. In speaking conversationally, we select the words we use to fit the ideas we have in mind and, as we speak, the mind automatically emphasizes certain ideas and subordinates others. This is evident to our listeners by the vocal variety we use in speaking. In the oral reading process, the author has selected the words he wishes to use and unless we think the ideas as we read these words, there will be little or no vocal variety. It is this variation in pitch, quality, rate and force which shows that we understand the meaning on the printed page and are eager to share these ideas with our audience.

There are no rules for emphasis. The right words for us to stress are those which will cause the listener to get the impression the author wished to create. The less important words in a phrase should be subordinated to the more important and the less important ideas are subordinated to the more important ideas by means of variation in vocalization arising out of our thinking the idea as we express it. The uttering of the words should have the spontaneity of language being used for the first time in the communication of the ideas.

**Conversational Quality in Oral Reading**

Good oral reading sounds like talk. Such reading calls for a "conversational pattern," the ability to easily and quickly change pitch and inflection, vary loudness and rate and quality. Factors which make up conversational speech have been discussed in Chapter 7. We need only to state here that vocal variety in oral reading is valueless unless it reveals the meaning and the mood the author meant to convey. It is impossible for us to use conversational speech with our eyes glued to a book. We should look at our listeners frequently and note their response. If we are sincere in our desire to share the written ideas with our audience, we will look directly at them often to see whether we are succeeding. We will really communicate.

| Use of Body |

In reading as well as in speaking, physical and vocal responses should be simultaneous. As good oral readers we will use our bodies as well as our voices as we share ideas. Our eyes receive the symbols from the printed page and we interpret them audibly and visibly for our audience in terms of our past experience. Both body and voice respond to the ideas as we express them orally. As readers we must be sure our bodies as well as our voices are saying what the author meant. We must not say one thing with the words and another with our bodies; nor must we say one thing with our facial expression and another thing with the rest of our body. A good performer allows the ideas on the page to be reflected in his entire body. The movement should be slight, but the muscle texture, the sparkle in his eyes, the unity of his physical expression should reveal the meaning and motive of his reading. Factual material calls for a smaller amount of visible response than emotional material but there must be visible response present or the reader is not truly expressing the meaning and mood. Good posture and a body free to respond to the ideas are real requisites to oral reading.

What is said about use of body in oral reading does not imply that hand and arm gestures are appropriate. Oral reading is not acting and there should be no attempt to imitate the person who wrote the words. We should do the whole job with a voice and body which is distinctly ours. We should get the meaning of the passages for ourselves and then get it across to the listener. We should do this job primarily with our voices.

# Part B:  Appreciative Listening

Many of us cheat ourselves out of pleasant and profitable listening experiences. Early in life, for example, perhaps we developed an intense dislike for some highly affected person who was forever proclaiming his fondness for classical music, drama, or the reading of poetry. Repelled by his personality, we may well have labeled him "arty," effeminate, or eccentric, and have concluded that the sources of his pleasure must likewise be perverted and unmanly. Such pre-judging of these activities is tragic — the more so when traceable to an individual whose love for the arts was never real. Yet many a "practical" man has thus irrationally disavowed things "cultural." Great indeed would have been his gain had he open-mindedly investigated the esthetic experience for himself.

Actually the esthetic experience is inescapable no matter what form it takes: whether it is the sweep of Ben Hogan's golf club, a perfectly cast fly in a trout stream, or the artistically thrown curve of a winning baseball pitcher. These activities are far removed from the practical necessities of life, but they are emotionally stimulating — nearly as much as the finely articulated chromatics of a virtuoso pianist or an idea cleanly delineated and expressed by a painter's brush. To accept and respond to the pianist and the painter is merely to enlarge an activity we already accept when we respond to the perfection of the highly-trained athlete or the skill of the sports car body designer. Only by reverting to the level of a pig, content with mud wallow, food, and warmth, could a man actually divorce himself from esthetic appreciation.

When one denies himself the limitless pleasure of esthetic listening, the loser is always one's self; but still greater is the loser who chooses to deride verbally the thing rejected, for in so doing he merely reveals his own poverty of cultural experience. The winner is the enemy within ourselves, the feeling of inferiority when we try to get practical meanings out of activities never intended, perhaps to convey such meanings. It is true that in listening to music our pleasure may be heightened by a knowledge of instrumentation, harmony, facts about the composer, the performer, or the historical position of the composition. Such knowledge is not essential to our enjoyment, however, any more than knowledge of the history of fly casting is necessary to the enjoyment of that skill.

This is by no means to suggest that we should like all classical music, such poetry as "An Ode to My Lady's Eyebrow," or all abstract art. It does mean that practically all serious music — that practically all critically approved poetry — is a potential source of pleasure to someone; that there is nothing wrong in enjoying it; and that our failure to enjoy it results from our refusal to investigate and respond to it.

Pleasurable listening derives from complex sources. A bird call, for instance, may give us intense pleasure because it reminds us of summer, vacation, freedom, the out-of-doors, hunting, pleasant associations. On the other hand, we may take intellectual pleasure in being able to identify the bird, know its habits, and its life history. It is possible, of course, simply to enjoy the virtuosity of the bird — the music of its call. Similar factors may play a part in the enjoyment of music, in listening to the reading of drama, verse, even the diction of a foreign language we cannot understand intellectually.

As a nation we are much addicted to "soap operas" — plotless and never-ending serialized stories by radio and television. For reading matter we lean heavily upon comic books and magazines, fiction couched at a fifth-grade level of difficulty. We tend to answer any citicism of such entertainment by declaring that after all we have a right to like what we like. Whose business is it but our own? The answer is that of course what we like is our own business — that no one can legally or legislatively force us to change. Nevertheless, every college and school system is obligated to furnish its students with opportunities to increase in esthetic appreciation — with a chance to live more richly, deeply, pleasantly. As students, it is up to us to decide how fully we shall want to enjoy the opportunities given us.

In view of the fact that most of us are surrounded by cultural advantages, it is interesting to speculate on why our appetites for the esthetic are as limited as they seem to be. One wonders if the complex jargon often used to describe things cultural may not in itself serve as a powerful deterrent to the uninitiated. The following lines, for instance, may serve more to confuse than to clarify. They appeared in the printed program for a recent, university-sponsored concert by an internationally famous pianist.

> The First movement throbs with life, save for the brief moments when the second theme emerges (this, the loftiest thought of all appears but seldom); but this is a spiritual rather than a muscular vitality. The slow movement is indefinite- almost inarticulate, in fact; but only so it is imaginable that its vision could be made in the least substantial. The final Rondo, which follows the Adagio molto (which itself is called introduction) is only a little more kinetic.

The next day the music critic for the local newspaper, describing the concert, wrote as follows in his column:

It was not a subtle concert; every effect was etched and meaning wrought before one's eyes and ears. But such is the measure of the man and so prodigious his technique that he sweeps through the vainest of passages without sounding turgid or bombastic. In all his brilliance, he can follow a driving smash to deep court with a soft, arching lob that dangles delectably before it floats to earth. The whorls of notes which Rubinstein impels are not quickly diffused, but rather are silhouetted in neat array until the artist chooses to sweep them all away and hang new images.

To many, such writing is pure drivel. To others, it is inexcusable affectation. To all but the most seasoned and sophisticated of theater-goers it is completely frightening — and therein exists the source of the damage done by such language. What undergraduate, reading it, could help but develop a man-sized inferiority complex toward classical music? Let us scoff at the rhetoric, however, not at the music.

The student fortunate enough to survive the language barrier to appreciative listening is likely to encounter a second mystery if he looks for advice on how to strengthen his appreciative powers. Regardless of whether they are discussing music, drama, speech, or oral reading, analysts of appreciative listening are prone to talk about three levels or planes of appreciation.

The lowest level is usually labeled "sensuous." At this plane the hearer presumably "enters fully into the presentation itself" to take delight in sound; to be carried away to a land of dreams. The second level is described as a combination of subjective and objective reaction to the presentation. The hearer is said to respond partly at an emotional and sensuous plane; but also to respond objectively at times, with some intellectual consciousness of the techniques employed by the producer. The highest level is reported as one at which the hearer is conscious of form or style alone. His response is to the intellectual, nonemotional and technical elements of the presentation.

The concept of three-level appreciation is probably more confusing than clarifying. The intensity of pleasure most of us receive seems always to depend upon three variables: our comprehension of the presentation, its quality, and the nature of the general listening situation. The happier the combination of these variables the greater the degree of our enjoyment. Most of the time, the majority of us need make no effort to separate the emotional and intellectual elements composing our appreciative experience.

The most important single fact about appreciative listening is this: The better we understand the thing we are hearing, the greater becomes our potential satisfaction and pleasure.

**We Have Much to Gain**

Appreciative listening can make very significant contributions to our lives. Let us briefly consider some of them.

*Increasing Our Enjoyment*

There is no need to apologize for the human desire for pleasure. Rather, we must try to increase our power to enjoy esthetic things during the years we spend in school. It is a notable fact that in addition to television reception students listen to radio broadcasts for more than two hours per day, on the average. One function of education is to increase our understanding of what is good in drama, music, and speech. If that obligation is met, selective listening to programs of increasingly high quality is certain to increase our enjoyment of life.

*Enlarging Our Experience*

A great deal that we learn during our lives must be through vicarious rather than personal experience. Appreciative listening to the stories of others extends our learning tremendously. Through radio and television we can acquire reasonable familiarity with scores of places and situations which would otherwise remain a mystery to us.

*Improving Our Language*

The best way known to develop language facility is by extensive listening to those who speak well. If we wish to improve our vocabularies and language usage, the most important effort we can make is to associate consistently with individuals whose speech we wish to emulate. Vocabulary growth, for example, depends largely on a careful noting of contextual clues to meaning whenever we hear or read new words. Fortunately radio and television, selectively used, can do nearly as much for language improvement as can personal association itself.

*Expanding Our Interests*

The fourth contribution of appreciative listening is well illustrated in the field of music. Throughout America in recent years our schools have organized and administered music-listening programs designed to improve the appreciative powers of our youth. The result has been outstanding. Today more of our young people than ever before in history recognize and appreciate melody, rhythm, harmony, and instrumentation.

With respect to poetry and drama there is widespread agreement among educators that the surest route to literary appreciation is through hearing good readers or actors. Although for several generations our schools have given some attention to appreciation of the drama, we still have much to learn in this area. Few of us, for example, seem to enjoy plays written in blank verse. In time, with a lift from radio and television, perhaps we shall come to enjoy the beauty and power of poetic speech as much as did Elizabethan England. Fortunately, students of our day need not depend upon the theater alone for good drama. Full-length recordings of Julius Caesar, Twelfth Night, Merchant of Venice, Macbeth, Hamlet, and other Shakespearean plays are now available. Newly recorded versions of scores of dramatic classics and contemporary plays are appearing each year.

*Decreasing Our Tensions*

Appreciative listening can help us to relax, to put aside personal worries and cares, to evade many mental or emotional disturbances which regularly beset us. To serve these purposes appreciative listening is incomparably superior to most other means conventionally employed; no drug or beverage obtainable can match its wholesome effects.

**Educators Are Concerned**

School people have always been concerned, apparently, with the development of esthetic appreciation. From time to time their concern has been given expression. One of the Seven Cardinal Principles of Education, for example, calls for "worthy use of leisure." Such a concept distinctly involves both the creation and appreciation of items of esthetic character. To develop an appetite for esthetic appreciation and to increase the satisfaction that can be derived from it are two very proper concerns of education.

Fortunately, appreciation lends itself to speeded development. The following declaration of The National Council of the Teachers of English firmly supports this conviction, and in addition points to ways in which appreciation of literature, music, drama, and art can be developed.

Standards of appreciation of literature can be developed effectively through listening to oral reading by both teachers and pupils, to radio and stage plays, and to the motion pictures. At the same time such productions can add immeasurably to the pupil's appreciation of the spoken language.

Listening to a play or to poetry leads naturally to discussion of the ways in which effects are achieved. This opens the entire field of listening for appreciation of literature and speech. . . .

Such films as Oliver's Henry V and Hamlet, the many recordings of Shakespearean plays and scenes by Maurice Evans, John Gielgud, and the Mercury Theatre Company, and such modern dramatic classics as Death of a Salesman, Peter Pan, and The Consul offer rich opportunities for developing criteria of judgment in appreciating this art-form. . . .

Listening for the beauties of the spoken language, whether they exist in the lecture of a brilliant teacher, in a poem by a classical or a contemporary author, in the dialogue of a master novelist or playwright, must be acquired.

Few indeed are the educators who fail to recognize the influence of listening upon the improvement of oral expression. As children, obviously we learn our language by listening. When we start to school we bring with us the language of our immediate environment. If good English is spoken in our homes, our progress in both school and later adult life is made much easier. Without exception, however, proper aural classroom experiences serve to enlarge our vocabularies, improve our pronunciation, increase the accuracy with which we choose and use words, and refine our abilities to speak fluently, correctly and confidently. Again, appreciation and refinement start with understanding and are deepened through pleasant, meaningful experience.

| | |
|---|---|
| **Steps to Appreciative Listening** | It is often debated whether we enjoy pure sound itself, or whether it is the things we associate with sounds that give us pleasure. Such discussion is largely academic. How could we ever |

determine which source provides the greater enjoyment to the hearer?

Although it is extremely doubtful that the development of appreciation comes in three specific stages, it seems likely that some kind of chronological sequence does operate. Apparently this kind of pleasure normally grows through (a) perceiving some kind of esthetic production which stirs an emotional response within us; (b) identifying the cause and the effect of our emotional arousal; and (c) re-creating the experience. In any case there are five steps which we can voluntarily take, if we will, to enhance life's meaning and satisfaction through improving the degree to which we can enjoy things esthetic. Let us consider them in turn.

**Identifying the Things We Like Most**

What leisure-time listening do we enjoy most of all? It is rather amazing that many of us actually have never taken the trouble to identify the things we most like to hear. To set them down on paper is an eminently sensible step. The chief reason we never seem to have time enough to do the things we like most is that we have not taken time to identify them. Once identified, such items can be regularly included in our daily routine.

**Verifying Why We Like Them**

Appreciation is acquired. The things we enjoy must be, first of all, things we have experienced. Having heard something we thoroughly enjoyed, the wisest step we can take is to ask ourselves why. Through deliberate self-introspection we may well gain a self-knowledge otherwise unattainable.

We need feel no fear of what such procedure will reveal. "Art for art's sake" is largely pure nonsense. As infants we crave for nothing esthetic; music and art then have incomparably less appeal to us than do sugar, warmth, or perhaps a stomach full of warm milk. If self-analysis reveals that our esthetic appetites seem tied to matters quite organic, that should be no matter for dismay. Rather, on the basis of such insight we can then build soundly for an intensification of our own esthetic pleasures.

**Noticing How They Affect Others**

Once we discover what things we like most and verify the sources from which we derive them, we are ready to search for new — and perhaps better — sources of these pleasures. It will take little exploration to reveal that many people we know and respect have the same esthetic appetites as we, but satisfy them through different media entirely. This is important! We are now ready to expand the number and range of the sources giving us listening pleasure.

**Exploring Curiously**

Now we must go in search of new esthetic expression. In our possession is the one attribute most necessary to expanded appreciative listening — intellectual curiosity. Our chief need is to give the new medium a chance. To do this we shall need to meet the new art-form halfway. What if understanding is a bit difficult at first? We must make a positive effort to understand. Occasionally we need to tackle the difficult for our own good; otherwise, how can we make the most of the cultural heritage which is ours? The worthwhile always involves an effort — and the effort required for understanding music and the arts generally is just as demanding as that needed in any other field of endeavor. If we sit completely relaxed and passive, saying only "Amuse me!" we shall in time become more vegetable than human — insensible to the very best in life.

*Reading and Consulting*

After each new esthetic experience we can study the new art-form, discuss it with others, and return for new perceptions which should add continually to our understanding. Given reasonable constancy of quality and situation, each return to a truly great poem, drama, or piece of music should intensify the pleasure we received when it first became a part of our experience. How many friends can be depended on so confidently? Our primary need is merely to possess curiosity — or to put ourselves in situations calculated to stir curiosity within us.

Appreciative listening, then, depends chiefly upon our willingness to learn. Possessed of that attribute, it is not difficult to increase rapidly our ability to understand ourselves — our likes and dislikes. It depends further upon our conscious, voluntary endeavor to deepen our understanding by broadening the range of experiences potentially affording us pleasure. A richer, finer, fuller life is ours all for the most modest and satisfying kind of effort. The fact that we shall develop a new sympathy and appreciation for the tastes of many of our associates in making this effort is a by-product which is all pure profit.

# CHAPTER 10

Speaking
and
Listening . . .

# . . . the personal pathway

The aim of the preceding chapters has been to help us, as students, begin a deeper understanding of the oral and aural communication processes so that we might gain some measure of success in our ability to exchange ideas, experiences, and feelings with others. We did not approach this speech course without any training in speaking and listening; all have practiced both since birth. It is obvious, however, that all have not developed these skills to the same extent. The environments out of which we come, family and community, have either favored or hindered our development of effective communication skills. Be that as it may, everyone through conscious study and practice can improve his ability to speak and to listen.

This course does not complete our attention to these matters. As we proceed through our college years and then on through our vocational careers, it should be our purpose to continue an examination of the communication problems which face us and to build on our previous experiences in such fashion that we improve in effectiveness. Many of us will continue our training through other formal courses in speech and listening training. Most colleges and universities offer courses in persuasion, discussion, interpretation, dramatics, debating, radio and television, and speech correction. We will participate in these according to our needs, interests, and time available.

There is no single skill of man of more importance to mankind in general than that of interpersonal communication. It is of prime importance in a society operating under a democratic form of government. The leaders in such a society must be able to express their ideas effectively and to understand the ideas of others. The multitudes in such a society must also be able and willing to speak their minds on public questions. These generalizations we do not deny even though we seem willing to accept rather unintelligent and irresponsible performances on the part of both groups. This would seem to call for more attention to the deficiencies in communication rather than to indicate a lack of importance of such skills.

Even in our day-to-day associations with others, our problems can be simplified with an improvement in communication skills. As a usual thing, misunderstandings become serious because two or more persons either spoke poorly or listened poorly. Mountains frequently become molehills when the communication gets straightened out. Each of us has had many experiences of this sort.

In a very practical way, our personal success in almost any endeavor will depend upon our ability to speak well and to listen efficiently. Most of our respected and influential leaders of today would tell us that a part of their success lies in their ability to communicate easily and effectively with individuals or with groups. Moreover, they would also tell us that their success in communication did not come easily. Maturation in speaking and listening takes a long period of time spent with many such experiences. Wishful thinking will not produce results here any better than with any other achievement. Study and practice will produce results for anyone who really wishes to improve his speaking and listening ability.

Each of us must start from where he is. It may be that a good many years will pass before we are able to talk with others as we would like. The multiplicity of detail in the final accomplishment must not keep us from making the start. Improvement in one part of the communication act added to another and another will begin to show. Sooner than we think we will be able to listen and to speak in a way that will meet our own requirements as well as the requirements of others.

Our adult lives of much listening and speaking are just getting under way during our college years. Our training in speaking and listening, in the formal and informal situations, should have established certain sound principles for practical communication performances. Without question, we should have learned there is a time to speak and a time to be silent. We should know by now that, except for light social conversation, our speaking time is directed to teaching and influencing others and our listening time is directed to learning from others.

As a speaker we must assume our proper responsibility for what we say. We must know what we are talking about and why we are talking about it. In addition, we must be responsible for the communication purpose: we speak to others in terms that can be understood, in terms of a frame of reference which will permit understanding.

As a listener we also must assume our share of the communication burden. It is up to us to acquire an amount of general knowledge and an interest in new information which will permit us to understand what is spoken to us, to know enough to listen. We must have a purpose in listening just as we have a purpose in speaking and we must learn to do that job well.

P
A
R
T **II**

# Speaking
# and
# Listening . . .

# . . . assignments

Part I of this book has dealt with a body of theory applicable to speaking and listening, the complimentary parts of the process of oral communication. A course in speaking and listening, however, must do more than disseminate a body of subject matter about the skills involved in the process. The students in the course must be given an opportunity to demonstrate their individual ability to speak and listen effectively.

Part II of this book is designed to facilitate actual practice in the two skills. Eight assignments have been worked out completely and nine others suggested. The number of guided practice exercises suited to a term of work will depend considerably upon the size of the class and the length of the term. Most of the class time should be spent with these student performances and the critiques of them.

Six extra speech evaluation blanks and six extra oral reading evaluation blanks are included at the end of Part II. These are for those extra exercises which will be possible where classes are small.

# Roll of Classmates

An alphabetical listing of the students in the class will help each student learn his classmates by name quickly. Each student should cooperate in this getting acquainted assignment.

| | |
|---|---|
| 1. ................................ | 16. ................................ |
| 2. ................................ | 17. ................................ |
| 3. ................................ | 18. ................................ |
| 4. ................................ | 19. ................................ |
| 5. ................................ | 20. ................................ |
| 6. ................................ | 21. ................................ |
| 7. ................................ | 22. ................................ |
| 8. ................................ | 23. ................................ |
| 9. ................................ | 24. ................................ |
| 10. ................................ | 25. ................................ |
| 11. ................................ | 26. ................................ |
| 12. ................................ | 27. ................................ |
| 13. ................................ | 28. ................................ |
| 14. ................................ | 29. ................................ |
| 15. ................................ | 30. ................................ |

# Speaking
# and
# Listening . . .

# . . . use of
# the exercises

The fifteen exercises in speaking and listening were designed as sample exercises rather than a comprehensive set to be followed meticulously by all oral communication classes. You will notice, for example, that exercises two and three are not repeated in the set of fifteen. It would certainly be appropriate to repeat both types in order to allow demonstration of improvement over the first performance. Even the twelve assignments involving "external problems" is in no sense an exhaustive list. Imaginative students and instructors will no doubt select other problems than those considered here because of greater interest to the group.

The first three assignments are recommended as good "first" exercises, but beyond that no specific order is necessarily prescribed. Variation in type of exercise does much to hold interest. Mixing the free discussion, oral reading, and speaking exercises will give needed practice in all three forms and provide the spice that change in routine allows. The instructor's brief lectures of from three to five minutes as the occasions arise will also provide profitable interludes. Class criticisms of the individual and group performances become an important part of each class hour also.

Each student performance should be a test of improvement over previous ones. The rating scales which accompany each assignment exercise provide a guide for the instructor's criticism and a program of study for the student. The weaknesses pointed out should be remedied in future performances; the strengths noted should provide the encouragement to work for total improvement.

The time limits for the separate performances should be adhered to rigidly. Class time is precious time. A timekeeper should indicate to each performer when he has used his share of that time. After the first week, the instructor should use some method other than roll call to check upon attendance if records of this nature must be kept.

# Assignment Exercise Number 1

*Autobiographical Speech*

The best approach to training in speaking and listening is to get started in guided practice at once. It might seem logical to study all about the techniques before stepping to the platform. We can't wait for that, however. We will learn better and faster by practicing as we go.

A speech and listening class becomes a well-knit unit of students endeavoring to improve the speaking and listening skills of every individual in that unit. The idea of cooperation in this enterprise between student and student, and instructor and student, should be heavily emphasized. Some competition is necessary for best motivation but competition is not the primary motivating factor. A speaking and listening class is somewhat unique among other college classes in this respect.

**Purpose of the Assignment:** Because of this close working arrangement, members of the class need to know about one another. In order to begin that acquaintance this autobiographical speech has been designed. For each individual the main purpose of his speech should be to give something of his background that other students might know him better and to learn something about the background of every other individual in the class. A second purpose will be to make the first speech and "get the feel" of standing before and talking to an audience.

This is not a difficult speech from the standpoint of gathering materials. Since each speaker will be talking about himself and points in his past history, he will have more data than can be used. A more difficult part of the assignment will be that of working originality into the presentation. A good introduction to the discussion of the points to be covered will be of particular importance.

**Procedure:** Each speaker should jot down in mind or on a 3 x 5 card the points to be covered in his talk. Somewhere in the introduction the first and last name should be spoken clearly. The rest of the talk can be about such things as the home town, favorite sports, significant autobiographical facts or incidents, and the reason for coming to this particular college or university.

Do not consider this an insignificant performance. Since this is the first class exercise, it is very important that the job be done well. List many items, more than can be used, in preparing for the speech, then cull them down to those that will leave the audience with something important and interesting to remember.

As each speaker prepares data about himself, he should not feel that he will be ill-mannered or boastful because he is talking about himself. Every speaker on this assignment must be talking about himself, but it need not be in bragging fashion.

The preparation should be in terms of adhering strictly to the time limits imposed by the instructor. One of the important things to learn about speech making is a respect for time limits. The preparation should also be in terms of ease in manner and use of voice. The conversational tone, as used in speaking with small groups of friends, serves best. There is no hurry. Take the time needed to make the speech and walk easily to the seat.

**Listening Exercise:**

The primary purpose of the listener in this exercise is to form an association of names and faces. The association can be promoted by writing down each name when it is given by the speaker (the instructor will carefully refrain from calling names) and recording some brief notation about the appearance of the speaker or something that he said. The important ability to learn names and faces cannot be overstressed.

The second purpose of the listener is to help the speaker by giving alert and careful attention at all time. The listener's job in this exercise, and in all others, is to gather all the information possible from the performance. This gleaning process goes beyond the verbal ideas presented; it involves attitudes, purposes, and interests. Listening is a full-time activity.

**Written Exercise:**

Fill out carefully the Guidance Questionnaire at the end of this exercise and hand it to the instructor when he calls for it.

## GUIDANCE QUESTIONNAIRE

Student's name ........................... .............

## DIRECTIONS

The purpose of this questionnaire is to provide the instructor with information which will help him in advising students in this Oral Communications course. Fill in all the items accurately. Tear out and turn in to the instructor.

1. Age ................ Class in School ..... ............. Major .......................

2. Home address ....................................................................

3. Were you reared on a farm? ................. Small town? ..................
   City over 5,000? ........................ Over 20,000? ..................

4. Does either of your parents do much public speaking?
   Father. Much .............. Occasionally ............... Rarely ...............
   Mother. Much .............. Occasionally ............... Rarely ...............

5. Would you say the quality of English spoken in your home is good
   ...................... fair ..................... poor ..................... ?
   Would you say the quality of English spoken by your childhood play-
   mates was good ................. fair ................... poor ...................?

6. Check with an X if you have ever:
   a. stuttered ........................    d. had any difficulty with speech ...
   b. lisped ........................    e. had a hearing loss .....................
   c. spoken with an accent .......    f. had difficulty in reading .........

7. Do you read a daily newspaper? Daily ........... Occasionally ...........
   Seldom ...............
   Do you read the front page of the newspaper? Yes .......... No ..........
   The editorial section? Yes ................ No ................
   How many books (fiction and nonfiction but not class texts or ref-
   erences) did you read last year? 0 ...... 1-3 ...... 4-6 ...... 7 or more .....
   What magazines do you read regularly? ...................................
   ...........................................................................

8. What subjects in school have you found most interesting? ................
   ...........................................................................

Indicate a first and second occupational choice. (1) .............................

(2) .........................

9. Did you take a speech course in high school? Yes ............ No ............

If yes, what course or courses? ..................................................................

Have you had a part in a high school play? Yes ............ No ............

Enter any high school speaking contests? Yes ............... No ...............

If yes, what type? ....................................................................................

How much time in English courses was spent in a study of speech?

Much ......................... Some ......................... None .........................

10. How you you rate yourself as a speaker?

Very good ........ Good ........ Average ........ Poor ........ Very poor ........

What do you consider your most serious problem in speaking? ............

..................................................................................................................

Have you ever worried about having to take a course in speech?

Yes ......................... No .........................

Do you take pride in your accomplishments? Frequently .....................

Occasionally ..................... Seldom ......................... .........................

In what accomplishments have you found the greatest satisfaction?

11 Indicate where you have traveled .......................................................

..................................................................................................................

Indicate your hobbies, recreational interests, athletic interests ............

..................................................................................................................

..................................................................................................................

12. Check the traits which you feel describe you.

a. shy ........                    g. thorough ........

b. socially sensitive ........      h. impulsive ........

c. self-conscious ........          i. observant ........

d. courteous ........               j. neat ........

e. friendly ........                k. respectful ........

f. determined ........              l. tactful ........

13. Write a short paragraph describing your reactions towards the need of a speech course in college.

# INSTRUCTOR EVALUATION OF DELIVERY

Student's name .......................................

(This evaluation sheet will be checked by the instructor and returned to the speaker. Tear it out and hand it to the instructor before making the speech.)

*Language*

|  | Above Average | Average | Below Average |
|---|---|---|---|
| 1. Sentence structure | ( ) | ( ) | ( ) |
| 2. Vocabulary | ( ) | ( ) | ( ) |
| 3. Fluency | ( ) | ( ) | ( ) |

*Body*

|  | | | |
|---|---|---|---|
| 1. Neatness | ( ) | ( ) | ( ) |
| 2. Posture | ( ) | ( ) | ( ) |
| 3. Facial expression | ( ) | ( ) | ( ) |
| 4. Gestures | ( ) | ( ) | ( ) |
| 5. Eye-contact | ( ) | ( ) | ( ) |

*Voice and Voice Usage Analysis*

I. Pattern

( ) A. Conversational

( ) B. Unconversational

II. Pitch

( ) Very pleasant

( ) Not unpleasant

( ) Too high

( ) Too low

( ) Too monotonous

III. Rate

( ) Excellent variation

( ) Adequate variation

( ) Too fast

( ) Too slow

( ) Too monotonous

IV.  Loudness                              V.  Quality

    (  )  Excellent  adjustment              (  )  Very  pleasant

    (  )  Average  adjustment               (  )  Not  unpleasant

    (  )  Too  loud                         (  )  Nasal

    (  )  Too  weak                         (  )  Harsh

    (  )  Too  monotonous                   (  )  Hoarse

                                      (  )  Breathy

*Pronunciation  and  Articulation*

|                              | Good | Average | Poor |
|------------------------------|------|---------|------|
| 1.  Pronunciation            | (  ) | (  )    | (  ) |
| 2.  Articulation             | (  ) | (  )    | (  ) |
| 3.  General  oral  accuracy  | (  ) | (  )    | (  ) |

4.  Specific inaccuracies ............... for ..............., ............... for ...............,

        ....................... for ......................, ....................... for .......................,

        ....................... for ......................, ....................... for .......................,

        ....................... for ......................, ....................... for ....................... .

# Assignment Exercise Number 2

*Informal Discussion*

Sometimes the approach to public performance in the speaking situation is softened by the group approach. When several persons cooperate in a performance, the pressure on each individual is reduced in relation to the size of the participating unit. Informal discussion groups can, therefore, serve the double purpose of providing experience in the frequently used panel discussion technique and easing the pressures of the platform situation for those who have some fear of facing an audience. Several informal discussion exercises should be planned as a part of the schedule of student performances.

**Purpose of the Assignment:**

The ability to carry on free discussion in the informal discussion assignment as planned in this exercise is the same as needed to carry on a healthy conversation. Conversation is, of course, the most common type of oral communication. We use it in a friendly way to pass the time of day and to share experiences but frequently we use it in a serious attempt to gain or give information and to convince or be convinced.

To state the purpose simply, it is the aim of this assignment to provide an experience in which students can participate cooperatively in the development of a topic. On each specific topic chosen, a panel will assume the responsibility of development for a set period which will then be followed by active audience cooperation.

**Procedure:**

The class should be divided into groups of from four to six members and each group should select a specific topic for development in the free discussion pattern. Each member of the groups should prepare himself to participate as a speaker as well as a listener. Some of the groups should select a leader to open the discussion, give some direction to it, and close it. Others should avoid the formal selection of a leader. After the groups have performed a judgment can be made about which method works best in the classroom situation.

Each panel should be seated in an almost closed circle with the open part facing the audience. Such a seating arrangement makes the panel semiprivate and promotes the individual speaker's attention to the other panel members rather than to the audience. At the close of the panel performance, the circle should be opened up so that all members face the audience.

The various groups should select their topics for discussion several days ahead of the performance date. Once that topic is selected, the groups need not meet as a unit until they are called before the class by the instructor. During those days preceding the classroom performance, each member of the group will be preparing himself for the coming exercise.

He will prepare by discussing the selected topic with other students and friends in an attempt to unveil the various directions a discussion of the topic might go. In addition, he will inform himself about the topic by reading from books or magazines available in the library. The drive by the student in this preparation period will be to inform himself on the details of the topic, to develop an interest in the subject matter to the extent that he wants to talk with others about it, and to consider the best ways of presenting what he has to say. If all members of the panel will so prepare, the presentation will be of interest and importance to the audience.

**Listening Exercise:**

The part of the class not in the performing panel will watch and listen with a critical eye and ear to the standard of the performance as well as to the specific ideas presented. The audience will be concerned as to whether the topic development seemed like free discussion or like a series of little speeches. They will judge whether the discussion had an element of spontaneity or whether it sounded "cut and dried." They will check as to whether all members of the unit had an adequate share in the speaking and as to whether panel members were good listeners when they were not speaking.

The audience will also judge the value of the ideas presented and the relation of the ideas to the total development of the topic. Ideas not clear or points not well taken will be noted by the listeners so that either questions or statements can be made to the panel when the discussion is opened to all. Finally, the audience will listen in order to rank the five best over-all performers in the free discussion exercise and the five who did better than expected as judged by the previous exercise.

**Written Exercise:**

Complete the blank on the following page and turn in to your instructor at the completion of the exercise.

Student  ................................................

## EVALUATION OF FELLOW STUDENTS

Directions: Rank the five classmates who in your estimation did best in the free discussion exercise, the best performer receiving rank one, the scond best rank two, etc. Establish a similar ranking for five students who did better than you expected from your previous acquaintance with them.

OVER-ALL SPEECH
PERFORMANCE

MOST SPEECH
IMPROVEMENT

*Name of Classmate*:

*Name of Classmate*:

1.

1.

2.

2.

3.

3.

4.

4.

5.

5.

(The blank space below and the back of this sheet may be used for keeping notes on the performances heard.)

Student ...........................................

## INSTRUCTOR EVALUATION OF PERFORMANCE

Directions: The student will place his name on this sheet perior to his performance, tear it out, and hand it to the instructor. The instructor will return it to the student at the next class meeting.

I. Content

    A.   Quantity

    B.   Quality

II. Delivery

    A.   Directness

    B.   Cooperation

    C.   Fluency

Suggestions for improvement:

# Assignment Exercise Number 3

*Oral Reading*

Many skill activities seem easier to do than they really are. Oral reading is one of these. Reading from the printed page seems so easy when the skilled person does it; however the effective performance is actually more difficult than the task of speaking extemporaneously on familiar topics. All speaking and listening courses should plan several assignments devoted to oral reading of both prose and poetry which involve humorous as well as serious themes.

**Purpose of the Assignment:** The purpose of the reader always is to interpret the full meaning of the selection to the audience. This interpretation involves emotional as well as informational content. The performance therefore involves much more than the mechanical process of reading the words without expression. Too much of the oral reading we hear is of this sort and the audience suffers when it is done this way.

The skills of oral reading are different enough from those of extemporaneous speaking to deserve special attention. You will give attention to the development of the separate factors in this and future oral reading assignments. Three of the skills extremely important to speaking and oral reading will receive attention in the present assignment.

The element of eye-contact, so vital in all speech activities, is particularly difficult to achieve in oral reading. It must be secured by the effective reader. Articulation and pronunciation, also important to communication of ideas in oral materials, deserve early attention. Old habits have been destroyed and new ones put into use. For this first reading assignment these three matters — eye-contact, articulation, and pronunciation — should receive paramount attention. Remember that in any oral performance you are trying to communicate meaning. The attention to eye-contact, articulation, and pronunciation is stressed for that purpose.

Reading for an audience should become an enjoyable performance for you once you have mastered the skills needed. The authors feel that training in oral reading is fully as important as training in other speech activities and so deserves adequate practice for the development of effective habits. The opportunities for oral reading will be many in the mature life of most individuals. You will never regret the skill gained through practice.

**Procedure:**
When your name is called, proceed to the front of the room and read the material you have selected to your classmates. This selection should be simple expository or descriptive content about any subject of your choice. After you have made a selection of material, it would be well to look up the pronunciation of any words about which you are not sure. Try to pick a topic which is interesting to you and which you feel will be interesting to the class.

Read with an attempt to interpret the meaning of the selection and be particularly careful with articulation and pronunciation. Take all the time you need. Read out clearly and distinctly, so that all can hear without straining. Get as much eye-contact as you can.

**Preparation:**
It would be well for you to study the chapter in this text devoted to oral reading and to follow such advice as seems pertinent to the present performance. If you have an opportunity to try out your selection on a roommate or member of your family, it should be taken. Without question you should practice your selection privately a good many times before you bring it to the classroom audience.

**Listening Exercise:**
As you listen to your classmates read from the printed page try to be attentive. Be prepared to comment upon the strong and weak elements in the performances you hear. Compare your classmates in their ability to read orally. Compare their performances with your own.

**Written Exercise:**
Place the performers in one of three categories and turn your evaluations in to the instructor. The three categories of performance are 1) above average, (2) average, and (3) below average.

## INSTRUCTOR EVALUATION OF DELIVERY

Pronunciation and Articulation       Student ........................................

|   |   | Good | Average | Poor |
|---|---|------|---------|------|
| 1. | Pronunciation | ( ) | ( ) | ( ) |
| 2. | Articulation | ( ) | ( ) | ( ) |
| 3. | General oral accuracy | ( ) | ( ) | ( ) |

4. Specific inaccuracies ............... for ..............., ............... for ..............., 

............... for ..............., ............... for ............, ,............... for ..............., 

............... for ..............., ............... for ..............., ............... for ............. ,

Voice and Voice Usage

I. Pattern

    ( )   A.   Conversational

    ( )   B.   Unconversational

II. Pitch

    ( )   Very pleasant

    ( )   Not unpleasant

    ( )   Too high

    ( )   Too low

    ( )   Too monotonous

IV. Loudness

    ( )   Excellent adjustment

    ( )   Average adjustment

    ( )   Too loud

    ( )   Too weak

    ( )   Too monotonous

III. Rate

    ( )   Excellent variation

    ( )   Adequate variation

    ( )   Too fast

    ( )   Too slow

    ( )   Too monotonous

V. Quality

    ( )   Very pleasant

    ( )   Not unpleasant

    ( )   Nasal

    ( )   Harsh

    ( )   Hoarse
(Breathy)

Body

|  | Above Average | Average | Below Average |
|---|:---:|:---:|:---:|
| 1. Neatness | ( ) | ( ) | ( ) |
| 2. Posture | ( ) | ( ) | ( ) |
| 3. Facial expression | ( ) | ( ) | ( ) |
| 4. Eye contact | ( ) | ( ) | ( ) |

# Assignment Exercise Number 4

## Communication Problems

Speaking and listening courses have been severely criticized for permitting students to deal with unimportant subject matter in their speech performances. This criticism has some merit. The authors of this text agree that there are sufficient important problem areas to make it unnecessary for a speaker to waste his time in preparation and his classmates' time in listening to "How to Shine a Pair of Shoes." The point of maturity in students even at the high school level would seem to warrant speech content of an important nature.

With this idea in mind, the following twelve assignment exercises deal with some of the important problems which have always faced mankind. Students and instructors should decide which of these or others like them would be profitable for class use. Experience indicates that guided practice exercises in extemporaneous speaking work best when all members of the class are considering various phases of the same general problem. This technique permits considerable breadth and depth in permeation of a problem which should avoid the criticism noted. Some of the informal discussion assignments may use these or other "eternal problems" as topics also.

**Purpose of the Assignment:** The subject matter area of "Communication Problems" is a large one. In addition to the problems of transmitting ideas from individual to individual or from individual to group, there are those involving the mass media of communication: the press, radio, and television.

As society grows more complex, the effect of the mass media assumes a more important place in our lives. Such mass media as radio and television are so relatively new in the history of mankind, that a full accounting of their power cannot be readily assessed. We do know that the communicative power of the mass media is tremendous in its effectiveness in the job its manipulators desire. Many of us are completely disgusted with the methods as well as the excessive use of advertising in all the mass media. Many magazines devote more than half of their space to advertising; television is going in the same direction. Much of this advertising is designed to impress the most naive of our populace; the rest of us have to listen to it. We are listening to radio and television to the extent that we must come to grips sooner or later with the extent of their influence upon society as a whole.

The whole range of problems involved in the area of communications makes this an interesting and important assignment for study. The suggested topics for this subject area are not meant to be inclusive or even the best ones for discussion. A reading of this list might serve, however, to suggest many additional and even better topics. Certainly there will be an adequate range of speech topics available to all.

|  |  |
|---|---|
| **Procedure:** | You will prepare for classroom delivery a five-minute speech in which you discuss a specific problem grounded in the general sub |

ject of communication. The list of topics given below may suggest a problem of interest to you or, better yet, reading in the subject area should produce a specific topic of your own selection and provide the materials for the development of that topic.

At the library, you should pursue the Reader's Guide to Periodical Literature, the card catalog, and other such sources for the documentary materials needed to support your point of view. Your job will be to analyze with care the materials you locate and to select carefully those pieces of evidence which will substantiate your stand on the issue selected.

For this first speech, you should divide the body of the talk into three parts: (1) Analysis of the problem, (2) Cause or causes of the problem, and (3) Solution to the problem. A brief introduction should be devised for the speech opening and a simple conclusion should be designed for the close. Be sure that you back up your generalizations with evidence. The quality and quantity of your documentation will help make or break the effectiveness of your talk. Statements without proof will do little to secure belief.

Once the speech materials have been organized in the pattern described, practice in delivery remains as a final polishing procedure prior to the classroom presentation. If your roommate or other friend will listen to a practice period, take advantage of him and have him listen. If you cannot secure this type of help, listen to yourself. Practice periods are essential for improvement in fluency and for checking out the timing on the speech. You are duty-bound to keep your talk within the time limits set by your instructor.

**Listening Exercise:**

As you listen to the speeches by your classmates, keep a few brief notes on each. These will enable you to make an important contribution during the criticism period if you are called upon for comment. In addition to notes on the contents of the speech, you should indicate your evaluation of the speech delivery. Both strong and weak points should be noted. You may find it impossible to make a satisfactory critique unless you keep a record of this type. Many instructors will call for six or seven classroom speeches prior to asking for class criticism upon each individual performance or for criticism of the group of speakers as a whole.

**Written Exercise:**

Prepare two multiple choice questions with four options or choices for each related to your talk. One of these should deal with an important fact presented in your speech and the second with the central idea. The questions can be used by the instructor for developing listening examinations for the class. The instructor will have the prerogative of improving the form but not the substance of the questions submitted. Prepare these questions with great care.

Complete the form "Composing the Speech" and give it to the instructor after you have made your classroom presentation.

**Suggested Topics:**

Problems in Communication

1. Deterioration of television
2. Thought control through the mass media
3. Editorializing the news
4. Breakdowns in industrial relations
5. Marital misunderstandings
6. Need for upward communication in industry
7. Depth psychology: the evils of hidden persuaders
8. Filth in modern novels
9. Communication barriers between parent and child

10. The village "vidiots": television addicts
11. The "hot line" to the Kremlin
12. Pay television
13. The educational television fiasco
14. The tragedy of poor classroom lectures
15. Communication breakdown in international diplomacy
16. Communication incompetence of ministers
17. Communication problems of the eggheads
18. The sad picture in modern advertising
19. Tabloid journalism
20. Freedom of reader from the press
21. Too much "classified" information
22. Costly breakdowns in interpersonal communication
23. Failure in political campaigns
24. Language barriers to communication
25. The cost of excessive advertising

Composing the Speech

Sources of materials:

1. ................................................    4. ................................................

2. ................................................    5. ................................................

3. ................................................    6. ................................................

Outline form:

I. Introduction

    A. Attention device: ................................................

    B. Transition sentence: ................................................

Il. Contract: ................................................

................................................

III. Discussion

    A.

        1.

        2.

    B.

        1.

        2.

    C.

        1.

        2.

IV. Conclusion:

    A. Summary or other method

    B. Response sought: ................................................

................................................

    C. Methods used to get response: ................................................

................................................

Evaluation Report

Speaking

I. Composition

    A. Introduction

    B. Contract

    C. Discussion

    D. Conclusion

II. Delivery

    A. Directness

    B. Animation

    C. Vocal variety and control

    D. Fluency

Strongest factor as a speaker:

Weakest factor as a speaker:

# Assignment Exercise Number 5

*Educational Needs*

Education is under fire today as it always has been to a certain extent. The race for world domination by governments with competing ideologies has focused our attention in recent years on our system of education, however, as has rarely been done heretofore. The whole range of the educational process from kindergarten to postdoctoral work is being scrutinized severely.

Everybody seems agreed that all educable youngsters should be given an opportunity to secure an education to the limit of their abilities and in the direction of their interests and potential. Many adults are now seeking further education than that provided in their elementary, high school, and college training periods. The community junior college system springing up in many states is an atttempt to bring higher education to those of little means and to those adults who cannot leave employment to go to some distant college or university. Special adult evening schools are being operated for those who need elementary training in the fundamental subject matter areas of reading, writing and mathematics. Technical training classes are being opened for students, both teen-agers and adults, all over the nation.

All of us have gone through an educational program which has lead to our present college career. Many will not complete a four year college degree, but others will do so and then go on for graduate work. In that progress up the educational ladder, we have formed certain convictions about the system of education as we experienced it. Moreover, our interest in education will not wane with the completion of our formal contact with schools, teachers, and classes. The progress of our children through an educational system will probably center our interest on these matters to an even greater extent.

**Purpose of the Assignment:** The purpose of each of the twelve extemporaneous speaking assignments is to provide subject matter of a serious nature for your practice speeches. The authors have no intention of taking over the work of the social scientists by suggesting these or other topics as the general subject matter for the classroom speeches. We do feel, however, that in preparing speeches on these several subject areas you will improve your knowledge about the areas and form tentative convictions about how certain problems might best be met.

All the areas selected are worthy of study and the speech you design on some problem in the individual area should be worth the time of your classmates in listening to it. We will all profit in the experience. As the speaker you will have confidence in your subject matter content for your practice in the art of extemporaneous speaking. The listeners will have the benefit of many hours of study and research as they listen to each fellow student.

**Procedure:**

Select a problem in education that has some particular interest for you. The topics listed at the close of this assignment may state a problem of which you have already been vaguely aware. If so, use it. Check all library reference aids for books and articles which deal with this particular problem. Read as widely as time permits but not past the time that will allow speech preparation and sufficient practice in delivery prior to your assigned class hour for presentation.

Again you will build the body of your speech with a three part division. The first part should state the problem clearly in such a way that all your listeners will agree that it is a real and serious problem. The second part should suggest at least one solution to the problem and the third part should indicate what will happen as a result of the acceptance of the solution.

The solution does not have to be an original piece of thinking. Perhaps it has already been tried and found successful. If so, your argument becomes one of asking for a wider acceptance of a tried solution. This type of argument has many strengths. Throughout the body of your speech interlace your generalizations with cogent reasoning and evidence in the form of facts, statistics, and authority.

**Listening Exercise:**

Every speech should have four distinct parts: (a) introduction, (b) contract, (c) body, and (d) conclusion. The introduction makes the opening contact with the audience and leads to the statement of the contract, the specific purpose in giving the speech. The body develops the contract and leads to the conclusion. As you listen to your classmates make speeches on some topic connected with education, try to locate the single sentence statement expressing the purpose of the speaker. During the criticism period include your evaluation of the clarity and exactness of this contract statement as well as those of other elements in the presentation.

**Written Exercise:**

As with all your extemporaneous speeches, you should build for your instructor two multiple choice questions over the speech which you deliver. One should deal with an important fact used in your speech content and the other with the central ideas you wished your listeners to accept.

**Suggested Topics:**

## EDUCATIONAL PROBLEMS

1. Incompetent teachers
2. Inadequate classrooms
3. Built-in weaknesses of large universities
4. Built-in weaknesses of small colleges
5. Excesses of progressivism
6. Horse and buggy school equipment in the space age
7. Disappointments in educational television
8. Inadequate sex education for our youth
9. Failure to identify and reward good teachers
10. Overemphasis upon athletics
11. Anti-intellectualism
12. Inadequate portion of the tax dollar devoted to education
13. Inadequate provision for gifted and handicapped children
14. Overreliance upon personality test scores
15. Undersized school districts
16. Unqualified personnel on local school boards
17. Inadequate high school curriculums
18. Failure to use physical plants the year around
19. Inadequate programs for continuation study by adults
20. Widespread use of uncertified teachers
21. Outworn traditionalism in education
22. Disciplinary problems
23. Inbreeding of staff at the university level
24. Tremendous inequalities in educational opportunity
25. Problems related to school integration

Composing the Speech

Sources of materials:

1. .................................................... 4. ....................................................

2. .................................................... 5. ....................................................

3. .................................................... 6. ....................................................

Outline form:

I. Introduction

    A. Attention device: ....................................................

    B. Transition sentence: ....................................................

II. Contract: ....................................................

    ....................................................

III. Discussion

    **A.**

        1.
        2.

    **B.**

        1.
        2.

    **C.**

        1.
        2.

IV. Conclusion:

    A. Summary or other method

    B. Response sought: ....................................................

    ....................................................

    C. Methods used to get response: ....................................................

    ....................................................

Evaluation Report

Speaking

I. Composition

    A. Introduction

    B. Contract

    C. Discussion

    D. Conclusion

II. Delivery

    A. Directness

    B. Animation

    C. Vocal variety and control

    D. Fluency

Strongest factor as a speaker:

Weakest factor as a speaker:

# Assignment Exercise Number 6

*Problems with Food and Water*

Just as it was thousands of years ago, one of man's most urgent problems deals with providing himself with a variety of good and plentiful food and fresh, clean water. Both food and water must be in constant supply in order that life can be carried on from one day to the next. Food and water must be available in abundance for all animal life to flourish. In addition to its uses for animal sustenance, water is the cooling, purifying, and mixing agent for hundreds of manufacturing processes. Unless great care is taken, the wastes from these industries will ruin vast quantities of water in our lakes and running streams. The costs of water pollution run into untold millions each year.

As the world's population mounts ever higher, the problems of food and water become more and more acute. In the not too distant future, apparently we will be facing a real battle to produce enough food for the exploding human population. All of our presently known techniques for food production will not be sufficient to meet the needs of mankind. New resources and new skills of tapping them will have to be found. The world's oceans may provide the new source and modern chemistry may provide the techniques.

Fresh water, too, must be found in greater quantities and must be protected from contamination. Again the sea may provide the source, and a reduction in the cost of desalinization may provide pure water fit for man's needs. In addition, man must take greater care to preserve the water provided by nature. Waste and contamination must be eliminated.

**Purpose of the Assignment:**  A speech assignment on "Problems in Food and Water" has been included in the twelve for several good reasons. First of all, the problem has many tangents. All that man has done — the development of the elaborate and complicated systems of industry, transportation, and government — has been an outgrowth of his need for food and water. Labor and sacrifice have attended his efforts to satisfy these basic needs of human sustenance. A study of these problems will provide subject matter of wide range, most of it interesting.

Second, we will be dealing with a real problem and not an academic one. Man is little closer to the solution of these problems than when he first discovered that soil would grow food if properly tilled and planted. In some respects, we are in worse shape now than man was thousands of years ago. Our water supply has only recently become a problem in much the same proportion that food has always been a problem.

Finally, it is a problem in which everyone has a vital interest. "In the sweat of thy face shalt thou eat bread" ties most of us to this matter of food and water in one way or another. If not in a personal way because of someone's foresight, we must be concerned with these problems because of group interest. These are problems that our governments, local and national, must face in an ever widening variety.

**Procedure:**

Specific topics from a general subject field will have widely different appeals as viewed by individuals seeking a classroom speech subject. There is little chance that any one of the topics listed following will turn out to be an overwhelming favorite and thus be overworked. Try to pick a topic of interest to yourself and one which you feel can be developed into an attractive talk for your classmates.

Select your own pattern of organization for this talk. It would be well to refer to Chapter 5 for a review of speech organization after you have selected the materials which you expect to use in your speech. Use that pattern or organization which seems to fit your materials best.

**Listening Exercise:**

In this exercise your classmates have been instructed to select their own pattern of point organization in the development of their speeches. As you listen to each talk given in class, try hard to identify the point arrangement pattern followed by the speaker and to anticipate each point the speaker develops before it is made clear. This will constitute a deliberate attempt on your part to practice the first ingredient skill in concentration — that of anticipating each point being made. In speech critiques be sure that a portion of your comment is upon how wisely and how clearly the speaker chose and followed a point arrangement pattern.

**Written Exercise:**

Prepare two multiple choice questions over the speech which you deliver in the class.

**Suggested Topics:**

1. Our growing water shortage
2. Soil depletion and hunger
3. The world's decreasing supply of crop land
4. Control of storms
5. Should the little farmer in America "get out"?
6. Land-use evils
7. Drinking water from sea water
8. Use of dams
9. Can wasteland be restored?
10. Food and salt water
11. Is birth control the answer?
12. Should we trade with hostile nations for items we need?
13. Has the soil bank idea proved a fiasco?
14. Will farm subsidies eventually destroy the American farmer?
15. The evils of strip mining
16. The evils in farm-to-city migration
17. Are strip cropping, terracing, and crop rotation the answer?
18. Malnutrition in a land of plenty
19. Missionaries versus agricultural experts
20. Are professional farm managers the answer?
21. Can the United States afford farm subsidies?
22. Can any one of us have a real future in American agriculture?
23. Flood damage — present and future
24. Fluoridation problems
25. Water pollution problems

## Composing the Speech

Sources of materials:

1. ................................ 4. ................................
2. ................................ 5. ................................
3. ................................ 6. ................................

## Outline form:

I. Introduction

    A. Attention device: ................................................

    B. Transition sentence: ................................................

II. Contract: ................................................

................................................ ................................................

III. Discussion

    A.

        1.
        2.

    B.

        1.
        2.

    C.

        1.
        2.

IV. Conclusion:

    A. Summary or other method

    B. Response sought: ................................................

................................................

    C. Methods used to get response: ................................................

................................................

Evaluation Report

Speaking

I. Composition

    A.   Introduction

    B.   Contract

    C.   Discussion

    D.   Conclusion

II. Delivery

    A.   Directness

    B.   Animation

    C.   Vocal variety and control

    D.   Fluency

Strongest factor as a speaker:

Weakest factor as a speaker:

# Assignment Exercise Number 7

*Family Problems*

The family remains the basic unit of society and sociologists quite uniformly agree that a decadent civilization would result if the integrity of home and family were destroyed. Newspaper headlines might tend to make us feel that marriage has become a very unstable institution and that the home is rapidly deteriorating in America. Such, however, is not really the case. While we must admit that divorces and other domestic troubles have created rather serious family problems, the great bulk of our marriages do endure and there is little likelihood that we shall abandon the home as the foundation stone of civilized life. This is not to say that all is serene and right in our homes. All sorts of uncertainties threaten the family as a social group.

These uncertainties are involved with the unemployment of fathers and the employment of mothers and children. Poor living conditions, whatever the reason, create instability in family life. Lack of personal respect, children for parents and parents for children, makes unstable conditions more precarious. Undesirable personality characteristics, oversensitivity to personal slights, ungovernable tempers, and downright selfishness ruin ideal home and family relationships.

We must all be concerned about any dangers to the home. If the home as the basic unit of the community is in danger of deterioration, the community itself will also deteriorate. These ill effects must necessarily affect the nation of which the communities are a part. Social and economic problems which create a danger for the home and family must be solved in order that our nation might make progress. Our present concerns about the home and the communities made up of homes is not amiss.

**Procedure:**

Young men and women of college age have already given considerable thought to matters of marriage and family living. It is not unlikely that many have formed definite convictions about family life which must ultimately affect their own marriage and home establishment. These convictions, if presented as a speech to one's classmates, should provide a talk worth making and one worth hearing.

It may be easy to quip one's way through a subject area of this nature. If you do that, you have lost the opportunity to present a talk of quality on a subject that is everything but frivolous. Should you not have a topic under "Family Problems" of your own pre-established choice, take one of those from the list of twenty-five and see what material the library will offer on that topic. Both books and magazines should provide tremendous quantities of material on many of the topics suggested.

After you have selected the topic and located more material than you need for a five minute speech, select an organization pattern for its presentation. It would be well to use a pattern type other than that used for the previous speech, although the speech purpose and the available material will govern this selection of organizational pattern to some extent.

Try to build an exceptionally interesting and attractive introduction for this talk. It would be well to devise three or four separate introductions for the talk and then to pick that which seems the best after the speech has been practiced with each one.

**Listening Exercise:** As your classmates speak during this class exercise, listen very carefully to the development of the introduction. Compare each one to your own in effectiveness. In critiques, be sure to comment upon the introduction as well as upon other points.

**Written Exercise:** In addition to the two questions built upon your own speech, submit an additional two built upon the instructor's or classmates' remarks made during the critique periods.

**Suggested Topics:**

Family Problems

1. Broken homes
2. Oversized families
3. Childless couples

4. Mixed-faith marriages
5. Unwed mothers
6. Hatred of brother and sister
7. Hatred of father or mother
8. Parental support of married children
9. Teen-age marriages
10. Homeless children
11. Oversheltering of children
12. Serious mismanagement of orphanages
13. Family budget problems
14. Home conditions leading to juvenile delinquency
15. The loss of family unity
16. Inadequate marriage counseling
17. Ineffective juvenile courts
18. Inadequate youth activity programs
19. Working mothers
20. The influence of Hollywood immorality
21. Infidelity
22. Juvenile street gangs
23. Dependent oldsters in the home
24. Leisure time in modern life
25. Finding a mate

Composing the Speech

Sources of materials:

1. ........................................ 4. ........................................

2. ........................................ 5. ........................................

3. ........................................ 6. ........................................

Outline form:

I. Introduction

    A. Attention device: ........................................

    B. Transition sentence: ........................................

II. Contract: ........................................

........................................

III. Discussion

    A.

       1.
       2.

    B.

       1.
       2.

    C.

       1.
       2.

IV. Conclusion:

    A. Summary or other method

    B. Response sought: ........................................

........................................

    C. Methods used to get response: ........................................

........................................

Evaluation Report

Speaking

I. Composition

    A. Introduction

    B. Contract

    C. Discussion

    D. Conclusion

II. Delivery

    A. Directness

    B. Animation

    C. Vocal variety and control

    D. Fluency

Strongest factor as a speaker:

Weakest factor as a speaker:

# Assignment Exercise Number 8

*Problems Related to Religion*

Religion and the church have a great deal to do with the ideals of a people. Religion is a matter of faith that a higher power than man is in ultimate control of the universe. The church is the institution which teaches this belief in God. Although many persons may have become deeply religious without direct association with any church, most persons arrive at their beliefs about religion through the organized efforts of some church. Although religion is not the same as morality the finest moral codes have grown, developed, and continued to live because of the efforts of religious groups — Buddhists, Christians, Hindoos, Jews, and others.

Religion has played an important role in America since early Colonial times. Many problems and conflicts have arisen over the differences among the various religious groups. These differences were stressed not so much because of differing ideals but because of differing interpretations of the Scripture. It is sometimes difficult, for example, to know which Protestant service is being presented on television or radio because the services are so much alike. Even though we belong to no specific sect ourselves, we can't very well avoid the everyday problems which are related to religion. Problems dealing with religious toleration, religious freedom, the separation of church and state are age-old and they affect us all.

Whether or not we belong to a church, we need to come to certain decisions about our own philosophy of life. We must set our own standards of conduct and we cannot depend upon a community to tell us what we ought to do. Our conduct must be such that all will benefit from it. If what we outline as a high standard of conduct happens to coincide with the teachings of the great religious leaders of past and present, we need not be alarmed by our thinking. Perhaps that is a fair indication we have found the truth.

**Procedure:**

The selected list of topics touch only a few of the problems directly related to religion. Some of those named are more nearly related to what has been called morality. The church, however, has become so closely related with guiding our individual lives that problems of this type are quite naturally included. "Cheating in the classroom" falls in this category. It has to do with a measure of conduct clearly described in the Ten Commandments. Other topics dealing with standards of conduct will occur to you. If you have a particular interest in some problem of this type, please use it as your speech topic.

It would be well to consult the usual sources of information either before or after selecting a specific topic. Current magazines will let you know what topics of a religious or moral nature are being discussed now. A reference to a recent article will give you an easy entry to your topic.

It would be wise to get a preview criticism on this speech from your roommate or other friend. Their recommendations may enable you to strengthen the weak spots and smooth out the total performance. Encourage your critic to be severe.

**Listening Exercise:**

As you listen to each talk given in class, try to identify quickly the point arrangement pattern being followed by the speaker and to anticipate before it is made the identity of the next point to be developed. Make every effort to classify the kinds of material used to support each point. In this way you will be practicing several ingredient skills of listening concentration. As you make your speech critique, let the speaker know you were noting and evaluating his point supporting material used by commenting upon that feature of his speech as well as upon other details.

**Written Exercise:**

Hand in the usual multiple choice questions built upon the material used in your speech.

**Suggested Topics:**

Religious Problems

1. Problems of conscientious objectors
2. Shortages in religious leadership
3. Persecution of small religious minorities
4. The effects of space travel upon religion
5. Apparent conflicts between science and religion

6. The search for a personal philosophy of life
7. Financial problems of our churches
8. Housing problems of our churches
9. Apathy in the church school
10. Difficulties in achieving interdenominational cooperation
11. Religious intolerance
12. Curtailment of freedom of religion
13. Religious quackery
14. Problems of the atheist
15. Problems of the agnostic
16. The economic burden of the church in regions of little wealth
17. Slow world-wide acceptance of the principles of Christianity
18. Separation of church and state
19. Censorship of literature and art by the church
20. Tax support of church schools
21. Conflict of good and evil within each man
22. Evangelism: Boon or Bane?
23. Cheating in the classroom
24. Failure of churches to provide moral leadership
25. Unethical practices in raising money

Composing the Speech

Sources of materials:

1. ........................................   4. ........................................

2. ........................................   5. ........................................

3. ........................................   6. ........................................

Outline form:

I. Introduction

   A. Attention device: ........................................

   B. Transition sentence: ........................................

II. Contract: ........................................

........................................

III. Discussion

   A.

      1.
      2.

   B.

      1.
      2.

   C.

      1.
      2.

IV. Conclusion:

   A. Summary or other method

   B. Response sought: ........................................

........................................

   C. Methods used to get response: ........................................

........................................

Evaluation Report

Speaking

I. Composition

    A.   Introduction

    B.   Contract

    C.   Discussion

    D.   Conclusion

II. Delivery

    A.   Directness

    B.   Animation

    C.   Vocal variety and control

    D.   Fluency

Strongest factor as a speaker:

Weakest factor as a speaker:

# Assignment Exercise Number 9

*Transportation Problems*

Assignment number nine and the six assignments following may be developed for exercises in extemporaneous speaking or in informal discussion. However they are used, accompanying exercises in listening should be made.

## Suggested Topics:

Transportation in Problems

1. Wasted production time through nonproductive travel
2. Impractical design and horsepower in American cars
3. The high cost of transportation
4. Inadequacies of American highways
5. Unfair preferential treatment given trucks as compared with trains
6. Toll road: good or bad?
7. Widespread pollution of air by fuel-burning vehicles
8. Nonstandardized signs, signals, and regulations between states
9. Inadequate transportation facilities for settling other planets
10. The parking problem
11. Radioactive gases in space
12. Poor railway passenger service
13. Tension created by meeting tight travel schedules
14. Slowness in providing one-man airships
15. The death toll of our highways
16. The licensing of unfit drivers
17. Inadequacies of control over air traffic
18. Graft related to land condemnation for highways
19. Exorbitant freight rates
20. Strikes in the transportation industry
21. Oversized trailers on our highways
22. Inefficient traffic management in cities
23. Teen-age driver problems
24. Car insurance and high garage bills
25. Need for control over pleasure boating

Composing the Speech

Sources of materials:

1. .................................... 4. ....................................

2. .................................... 5. ....................................

3. .................................... 6. ....................................

Outline form:

I. Introduction

   A. Attention device: ....................................

   B. Transition sentence: ....................................

II. Contract: ....................................

      ....................................

III. Discussion

   A.

     1.

     2.

   B.

     1.

     2.

   C.

     1.

     2.

IV. Conclusion:

   A. Summary or other method

   B. Response sought: ....................................

      ....................................

   C. Methods used to get response: ....................................

      ....................................

Evaluation Report

Speaking

I. Composition

    A. Introduction

    B. Contract

    C. Discussion

    D. Conclusion

II. Delivery

    A. Directness

    B. Animation

    C. Vocal variety and control

    D. Fluency

Strongest factor as a speaker:

Weakest factor as a speaker:

# Assignment Exercise Number 10

*Housing Problems*

## Suggested Topics:

Problems in Housing

1. Deficiencies in the Federal Housing Administration
2. Overinvestment in houses
3. Transportation problems related to suburban living
4. Tenements and slums: national disgrace
5. Minority clannishness in housing
6. Drawbacks in buying an old house
7. Bad planning of commercially zoned areas
8. Inadequate provision of parks and playgrounds
9. The urgent need for bomb and storm shelters
10. Sanitation problems around the world
11. Poor quality of building materials
12. Factory location versus differences in tax loads
13. Architectural monstrosities
14. Problems of two or more families under one roof
15. Disadvantages in renting a home
16. The evils in homestead exemption
17. Problems in financing a home
18. Geographic errors in selection of homesites
19. Exorbitant hotel and motel rates
20. Inadequate school construction
21. Unethical bank financing practices
22. Insect and rodent damages to homes
23. Are today's subdivisions tomorrow's slums?
24. The need for decentralization of any big cities
25. Housing problems of married students

Composing the Speech

Sources of materials:

1. ................................................    4. ................................................

2. ................................................    5. ................................................

3. ................................................    6. ................................................

Outline form:

I. Introduction

    A.  Attention device: ................................................

    B.  Transition sentence: ................................................

II. Contract: ................................................

    ................................................

III. Discussion

    A.

        1.
        2.

    B.

        1.
        2.

    C.

        1.
        2.

IV. Conclusion:

    A.  Summary or other method

    B.  Response sought: ................................................

    ................................................

    C.  Methods used to get response: ................................................

    ................................................

Evaluation Report

Speaking

I. Composition

    A.  Introduction

    B.  Contract

    C.  Discussion

    D.  Conclusion

II. Delivery

    A.  Directness

    B.  Animation

    C.  Vocal variety and control

    D.  Fluency

Strongest factor as a speaker:

Weakest factor as a speaker:

# Assignment Exercise Number 11

*War and Peace*

## Suggested Topics:

Problems of War and Peace

1. Tremendous costs of national defense
2. Nonproductivity of military hardware
3. Inexcusable waste in the military services
4. Problems of the "have-not" nations
5. Excessive spirit of nationalism
6. Inadequate power of the United Nations
7. Inadequacy of defense against modern weapons
8. Horrors of biological warfare
9. Dangers of attack from outer space
10. Inherent weaknesses in international police forces
11. The serious need for an international language
12. The serious need for international currency
13. The serious need for international law
14. The serious need for international courts
15. The serious need for a truly international university
16. Heightened tensions through population increases
17. Areas of constant international friction
18. Inherent evils in psychological warfare
19. Alien political philosophies
20. Religious differences which cause war
21. Racial differences which cause war
22. The struggle to perpetuate colonial empires
23. Isolationist trade policies
24. Universal military training
25. Compulsory ROTC

Composing the Speech

Sources of materials:

1. ...................................... 4. ......................................

2. ...................................... 5. ......................................

3. ...................................... 6. ......................................

Outline form:

I. Introduction

   A. Attention device: ......................................

   B. Transition sentence: ......................................

II. Contract: ......................................

......................................

III. Discussion

   A.

      1.
      2.

   B.

      1.
      2.

   C.

      1.
      2.

IV. Conclusion:

   A. Summary or other method

   B. Response sought: ......................................

......................................

   C. Methods used to get response: ......................................

......................................

Evaluation Report

Speaking

I. Composition

    A.   Introduction

    B.   Contract

    C.   Discussion

    D.   Conclusion

II. Delivery

    A.   Directness

    B.   Animation

    C.   Vocal variety and control

    D.   Fluency

Strongest factor as a speaker:

Weakest factor as a speaker:

# Assignment Exercise Number 12

*Crime and Corruption*

**Suggested Topics:**

Problems of Crime and Corruption

1. Crime, horror, and obscenity in modern publications
2. Capital punishment
3. Is sterilization of the habitual criminal the answer?
4. Excessive restrictions on classroom punishment
5. Sale of liquor to minors
6. Drug traffic
7. Easy pardons and paroles
8. Integration of hardened criminal and first offender
9. Uncontrolled gambling
10. The problem of prostitution
11. The sale of "protection"
12. Truancy and petty crimes
13. Corruption and bribery in government
14. Corrupt judicial officials
15. Widespread breaking of speed laws
16. The cost of crime
17. Dishonesty and racketeering in labor unions
18. Unjust treatment of minorities
19. Drinking drivers
20. Correction versus punishment
21. Overcrowded court dockets
22. Wealth and its unfair influence upon justice
23. Inadequate recruitment and support of law enforcement officers
24. The suicide problem
25. Medieval methods still practiced in some prisons

Composing the Speech

Sources of materials:

1. ............................................. 4. .............................................

2. ............................................. 5. .............................................

3. ............................................. 6. .............................................

Outline form:

I. Introduction

   A. Attention device: .............................................

   B. Transition sentence: .............................................

II. Contract: .............................................

   .............................................

III. Discussion

   A.

      1.
      2.

   B.

      1.
      2.

   C.

      1.
      2.

IV. Conclusion:

   A. Summary or other method

   B. Response sought: .............................................

   .............................................

   C. Methods used to get response: .............................................

   .............................................

Evaluation Report

Speaking

I. Composition

    A.  Introduction

    B.  Contract

    C.  Discussion

    D.  Conclusion

II. Delivery

    A.  Directness

    B.  Animation

    C.  Vocal variety and control

    D.  Fluency

Strongest factor as a speaker:

Weakest factor as a speaker:

# Assignment Exercise Number 13

*Health Problems*

## Suggested Topics:

Problems in Health

1. Exorbitant costs of medical and dental care
2. Inadequate medical care in rural areas
3. Artificial shortage of doctors
4. Inadequate hospital facilities
5. Drawbacks of group-care plans
6. The American Medical Association: Boon or Bane?
7. Our increasing problems of mental health
8. The common cold
9. Dangers of obesity
10. New diseases succeeding old ones
11. The high cost of dying
12. Eight o'clock to five o'clock doctors
13. Pesticides and health
14. Are mercy deaths the answer?
15. Reproduction by the weak and feeble-minded
16. Tension and job pressures
17. Cigarettes versus lung cancer
18. Inadequate time for sleep
19. Medical quackery
20. Pest and epidemic control
21. Inadequate food and drug protection
22. Inadequate physical development
23. Dangers in dieting
24. Radioactive threats to our lives
25. Our polluted air

## Composing the Speech

Sources of materials:

1. ........................................   4. ........................................
2. ........................................   5. ........................................
3. ........................................   6. ........................................

### Outline form:

I. Introduction

    A. Attention device: ........................................

    B. Transition sentence: ........................................

II. Contract: ........................................

    ........................................

III. Discussion

    A.

        1.
        2.

    B.

        1.
        2.

    C.

        1.
        2.

IV. Conclusion:

    A. Summary or other method

    B. Response sought: ........................................

    ........................................

    C. Methods used to get response: ........................................

    ........................................

Evaluation Report

Speaking

I. Composition

    A. Introduction

    B. Contract

    C. Discussion

    D. Conclusion

II. Delivery

    A. Directness

    B. Animation

    C. Vocal variety and control

    D. Fluency

Strongest factor as a speaker:

Weakest factor as a speaker:

# Assignment Exercise Number 14

*Problems Related to Government*

## Suggested Topics:

Problems Related to Government

1. Dictatorships which suppress human rights
2. Excessive regulation of agriculture
3. Excessive regulation of business
4. Excessive regulation of the individual
5. Usurpation by government of legitimate areas of private business
6. Overcentralization of government
7. The high cost of government
8. Inadequate control of monopolies
9. Inadequate control of conflicts in industry
10. Governmental interference with education
11. Voting problems of Negro citizens
12. Corruption of justice through wealth
13. Discrimination against religious minorities
14. Complexity of income tax reporting
15. Unequal opportunities for women in politics
16. Oversized state legislatures
17. Unequal representation of voters
18. Refusal to let the 18-year-old vote
19. Voter apathy
20. Bribery of governmental employees and officials
21. Overlapping units of government
22. The spoils system
23. Evils of seniority in governmental service
24. Unfair taxes
25. Nepotism in government offices

Composing the Speech

Sources of materials:

1. ........................................ 4. ........................................

2. ........................................ 5. ........................................

3. ........................................ 6. ........................................

Outline form:

I. Introduction

    A. Attention device: ........................................

    B. Transition sentence: ........................................

II. Contract: ........................................

    ........................................

III. Discussion

    A.

        1.
        2.

    B.

        1.
        2.

    C.

        1.
        2.

IV. Conclusion:

    A. Summary or other method

    B. Response sought: ........................................

    ........................................

    C. Methods used to get response: ........................................

    ........................................

Evaluation Report

Speaking

I. Composition

    A. Introduction

    B. Contract

    C. Discussion

    D. Conclusion

II. Delivery

    A. Directness

    B. Animation

    C. Vocal variety and control

    D. Fluency

Strongest factor as a speaker:

Weakest factor as a speaker:

# Assignment Exercise Number 15

*Making a Living*

## Suggested Topics:

Problems in Making a Living

1. The cost of strikes
2. Difficulties in finding the job we really want
3. Unjust pay scales
4. Special problems of overaged workers
5. The problem of obsolete training methods
6. The inadequate differential between salaries of college graduates and others
7. The urgent need for real craftsmanship
8. Should college students work part-time?
9. Unreliability of job aptitude and personality tests
10. The problem of incompetent workers' receiving union protection
11. Inadequate safety measures in certain lines of employment
12. The migratory worker
13. Working wives
14. The cost of preparation for making a living
15. Special problems of the colored worker
16. Special problems of workers with handicaps
17. The unscrupulous labor union leader
18. Drawbacks in incentive systems
19. The unscrupulous employer
20. The guaranteed annual wage
21. The inadequacy of present stock purchase plans for employees
22. Wasted human resources under early retirement plans
23. Problems related to automation
24. The necessity of working four months a year to pay our taxes
25. The competition between industry and government for trained manpower

Composing the Speech

Sources of materials:

1. ................................................ 4. ................................................

2. ................................................ 5. ................................................

3. ................................................ 6. ................................................

Outline form:

I. Introduction

   A. Attention device: ................................................

   B. Transition sentence: ................................................

II. Contract: ................................................

................................................

III. Discussion

   A.

     1.

     2.

   B.

     1.

     2.

   C.

     1.

     2.

IV. Conclusion:

   A. Summary or other method

   B. Response sought: ................................................

................................................

   C. Methods used to get response: ................................................

................................................

Evaluation Report

Speaking

I. Composition

    A.   Introduction

    B.   Contract

    C.   Discussion

    D.   Conclusion

II. Delivery

    A.   Directness

    B.   Animation

    C.   Vocal variety and control

    D.   Fluency

Strongest factor as a speaker:

Weakest factor as a speaker:

# Assignment Exercise Number 16

### *Oral-Reading — Poetry*

Poetry reading is more difficult than prose reading for most of us, but the satisfaction that comes from learning to do it well makes the effort worthwhile. Much poetry has a rhythm or meter which stands out vividly with careless oral reading. The experienced oral reader will reduce this natural rhythm until it all but disappears and is subdued to the extent that the listener's attention can be focused on the emotional and intellectual elements rather than on the rhythmical pattern. When the poetry is not written in poetic measures, it still possesses a mood which must be suggested by the reader. The reader must get the feel of this mood and bring it to the listener through the proper tonal response. These two elements make the oral reading of poetry more difficult than the oral reading of prose.

The selection for the oral reading performance is made in terms of the performer and the listening audience. The selection must suit the reader in that he must have had the background of experience which enables him to understand the emotional as well as the intellectual content. The selection must suit the listener by being within his realm of understanding also. The too familiar poetry should not be read for an audience.

Pick a selection or selections of poetry for this exercise which you feel you can interpret and which you feel will be of interest to the audience. Whatever you choose, prepare it well through extensive practice periods. Pick humorous or serious poetry, whichever you enjoy doing most and whichever you think you do best.

Evaluation Report

Oral Reading

I. Composition

    A.   Suited to reader

    B.   Suited to audience

    C.   Quality of selection

    D.   Interest to audience

II. Delivery

    A.   Directness

    B.   Animation

    C.   Vocal variety and control

    D.   Pronunciation and articulation

Strongest factor as an oral reader:

Weakest factor as an oral reader:

# Assignment Exercise Number 17

## Oral Reading — Informal Essay

The oral reader of prose attempts to communicate the meaning and motive of the author in the selection chosen. To do this he must use all the qualities of good conversational speaking. Phrasing becomes extremely important in gaining the conversational pattern but the variations in rate and pitch play their part also. If you are to share with others what you read from the printed page, you must be prepared to use your voice in the re-creating process.

A short essay or a cutting from an essay will serve as the selection for this exercise. The reading time should be no more than four minutes. With adequate preparation, the reader should be able to get considerable eye-contact with the audience. He should read at a pace which will allow the listener opportunity to reflect on what is heard.

Adequate practice ordinarily means reading through the selection twenty to twenty-five times. These readings should be out loud so that pausing and emphasis can be practiced. Textbooks for literature courses will contain essay selections. The library will contain many volumes of collected essays with selections suitable for classroom oral reading exercises.

Evaluation Report

Oral Reading

I. Composition

    A.  Suited to reader

    B.  Suited to audience

    C.  Quality of selection

    D.  Interest to audience

II. Delivery

    A.  Directness

    B.  Animation

    C.  Vocal variety and control

    D.  Pronunciation and articulation

Strongest factor as an oral reader:

Weakest factor as an oral reader:

Evaluation Report

Speaking

I. Composition

    A.   Introduction

    B.   Contract

    C.   Discussion

    D.   Conclusion

II. Delivery

    A.   Directness

    B.   Animation

    C.   Vocal variety and control

    D.   Fluency

Strongest factor as a speaker:

Weakest factor as a speaker:

**Extra Speech Rating Blank**

Evaluation Report

Speaking

I. Composition

    A.   Introduction

    B.   Contract

    C.   Discussion

    D.   Conclusion

II. Delivery

    A.   Directness

    B.   Animation

    C.   Vocal variety and control

    D.   Fluency

Strongest factor as a speaker:

Weakest factor as a speaker:

Evaluation Report

Speaking

I. Composition

    A. Introduction

    B. Contract

    C. Discussion

    D. Conclusion

II. Delivery

    A. Directness

    B. Animation

    C. Vocal variety and control

    D. Fluency

Strongest factor as a speaker:

Weakest factor as a speaker:

Evaluation Report

Speaking

I. Composition

    A. Introduction

    B. Contract

    C. Discussion

    D. Conclusion

II. Delivery

    A. Directness

    B. Animation

    C. Vocal variety and control

    D. Fluency

Strongest factor as a speaker:

Weakest factor as a speaker:

Evaluation Report

Speaking

I. Composition

    A.   Introduction

    B.   Contract

    C.   Discussion

    D.   Conclusion

II. Delivery

    A.   Directness

    B.   Animation

    C.   Vocal variety and control

    D.   Fluency

Strongest factor as a speaker:

Weakest factor as a speaker:

Evaluation Report

Speaking

I. Composition

    A.  Introduction

    B.  Contract

    C.  Discussion

    D.  Conclusion

II. Delivery

    A.  Directness

    B.  Animation

    C.  Vocal variety and control

    D.  Fluency

Strongest factor as a speaker:

Weakest factor as a speaker:

Evaluation Report

Oral Reading

I. Composition

    A.   Suited to reader

    B.   Suited to audience

    C.   Quality of selection

    D.   Interest to audience

II. Delivery

    A.   Directness

    B.   Animation

    C.   Vocal variety and control

    D.   Pronunciation and articulation

Strongest factor as an oral reader:

Weakest factor as an oral reader:

Evaluation Report

Oral Reading

I. Composition

    A.   Suited to reader

    B.   Suited to audience

    C.   Quality of selection

    D.   Interest to audience

II. Delivery

    A.   Directness

    B.   Animation

    C.   Vocal variety and control

    D.   Pronunciation and articulation

Strongest factor as an oral reader:

Weakest factor as an oral reader:

Evaluation Report

Oral Reading

I. Composition

    A.  Suited to reader

    B.  Suited to audience

    C.  Quality of selection

    D.  Interest to audience

II. Delivery

    A.  Directness

    B.  Animation

    C.  Vocal variety and control

    D.  Pronunciation and articulation

Strongest factor as an oral reader:

Weakest factor as an oral reader:

Evaluation Report

Oral Reading

I. Composition

    A.  Suited to reader

    B.  Suited to audience

    C.  Quality of selection

    D.  Interest to audience

II. Delivery

    A.  Directness

    B.  Animation

    C.  Vocal variety and control

    D.  Pronunciation and articulation

Strongest factor as an oral reader:

Weakest factor as an oral reader:

Evaluation Report

Oral Reading

I. Composition

    A.  Suited to reader

    B.  Suited to audience

    C.  Quality of selection

    D.  Interest to audience

II. Delivery

    A.  Directness

    B.  Animation

    C.  Vocal variety and control

    D.  Pronunciation and articulation

Strongest factor as an oral reader:

Weakest factor as an oral reader:

Evaluation Report

Oral Reading

I. Composition

    A.  Suited to reader

    B.  Suited to audience

    C.  Quality of selection

    D.  Interest to audience

II. Delivery

    A.  Directness

    B.  Animation

    C.  Vocal variety and control

    D.  Pronunciation and articulation

Strongest factor as an oral reader:

Weakest factor as an oral reader:

P
A
R
T
**III**

**Speaking
and
Listening . . .**

# . . . appendices

The consonant and vowel tables included in Part III are not for general classroom use. Those students who have particular minor deviations in pronunciation should be able to consult these tables for help. Students with gross deviations should be sent to the speech clinic for advice and guided practice.

The lists of frequently mispronounced words can be used for individual study on classroom exercises. The pronunciation and articulation exercise can be used in the same way. If each student can give an acceptable pronunciation for most of the 356 words in this list, how to pronounce words will no longer be a class problem.

The Teacher Rating Scale was included in the appendix as an encouragement to instructors to ask for this criticism. The authors of this book are convinced that students can help instructors improve their teaching through a serious and honest use of this rating scale.

# Speaking
# and
# Listening . . .

# . . . speech sounds
# of english

The speech sounds of English are roughly divided into two classes — consonants and vowels. The consonant sounds are those in which the breath stream is impeded or completely blocked while the vowel sounds are relatively unimpeded. Some consonants are voiceless but all vowels are voiced.

The consonant phonemes are twenty-five in number, if we include the two combinations t∫ (church) and dʒ (judge). All of the consonant sounds take place within the mouth, throat, or nose. The movements of the tongue, lips, jaw, velum, and throat modify the breath stream in such a way as to produce the individual sounds. The table following classifies the consonants as continuants (such as $f$ or $m$ which may be prolonged without change of quality), plosives (such as $p$ or $t$ which are exploded after the breath stream has been stopped), and glides (such as $r$ or $l$ which have a vowel-like quality but are gradually changed as the sound is produced). The symbols used are those of the International Phonetic Alphabet.

## ENGLISH CONSONANT SOUNDS

| | | | | |
|---|---|---|---|---|
| *m* | lips together | voiced | nasal emission | *m*ore |
| *n* | tongue against upper gum ridge | voiced | nasal emission | ta*n* |
| ŋ | rear of tongue pressed against velum | voiced | nasal emission | ri*ng* |
| *f* | upper front teeth resting on lower lip | voiceless | air stream between teeth and lip | laug*h* |
| *v* | same as for *f* | voiced | same as for *f* | *v*iew |
| θ | tip of tongue between front teeth | voiceless | air stream between tongue and teeth | pa*th* |
| ð | same as for θ | voiced | same as for θ | *th*e |
| *s* | tongue tip raised toward upper gum ridge | voiceless | air stream over tongue tip | *s*ell |
| ʃ | flattened tongue raised toward hard palate | voiceless | air stream forced between tongue and hard palate | *s*ugar |
| ʒ | same as or ʃ | voiced | same as for ʃ | u*s*ual |

**Plosives:**

| | | | | |
|---|---|---|---|---|
| *p* | lips together | voiceless | lips forced apart | *p*ay |
| *b* | same as for *p* | voiced | same as for *p* | *b*oy |
| *t* | tongue pressed against upper gum ridge | voiceless | tongue tip forced away | *t*o |
| *d* | same as for *t* | voiced | same as for *t* | *d*o |
| *k* | throat muscles contract | voiceless | throat muscles release | lo*ck* |
| *g* | same as for *k* | voiced | same as for *k* | *g*ot |
| *t*ʃ | same as for *t* and ʃ | voiceless | same as for *t* and ʃ | spee*ch* |
| *d*ʒ | same as for *d* and ʒ | voiced | same as for *d* and ʒ | pa*ge* |

**Glides:**

| | | | |
|---|---|---|---|
| r | tongue against upper side teeth | voiced | *r*un |
| l | tongue not pressed against upper side teeth | voiced | *l*et |
| j | tongue tip behind lower front teeth | voiced | *y*ou |
| hw | tongue pulled back; lips rounded | voiceless | *wh*y |
| h | tongue flat, throat muscles tensed | voiceless | *h*ow |

## ENGLISH VOWEL SOUNDS

*Vowels and Diphthongs*

The vowels of our English alphabet (a-e-i-o-u) when analyzed phonetically make up approximately sixteen different phonemes plus six combinations or diphthongs. For instance, the *a* is articulated differently for the words *a*te, *a*bove, f*a*t, and f*a*ther; the *e* in *e*at differs from the *e* in g*e*t. Each of the five vowels of the alphabet thus represent several different phonemes. The spelling does not accurately portray the phonemes as received by the ear when the sound is produced. The table which follows classifies the vowel phonemes of American spoken English. The diacritical marks and the IPA symbols are listed for each vowel sound.

**Vowels:**

| | | | | | | |
|---|---|---|---|---|---|---|
| ē | i | as in *e*asy | | ŏŏ | ʊ | as in b*oo*k |
| ĭ | ɪ | as in *i*t | | ōō | u | as in r*u*le |
| ĕ | ɛ | as in *e*ver | | û | ɝ | as in c*ur*b (stressed syllables) |

ă    æ    as in h*a*t                    û    ɚ    as in p*ur*sue
                                                   (unstressed syllables)

ŭ    ʌ    as in l*o*ve (stressed            ɜ    as in b*ir*d (South
          syllables)                             and East)

ȧ    ə    as in *a*bove                     ɒ    as in c*o*llege (East)

          (unstressed syllables)

ä    ɑ    as in c*a*lm                 ō    o    as in m*o*tel
                                                   (unstressed syllables)

ô    ɔ    as in *o*ff                   ā    e    as in v*a*cation
                                                   (unstressed syllables)

## Diphthongs:

ī    aɪ    as in *i*ce                 ō̆    ou    as in *o*bey

ou   au    as in *ou*t                 oi   ɔɪ    as in t*oi*l

ā    eɪ    as in *a*te                  ū    ju    as in *u*se

## RULES FOR PRONUNCIATION

There are many exceptions to any rule of pronunciation. However, the following rules may be of some value:

(1) The letter *n* when preceded by *m* or *l* in the same syllable is usually silent. (hymn, kiln)

(2) When the letter *l* is preceded by *a* and followed by *m* in the same syllable, the *l* is usually silent. (palm, calm)

(3) The *t* if preceded by *s* or *f* in the endings *tle* and *ten* is usually silent. (bustle, often)

(4) When nouns and verbs have the same spelling, the noun is usually accented on the first syllable and the verb on the second. (contract) Notice that as the accent changes the first vowel undergoes change too.

(5) Most *ile* endings in words of more than one syllable are pronounced with a short *i*. (Virile, juvenile)

(6) The final *s* of most third person singular verbs following a voiced consonant is pronounced *z*. (runs, calls)

(7) The final *s* of the third person singular which follows a voiceless consonant is usually pronounced *s*. (works, hits)

(8) The *s* of the plural noun is pronounced *s*, if the final consonant of the singular form of the noun ends in *k, t, p, f*, or voiceless *th*. (dots, tops) Most other nouns form the plural by adding the *z* sound. (lungs, hams)

(9) When the infinitive form of the verb ends in *d* or *t*, the *e* of the suffix *ed* is pronounced. (benefited, raided)

(10) When the suffix *ed* is added to an infinitive ending in a voiceless consonant, the *ed* is pronounced *t*. (shopped, clocked) When the infinitive ends in a vowel or voiced consonant, the *ed* is pronounced *d*. (called, worried)

## WORDS I TEND TO MISPRONOUNCE

| List of Words | Diacritical or Phonetic Marking |
| --- | --- |
| 1. | |
| 2. | |
| 3. | |
| 4. | |
| 5. | |
| 6. | |
| 7. | |
| 8. | |
| 9. | |
| 10. | |
| 11. | |
| 12. | |
| 13. | |
| 14. | |
| 15. | |
| 16. | |
| 17. | |
| 18. | |
| 19. | |
| 20. | |
| 21. | |
| 22. | |

## PRONUNCIATION PRACTICE LISTS

The short list of words on this and the following pages contains most of those which give students trouble. Check your pronunciation of these words with a dictionary if you are not sure of reputable usage.

| | | |
|---|---|---|
| abdomen | assidious | calyx |
| aborigines | atrocity | cambric |
| absorption | atrophy | canine |
| abstemious | attaché | capillary |
| absurd | authoritative | capricious |
| accuracy | avarice | carillon |
| actually | azure | caste |
| adamant | bacillus | catastrophe |
| adaptation | bade | cavalry |
| adjective | balk | celestial |
| admonition | balmy | cello |
| adversary | baptize | centrifugal |
| affectation | barbarous | cerebral |
| agenda | baste | chaff |
| agile | bathe | chaise |
| alias | bayou | chamois |
| alienate | beige | chasm |
| allege | bier | chaste |
| alma mater | blasphemy | chastise |
| almond | blatant | chef |
| amicable | bona fide | chemise |
| anaemic | bouillon | chic |
| annihilate | bourgeois | chicanery |
| antiquity | bravado | chivalrous |
| aperture | brethren | cholera |
| apropos | brimstone | christen |
| aquatic | bulwark | clique |
| arbiter | buoy | comparable |
| archives | bureau | concerto |
| ardor | burrowed | condolence |
| aria | bury | conduit |
| artifice | bustle | consommé |
| artisan | cache | conversant |
| ascertain | calculate | coupon |
| assay | calumny | credence |

critique
cuisine
culinary
cynic
dais
danseuse
data
debacle
debate
debauch
debris
debut
decade
decorous
defamation
defer
deficit
degradation
deign
deity
deluge
demise
demitasse
demoniacal
demonstrative
demur
depilatory
deposition
depot
desert
despot
desultory
devastate
diabetes
dilate
dilatory
diminution
diminutive
diphtheria
dirigible
discretion
disheveled

disputant
dissect
divan
diverge
docile
drought
duly
ecstasy
education
efficacy
elite
emaciate
embryo
emeritus
enamel
encore
ensemble
entails
entree
environment
epitaph
epitome
equitable
err
erroneous
espionage
étude
Eustachian
exaltation
examine
executive
exotic
experiment
façade
facile
facsimile
ferment
ferocity
fiasco
filet mignon
flaccid
foliage

forbade
forehead
formidable
fricassee
frivolous
fuchsia
fury
gala
gamut
gesture
gibbet
gigantic
gourmet
gratis
grievous
griped
groveling
guarantee
habitable
hacienda
halcyon
harbinger
harrow
height
heinous
hickory
homage
horizon
hostage
hypocrisy
ignominy
imbecile
impediment
impetus
impious
impotent
incognito
incomparable
indefatigable
indict
indigenous
indolent

infamy
ingratiate
inherent
inquiry
insidious
integral
interpolate
intrepid
iodine
isolate
isthmus
jocund
juvenile
kilometer
kimono
labyrinth
lamentable
larynx
latent
legate
length
liaison
lichen
ludicrous
luscious
magistrate
maintenance
mauve
medieval
meringue
mesa
meteor
mien
municipal
nestle
novice
nuptials
oblivion
ominous
omnipotent
orgy
palsy

particular
partner
pastoral
penalize
penury
perfume
persistent
placate
poignant
politic
popular
posthumous
potpourri
practicable
precedent
precinct
preface
preferable
prelate
prerogative
prevalence
prima facie
probity
protein
quaff
quartile
ravenous
recognize
recreant
regalia
reptile
reputable
reside
resin
respite
rotary
salon
satiate
savory
schism
scion
sedative

senile
servile
sequence
sieve
solace
soufflé
staccato
statistics
steward
stratagem
subpoena
surfeit
sustenance
taciturn
tapestry
temperate
textile
transient
travail
treatise
trespass
tyranny
ultimate
umbrella
unison
usurp
vagary
valiant
variable
vehemence
venom
victual
visage
wept
wheel
whisper
whistle
wring
yeast
zealous
zenith

# Pronunciation and Articulation Exercise Material

## The Welfare State[1]

The "welfare state," as that term has come to be applied to the United States, is a concept of economic organization in which the state or government plays an active and dominant role in controlling the economic system. It is one of several economic philosophies falling between the extremes of economic organizations — *laissez faire* on one side and communism on the other. *Laissez faire* is the concept of an economy in which private enterprise is completely unrestricted; communism embodies the concept of completely centralized authority. Other in-between philosophies of economic organization include state socialism and government regulation of the economy without the assumption of control. State socialism embraces public ownership and management of certain selected industries as evidenced in Great Britain today; government regulation of the economy permits the government to enforce the principle of competition, insure certain standards of performance, and carry on those activities generally believed to be beyond the competence of individual or group enterprises. Under the philosophy of regulation, the government cannot assume the direction of business management nor legislate a destruction of the competitive free-market system of private enterprise.

None of these types of economic organization exists in pure form in any country in the world. At the present time, the United States has in operation some exemplifications of all the philosophies mentioned. Some elements of our economy are completely free of regulation; some are completely under government ownership and control; some government action represents regulation of the economy short of control; and other government action attempts direct control of the economic organization. Measures of the latter type constitute what we have chosen to call the "welfare state" philosophy of economic organization. Briefly, the difference between the welfare state philosophy of control and the philosophy of regulation is that the first uses the coercive power of the state to control and administer the pro-

---

[1]The "reading ease score" of the above passage as determined by the Flesch formula classifies the material as difficult. This type of passage was chosen over the tongue twister, unique word sort of selection as a more realistic test of pronunciation and articulation skill. From various sources any instructor can supplement with as many other kinds of selections as needed.

duction and distribution of goods while the latter uses the coercive power of the state to guide and promote the principle of a free market.

The term "welfare state" may be confusing since many individuals assume that any other plan of economic organization must perforce be against the general welfare. The general welfare, however, is the goal of each of the types described, and our concern with any specific type is to judge whether it constitutes a good means to the ends sought. In this judgment, economics is not the only consideration. What of democracy? Complete *laissez faire* would lead to anarchy; complete government ownership and control would demand dictatorship. A discussion of the proposal that the American people should reject the welfare state does not imply, surely, that the advocates of the proposal must uphold the extreme of *laissez faire* nor does it demand that opponents of the proposal uphold a communistic dictatorship. The discussion must concern itself wtih the implications of *control* versus *regulation* of the economic organization of the country.

We must constantly keep in mind that the role of government in our present economy features elements of both philosophies as it seeks to improve the general welfare of its citizens and that an attack on those attempts of our government to *control* rather than *regulate* the production and distribution of goods and services does not constitute an attack on welfare activities of the government in such areas as education, housing, banking regulations, social security, national health insurance, and conservation programs. Such considerations are not applicable to this discussion because they do not necessarily involve the philosophy of *control* versus *regulation* of the production and distribution of goods in a free market economy and are no more a part of the "welfare state" than they are of any other type of economic organization.

The welfare state concept of economic organization is not, as some people are inclined to believe, a new proposal growing out of attempts of the government to combat the depression of the thirties. Since the period of the great depression was one of expanding governmental control over the economic system, that period of our history has come to be associated with the "welfare state" philosophy as though it were something entirely new. As a matter of fact, the concept of governmental control is very old. In the light of history, we cannot but recognize that a return to governmental control is a return to the rather general practices of government in the pre-technical civilizations. It may have worked fairly well in those primitive economies where the direction of authority could be very general. However, governmental control of production did not work well after a technical society was developed. During the seventeenth and eighteenth centuries France tried governmental control of the economy and made a miserable failure of the attempt. During the eighteenth century men began to embrace the philosophy that governmental officials could not successfully direct the economic system for the welfare of all concerned. Throughout the centuries of control by omnipotent states, the desire for security was paramount; in the briefer period of emancipation from governmental control over the economy, freedom for the individual was foremost.

During the later part of the nineteenth century, in this country at least, we began to look once more to the government for direction of certain segments of the economy. Therefore the expansion of governmental controls during the 1930's represents an accentuation in a drift of affairs which had occurred somewhat earlier in our history. This renewed interest in an old philosophy of economic organization had its effect in countries other than ours. Some nations accepted complete domination of the economic life by the government — as under communism, fascism, and nazism; since the war, Great Britain has accepted the hybrid system of state socialism. The United States has refused to accept communism and thus far has refused state socialism as the answer to her social and economic problems. During the Roosevelt administration a considerable amount of legislation of a *control* nature was adopted. Some of this legislation was adopted as recovery measures during the depression and a good proportion was produced in order to meet the exigencies of a war economy. Since the end of the war, however, the government has elected to keep a large portion of the controls and to consider them for permanent use.

## TEACHER RATING SCALE

Directions to Students: In order to secure information which may lead to the improvement of instruction, you are asked to rate your instructor on EACH of the items listed. Encircle a number for each item at the place which seems to you most appropriate for the instructor you are rating. The highest possible rating for an item is 10, the lowest is 0, with nine gradations between. Conceal your identity by typing your answers or by having a friend write what you direct.

### DO NOT SIGN YOUR NAME BUT PLEASE RATE EACH ITEM HONESTLY!

I. CLARIFICATION OF COURSE OBJECTIVES.

10   9   8   7       6   5   4       3   2   1   0

Objectives clearly de-    Objectives somewhat    Objectives very vague
fined.                    vague or indefinite.    or given no attention.

Remarks:


II. GENERAL ORGANIZATION OF COURSE.

10   9   8   7       6   5   4       3   2   1   0

Course exceptionally      Course satisfactorily    Organization very
well organized; subject   organized; subject       poor; subject matter
matter in agreement       matter fairly well       frequently unrelated to
with course objectives.   suited to objectives.    objectives.

Remarks:


III. KNOWLEDGE OF THE SUBJECT FIELD.

10   9   8   7       6   5   4       3   2   1   0

Knowledge of subject      Knowledge of subject     Knowledge of subject
broad, accurate,          somewhat limited and     seriously deficient and
up-to-date.               at times not             frequently inaccurate
                          up-to-date.              and out-of-date.

Remarks:

### IV. RANGE OF INTERESTS AND CULTURE.

| 10 | 9 | 8 | 7 | 6 | 5 | 4 | 3 | 2 | 1 | 0 |
|----|---|---|---|---|---|---|---|---|---|---|

Instructor has very broad interests and culture; frequently relates course to others.

Instructor has fair breadth of interests and culture; occasionally relates subject to other fields and to present day problems.

Instructor is narrow in his interests and culture; seldom relates subject to other fields or to present day problems.

Remarks:

### V. PRESENTATION OF SUBJECT MATTER.

| 10 | 9 | 8 | 7 | 6 | 5 | 4 | 3 | 2 | 1 | 0 |
|----|---|---|---|---|---|---|---|---|---|---|

Explanations are clear; makes good use of blackboard and other instructional aids.

Explanations at times not clear; makes some use of blackboard and other instructional aids.

Explanations frequently not clear; makes little use of blackboard and other instructional aids.

Remarks:

### VI. ASSIGNMENTS.

| 10 | 9 | 8 | 7 | 6 | 5 | 4 | 3 | 2 | 1 | 0 |
|----|---|---|---|---|---|---|---|---|---|---|

Clear, reasonable coordinated with the class work.

Occasionally indefinite and unrelated to class work.

Confused, often made late; with no relation to work of course.

Remarks:

### VII. ABILITY TO AROUSE INTEREST.

| 10 | 9 | 8 | 7 | 6 | 5 | 4 | 3 | 2 | 1 | 0 |
|----|---|---|---|---|---|---|---|---|---|---|

Interest among students usually runs high.

Students seem only mildly interested.

Majority of students inattentive most of the time.

Remarks:

## VIII.  MANNERISMS AND APPEARANCE.

10   9   8   7      6    5    4       3   2   1   0

| | | |
|---|---|---|
| Appearance pleasing; free from annoying mannerisms. | Mannerisms not seriously objectionable; sometimes untidy. | Constantly exhibits annoying mannerisms; slovenly in appearance. |

Remarks:

## IX.  EXAMINATIONS AND GRADING.

10   9   8   7      6    5    4       3   2   1   0

| | | |
|---|---|---|
| Fair and impartial, grades based on several evidences of achievement. | Partial at times; grades based on a few evidences of achievement. | Frequently shows partiality; grades based on very limited evidences of achievement. |

Remarks:

## X.  WILLINGNESS TO HELP STUDENTS.

10   9   8   7      6    5    4       3   2   1   0

| | | |
|---|---|---|
| Instructor exceptionally friendly; always willing to help students when he has time. | Instructor moderately friendly; usually willing to help students. | Instructor aloof or sarcastic and preoccupied; unwilling to help students. |

Remarks:

## XI.  RECOGNITION OF OWN LIMITATIONS.

10   9   8   7      6    5    4       3   2   1   0

| | | |
|---|---|---|
| Welcomes differences of opinion; honest in admitting when he does not know. | Moderately tolerant of different viewpoints; usually willing to admit when he does not know. | Displeased by opposite viewpoints; dogmatic and argumentative even when clearly wrong. |

Remarks:

## XII.   VOICE OF ARTICULATION.

| 10 | 9 | 8 | 7 | 6 | 5 | 4 | 3 | 2 | 1 | 0 |

Speaks clearly and distinctly; pleasant voice.

Words sometimes indistinct and hard to hear; voice somewhat unpleasant.

Words very indistinct; often impossible to hear; voice unpleasant.

Remarks:

## XIII.   SENSE OF HUMOR.

| 10 | 9 | 8 | 7 | 6 | 5 | 4 | 3 | 2 | 1 | 0 |

Enjoys a good joke (even when it is on himself); yet knows when to be serious.

Unpredictable; sometimes pleasant and happy; at other times downcast.

Poor sport; never sees the humorous side of any situation.

Remarks:

## XIV.   GENERAL ESTIMATE OF TEACHER.

| 10 | 9 | 8 | 7 | 6 | 5 | 4 | 3 | 2 | 1 | 0 |

Very superior teacher.   Average teacher.   Very poor teacher.

Remarks:

## XV.   IMPRESSION OF COURSE.

1. Favorable:

2. Unfavorable:

# Index